The Mind of the Nation

The Mind of the Nation

Völkerpsychologie in Germany, 1851–1955

Egbert Klautke

berghahn

NEW YORK · OXFORD

www.berghahnbooks.com

First published in 2013 by
Berghahn Books
www.berghahnbooks.com

Library of Congress Cataloging-in-Publication Data

Klautke, Egbert.
  The mind of the nation: Völkerpsychologie in Germany, 1851-1955 /
Egbert Klautke.
       pages cm
  Includes bibliographical references and index.
  ISBN 978-1-78238-019-1 (hardback) -- ISBN 978-1-78533-200-5
  (paperback) -- ISBN 978-1-78238-020-7 (ebook)
  1. Ethnopsychology--Germany--History. 2. National characteristics,
German--History--19th century. 3. National characteristics, German--
History--20th century. 4. Germany--Intellectual life--19th century. 5.
Germany--Intellectual life--20th century. I. Title.
  GN502.K55 2013
  155.8'2094309034--dc23

                                                      2013005576

British Library Cataloguing in Publication Data
A catalogue record for this book is available from the British Library

ISBN 978-1-78238-019-1 (hardback)
ISBN 978-1-78533-200-5 (paperback)
ISBN 978-1-78238-020-7 (ebook)

Contents

Acknowledgements

I would like to thank my colleagues Peter Zusi (London) and Eckard Michels (London/Berlin), who proofread the whole manuscript, for their criticism and corrections. Martyn Rady (London) and Uffa Jensen (Berlin) both read earlier parts of the text and provided equally helpful comments. The three anonymous readers who reviewed the typescript for Berghahn Books made valuable suggestions for the final revision of the text. I would like to thank Marion Berghahn and Ann Przyzycki DeVita at Berghahn Books for their support. While preparing and writing this study I have profited from discussions with A. Dirk Moses, Kiran K. Patel, Wolfgang Eßbach, Peter Schöttler, Mark Hewitson, and my colleagues at UCL's School of Slavonic and East European Studies. My thanks go to the conveners and the attendants of the seminar series that gave me the opportunity to present and discuss preliminary findings on the history of folk psychology: the seminar series of the Centre for the Study of Central Europe at UCL's School of Slavonic and East European Studies, organized by Richard Butterwick and Philipp Müller; the Modern German History Seminar at Oxford University, organized by Jane Caplan, Alexander Sedlmaier, Oliver Zimmer and Anna Menge; the Seminar Series on the History of the Psychological Disciplines of the British Psychological Society at University College London, organized by Sonu Shamdasani; the Modern German History Seminar at the Institute of Historical Research, University of London, at the time organized by Mark Hewitson, Eckard Michels, Rudolf Muhs and Cornelie Usborne; the German-French seminar series at the *Frankreich-Zentrum* of the Free University Berlin, organized by Anne Kwaschik and Peter Schöttler.

Some of the material used in Chapter 1 has appeared in an article published as 'The Mind of the Nation: The Debate about Völkerpsychologie, 1859–1900', in *Central Europe* 8.1 (2010), pp. 1–19; it appears here with permission of the editors.

Völkerpsychologie in Germany

Völkerpsychologie, or folk psychology, reflected some of the main currents within German academia in the nineteenth and early twentieth centuries. Its champions attempted to synthesize the empirical knowledge about the history and development of civilization that had been accumulated during the nineteenth century, and tried to construct an academic discipline that would reflect the rapid political, economic and cultural changes of their contemporary society, and explain these in a comprehensive way. The success of the sciences provided an irresistible model for such an enterprise, as did the national movement in Prussia and the subsequent founding of a unified German nation state under Prussian auspices. The optimism and the belief in progress that characterized liberal thinking in the nineteenth century underpinned the 'project' of folk psychology.

Today the original aims of the 'founders' of *Völkerpsychologie* have been thoroughly forgotten. Instead, the term is widely associated with simplistic prejudices and stereotypes that might be common amongst journalists and political propagandists, but unworthy of serious academic contributions. Historians and literary critics easily dismiss folk psychology as a pseudo-science that presented speculations about 'national characters' as serious scholarship. They see folk psychology as an example of the perversion of science for political reasons, and treat it as little more than a chapter of the abuse of scholarship for political purposes. Thus, the contribution of folk psychology to the history of the social sciences has been regularly underestimated or even ignored. Similarly, *Völkerpsychologie* has not been included in the pedigree of the social sciences, and has rarely been studied in detail. The original aims and objectives of its proponents have thus been frequently misunderstood.[1] Often, authors have followed the verdict of the social anthropologist Wilhelm Emil Mühlmann (1904–88), who, when writing the history of his own discipline, dismissed Wilhelm Wundt's *Völkerpsychologie* as an overambitious concept, which was conceptually flawed and thus deserved to be forgotten: '*Völkerpsychologie* did not deal with peoples, and was no psychology either.'[2]

The following study tries to correct the commonly held view that folk psychology was little more than political propaganda dressed up as a social science. It will present it as part of the wide-ranging debates that led to the formation of the social sciences, and follow the history of *Völkerpsychologie* in Germany from its beginnings in the 1850s to the 1950s. In order to cover such an extended period of time in a concise study, the focus will be on the main representatives of folk psychology, i.e., those authors who actively promoted and advertised it as a discipline. The first chapter will introduce the folk psychology of the philosopher Moritz Lazarus (1824–1903) and the linguist Heymann Steinthal (1823–99), who founded a specialized journal, the *Zeitschrift für Völkerpsychologie und Sprachwissenschaft* (*ZfVS*), to promote and establish their version of folk psychology. Lazarus and Steinthal were succeeded by the psychologist and philosopher Wilhelm Wundt (1832–1920), who published a massive ten-volume study on *Völkerpsychologie* from 1900 to 1920, the most detailed and comprehensive contribution to the field. As the best-known folk psychologist, Wundt will be the focus of the second chapter. In the 1930s the psychologist, journalist and politician Willy Hellpach (1877–1955), a former student of Wundt, revived the by then ailing approach when he published the only textbook on *Völkerpsychologie*, in an effort to accommodate himself within the Third Reich. Hellpach remained a dedicated folk psychologist until his death, personifying both the continuity and the demise of folk psychology after the Second World War. All three chapters will provide the necessary biographical background of the different generations of folk psychologists, introduce their approaches to the field, and look at the reception and appropriation of their folk psychology.

Such a careful reconstruction and contextualization will show that, even though the sometimes grandiose plans and expectations attached to folk psychology attracted severe criticism from the outset, folk psychology left its mark on the intellectual landscape of turn-of-the century Germany, as well as abroad, particularly in France, the United States, Eastern Europe and Russia. Central concepts of *Völkerpsychologie* were incorporated by sociologists, cultural and social anthropologists, and representatives of *Volkskunde* – all disciplines which, in contrast to folk psychology, became subsequently established at university level during the twentieth century. Even though folk psychology failed in this respect, questions posed and problems formulated by early folk psychologists have thus remained on the agenda of the humanities and the social sciences until the present day. Many of the questions and ideas that are nowadays associated with disciplines such as sociology, cultural anthropology and cultural studies were first raised by the representatives of folk psychology. The list of scholars who benefitted from the insights of folk psychology reads like a 'who's who' of the early social sciences: Ernest Renan (1823–92), Emile Durkheim (1858–1917), Martin Buber (1878–1965), Franz Boas (1858–1942) Georg Simmel (1858–1918) and Werner Sombart (1863–1941) were among those who were heavily influenced by Lazarus, Steinthal and Wundt, although they did not always acknowledge these intellectual debts. Renan's famous 'voluntaristic' definition of the nation, for instance, was based on a notion that was very similar to Lazarus's definition of the 'folk'; Simmel's pioneering works on cultural sociology were based around central concepts of the folk psychology of his teachers Lazarus and Steinthal; central pillars of Durkheim's sociology – 'social facts' and 'collective representations' – owed much to his reading of Wundt's *Völkerpsychologie*. Moreover, current concepts such as 'national identity' or 'national mentality' can be traced back to the debates about folk psychology and are directly related to the central concept of folk psychology, the idea of a unique 'folk spirit' or 'folk soul'.

When Moritz Lazarus coined the phrase *Völkerpsychologie* in 1851, he did not do so in an intellectual vacuum. Attempts to characterize other nations or peoples were then hardly new; indeed, some authors could easily trace the 'othering' of foreign nations back to the earliest records of history. Herodotus and Thucydides have thus been identified as the 'first folk psychologists', since the thinking of classical Greek philosophy depended on the asymmetrical basic concepts of 'Greeks' and 'barbarians'.[3] The idea of a 'national character', closely related to any version of folk psychology, became an integral part of Enlightenment philosophy, and was hence as common in Germany as in other European countries by the mid nineteenth century. The list of authors who wrote on 'national character' includes some of the most famous European philosophers: Giambattista Vico's (1668–1744) *Scienza Nuova*, the first attempt to establish a 'social science' in modern times, took the 'common nature of peoples' as its starting point.[4] Montesquieu's (1689–1755) *Esprit des lois* was based around the concept of national character, and Voltaire (1694–1778) and Jean-Jacques Rousseau (1712–78) followed him in this way.[5] Auguste Comte's (1798–1857) *Sociologie* did not differ in this respect.[6] David Hume (1711–76) wrote a short essay, 'On National Characteristics', in which he refuted popular anthropological theories of the eighteenth century that explained the peculiarities of nations as the result of the climate and natural living conditions.[7] As part of his *System of Logic*, John Stuart Mill (1806–73) had outlined a 'political ethology' or 'science of national character' that was to form the centre of a future social science. Indeed, Heymann Steinthal considered this the most accurate English translation of the German term *Völkerpsychologie*.[8] In Germany, Johann Gottfried Herder (1744–1803) had used the concept of an irreducible 'folk spirit' to counter the universal individualism of the Enlightenment philosophers. For him, the spirit of a people manifested itself in its culture, i.e. its language, customs, and mores; history represented the continuous development of individually different, but structurally similar nations which together formed a harmonic and pluralist universe.[9] Lazarus and Steinthal were well aware of this venerable tradition. In particular, they were heavily indebted to Herder and shared his belief in national progress as much as the assumption of a harmonic plurality of the different nations that constituted mankind. Their *Völkerpsychologie* can be seen as an attempt to continue the Herderian tradition and make it compatible with the modern, 'scientific' age.

In contrast to older traditions, then, Lazarus and Steinthal's aim was to build a new discipline that did not only incorporate a notion of 'national characters', but would be exclusively devoted to the study of the 'folk spirit' (*Volksgeist*). To them, the folk spirit was not only an important aspect of history, but its driving force. A complete and adequate understanding of the folk spirit would explain the historical development of mankind in its entirety. With hindsight, *Völkerpsychologie* as conceived by Lazarus and Steinthal in the mid nineteenth century appears as a quintessentially modern discipline, despite the archaic terminology they employed.[10] The core ideas of liberalism were fused in their concept of folk psychology: the belief in the primordial importance of the nation was combined with an admiration for the methodological rigour of the sciences. These notions were merged with the idea of universal progress, both material and moral, which was informed not only by philosophical study, but by their personal experience of Jewish emancipation, which coincided with their identification with Prussian and German culture and society.

A comprehensive history of *Völkerpsychologie* – in particular, a study that follows the reception and impact of this concept, and positions it in its historical context – has not been available yet.[11] This study will fill this gap, drawing on a wide range of original literature and specialized studies, which contain the scattered information on the representatives of German folk psychology, their readers, followers and critics. Lazarus and Steinthal have first and foremost attracted attention for their role in the Jewish reform movement in Germany, and as typical representatives of German-Jewish intellectuals in the nineteenth century. Their political-social views and personal experiences have thus been more thoroughly studied than their academic work.[12] More recently, however, their folk psychology has received increased attention. Lazarus in particular has been discovered as a forerunner of contemporary philosophy of culture, while the importance of Steinthal's linguistic works has been duly acknowledged.[13] In fact, their political-social views cannot and should not be separated from their academic work: the first chapter of this study will show how the idea of 'folk psychology' was intricately, and increasingly, related to Lazarus and Steinthal's Jewish experiences.[14]

Despite Wilhelm Wundt's standing and fame as one of the founders of modern psychology, his *Völkerpsychologie* has only received scant attention.[15] Only a few biographical studies on Wilhelm Wundt exist, none of which pays tribute to his role in German academia between the 1870s and 1920.[16] A full-scale academic biography of Wundt, along the lines of recent studies of other outstanding scholars such as Theodor Mommsen (1817–1903), Rudolf Virchow (1821–1902), Werner Sombart and Max Weber (1864–1920), which would look at this liberal mandarin as a typical personality of Imperial Germany, remains a desideratum.[17] In general historical literature, Wundt rarely makes an appearance, and in the few cases that exist, he is often misrepresented.[18] Knowledge of Wundt's personality and of his academic work, and in particular his *Völkerpsychologie*, has largely been restricted to historians of psychology, who have studied his contributions to the field from their particular vantage point i.e., the formation of psychology as an independent discipline, with a focus on the 'emancipation' of psychology from philosophy and its transformation into a scientific, experimental discipline. Wundt's *Völkerpsychologie*, in which he followed the traditional, hermeneutic methods of the humanities, did not fit into this 'grand narrative' of the history of psychology as a natural science, and has thus received limited attention. While there have been attempts to rehabilitate Wundt's folk psychology as an original version of contemporary cultural psychology, its historical context and impact have remained underexplored.[19]

Willy Hellpach's huge academic *œuvre* is largely forgotten today. Even authors who are more sympathetic towards folk psychology than the majority of intellectual historians have overlooked his contributions to the field, despite the fact that he was the author of the only textbook on *Völkerpsychologie*, which enjoyed considerable success and was reprinted three times during his lifetime, both during and after the Third Reich.[20] The only two specialized studies that focus on Hellpach's folk psychology present it as a shrewd attempt to criticize National Socialist ideology by using 'coded language'. A close reading and contextualization of Hellpach's folk psychology, however, reveals that such a sympathetic interpretation is not tenable.[21] Due to the wide coverage of his publications and the range of his interests, Hellpach appears in diverse historical contexts in the academic literature. As a popular and popularizing author he was at his best, able to comment on topics as diverse as religious reform, prostitution as a social problem, the effects of weather on the human psyche, or the pitfalls of parliamentary democracy. For instance, he has served Joachim Radkau in his study of the 'age of nervousness' as a 'seismograph' of the history of Wilhelmine Germany, on account of his contributions to the debate on 'neurasthenia' before the First World War. Accurately, Radkau claims that due to his relentless eclecticism Hellpach missed the chance to become a great scientist, but was a 'medium of his time'.[22] His main strength was the popularization of scientific research, and his best works were syntheses and introductory textbooks for which he made good use of his dual qualification as a medical doctor and a psychologist. Best known for his political career and as a political commentator and journalist during the Weimar Republic, Hellpach's idiosyncratic political views have been discussed controversially. While Christian Jansen sees Hellpach as an 'anti-liberal democrat' who came close to the 'conservative revolution' and the '*völkisch* movement' since he defined 'nations' (*Völker*) in an essentialist way as supraindividual and suprahistorical entities with their own specific character, a recent biographical study has defended Hellpach as a loyal democrat who stayed true to the principles of his party, the left-liberal DDP, even during the crisis of the Weimar Republic in the early 1930s. In this perspective, Hellpach is claimed for the democratic, anti-totalitarian tradition in Germany. While both these views have their merits, they remain too limited since they are not able to conceive Hellpach as a democratic politician whose views still overlapped to a large degree with the radical right in Germany, including Nazi ideology.[23] The third chapter in this study will show how Hellpach used folk psychology to accommodate himself within the Third Reich, and how easy it was for him to stick to his academic and political views after 1945.

The following study will follow the history of *Völkerpsychologie* from its 'invention' by Lazarus and Steinthal in the 1850s through to its ultimate demise in the Federal Republic of Germany in the 1950s. It will show that folk psychology needs to be taken seriously by intellectual historians because of the impact it had on the development of the humanities and the social sciences. In order to do so, ample room will be given to the reception of folk psychology, both within Germany and abroad. While there were only few active champions of folk psychology, it reached and influenced scholars and intellectuals that were or became much more famous than Lazarus, Steinthal, Wundt and Hellpach. All these champions of folk psychology hoped to find a way to study the 'mind of the nation' in an objective and academic way, and distanced themselves from political ideologies. This proved to be an impossible task: in each case discussed in the following study, political events intervened and changed folk psychology substantially. In the case of Lazarus and Steinthal, the growing anti-Semitism in of the 1870s and 1880s changed the meaning and direction of their folk psychology. The legacy of Wilhelm Wundt's folk psychology was determined by the First World War, and his contributions to the 'war of words' that accompanied it. Hellpach's folk psychology was his attempt to find an arrangement within the Third Reich; without the takeover of power by the Nazis, it would most certainly not have been written. Still, I will argue that despite the obvious problems in writing a purely academic and theoretical folk psychology that does not get entangled in political debates, the easy dismissal of folk psychology as little more than a political ideology is premature. The central problem that folk psychology addressed, namely the question of the nature or character of nations, has remained on the agenda of the humanities and social sciences, despite the apparent 'failure' of *Völkerpsychologie* as a discipline.

Note on Language

Writing on *Völkerpsychologie* in English poses specific problems of translation. It is almost impossible to translate the very term *Völkerpsychologie* accurately into English. The most literal translation, 'psychology of peoples', sounds particularly awkward and has never been used. Instead, since its introduction in the nineteenth century, the term has been rendered variously as 'folk psychology', 'ethnic psychology', 'ethnic anthropology', 'social psychology', or even 'race psychology'. All these possible translations – one could add 'national psychology' – do not quite catch the connotations of the German original and are thus more interpretations than translations. Importantly, all these options ignore the plural of *Völker* in the German original, which distinguished *Völkerpsychologie* from *Volkskunde* ('folklore') and implied the study of 'peoples' as nations, not the 'common people'. Historically, 'folk psychology' was chosen by the translator of Wilhelm Wundt's study *Elemente der Völkerpsychologie*, which earned him an angry comment from a British reviewer for the introduction of such a ghastly neologism. Furthermore, using the English term 'folk psychology' can lead to further misunderstandings since contemporary psychologists employ this term to describe lay-psychological reasoning, in contrast to academic psychology. Despite these problems, for pragmatic reasons, I will use 'folk psychology' in the following study. I do not imply that this is the best or most accurate translation, but will use it interchangeably with, and as a kind of placeholder for, the German *Völkerpsychologie*. The related terms *Volksgeist* and *Volksseele* will accordingly be rendered as 'folk spirit' and 'folk soul'. All composites that include the German term *Volk* or the adjective *völkisch* are potentially misleading in English translation; *Volkstum* creates even bigger problems and will be translated as 'nationhood'. Similarly, *völkisch* was a far more generic term before it became hijacked by the far-right and anti-Semitic *völkisch* movement. Despite this political use of the term, it should not, as has been done in a recent study on the Third Reich, be translated as 'racial' without any further explanation.[24]

Notes

1. See for instance H.-U. Wehler, *Nationalismus: Geschichte, Formen, Folgen* (Munich, 2001), p. 7, who refers to *Völkerpsychologie* as an aberration. T. Nipperdey, *Deutsche Geschichte 1866–1918. Band 1: Arbeitswelt und Bürgergeist* (Munich, 1990), p. 631, sees Wundt's *Völkerpsychologie* as a 'failure'.

2. W.E. Mühlmann, *Geschichte der Anthropologie*, second edition (Frankfurt am Main and Bonn, 1968), p. 120: 'Die Völkerpsychologie hatte weder mit Völkern zu tun, noch war sie Psychologie.' Few authors have noted that this text, originally published in 1948, served a purpose in whitewashing German anthropology during the Third Reich, including Mühlmann's own contributions. In his *Rassen- und Völkerkunde: Lebensprobleme der Rassen, Gesellschaften und Völker* (Braunschweig, 1936), Mühlmann had devoted a substantial chapter to *Rassen- und Völkerpsychologie*.

3. E. Beuchelt, *Ideengeschichte der Völkerpsychologie* (Meisenheim am Glan, 1974); more recently M. Cole, *Cultural Psychology: A Once and Future Discipline* (Cambridge, MA and London, 1996); see R. Koselleck, 'The Historical-Political Semantics of Asymmetric Counterconcepts', in idem, *Futures Past: On the Semantics of Historical Time*, trans. K. Tribe (New York, 2004), pp. 155–91.

4. G. Vico, *Grundzüge einer neuen Wissenschaft über die gemeinschaftliche Natur der Völker*, trans. W.E. Weber (Leipzig, 1822).

5. R. Romani, *National Character and Public Spirit in Britain and France, 1750–1914* (Cambridge, 2002).

6. C. Sganzini, *Die Fortschritte der Völkerpsychologie von Lazarus bis Wundt* (Bern, 1913), pp. 9–12, 21–24.

7. D. Hume, 'On National Characteristics [1777]', in idem, *Essays: Moral, Political and Literary*, ed. E.F. Miller (Indianapolis, n. d.), pp. 197–215.

8. J.S. Mill, *A System of Logic: Ratiocinative and Inductive* [1843], vol. 2, seventh edition (London, 1868), pp. 497–500; see H. Steinthal, *Philologie, Geschichte und Psychologie in ihren gegenseitigen Beziehungen: Ein Vortrag gehalten in der Versammlung der Philologen zu Meissen 1863* (Berlin, 1864), p. 76.

9. J. Echternkamp, *Der Aufstieg des deutschen Nationalismus, 1770–1840* (Frankfurt am Main, 1998), pp. 101–4; P. Zusi, '"Kein abgefallenes Blatt ohn Wirkung geblieben": Organicism and Pluralism in Herder's Metaphorics of Culture', in *Der frühe und der späte Herder: Kontinuität und/oder Korrektur*, ed. S. Groß and G. Sauder (Heidelberg, 2007), pp. 89–97.

10. Lazarus and Steinthal did not, however, as Helga Sprung has argued in an attempt to include them in the pedigree of 'scientific' psychology, employ 'quasi-experimental' methods. Cf. H. Sprung, 'Hajm Steinthal (1823-1899) und Moritz Lazarus (1824–1903) und die Ursprünge der Völkerpsychologie in Berlin', in L. Sprung and W. Schönpflug, eds, *Zur Geschichte der Psychologie in Berlin* (Frankfurt am Main, 1992), pp. 83–96, at p. 88.

11. Beuchelt, *Ideengeschichte der Völkerpsychologie*, is mainly interested in the school of 'culture and personality', which combined cultural anthropology with Freudian theories.

12. See in particular I. Belke, ed., *Moritz Lazarus und Heymann Steinthal: Die Begründer der Völkerpsychologie in ihren Briefen*, 3 vols (Tübingen, 1971–1986).

13. M. Lazarus, *Grundzüge der Völkerpsychologie und Kulturwissenschaft*, ed. C. Köhnke (Hamburg, 2003); I. Kalmar, 'The Volkerpsychologie of Lazarus and Steinthal and the Modern Concept of Culture', in *Journal of the History of Ideas* 48 (1987), pp. 671–90. On Steinthal see C. Trautmann-Waller, *Aux origines d'une science allemande de la culture: Linguistique et psychologie des peuples chez Heymann Steinthal* (Paris, 2006); W. Bumann, *Die Sprachtheorie Heymann Steinthals. Dargestellt im Zusammenhang mit seiner Theorie der Geisteswissenschaft* (Meisenheim am Glan, 1966).

14. See U. Jensen, *Gebildete Doppelgänger: Bürgerliche Juden und Protestanten im 19. Jahrhundert* (Göttingen, 2005); M. Bunzl, '*Völkerpsychologie* and German-Jewish emancipation', in H.G. Penny and M. Bunzl, eds, *Worldly Provincialism: German Anthropology in the Age of Empire* (Ann Arbor, MI, 2003), pp. 47–85.

15. C.M. Schneider, *Wilhelm Wundts Völkerpsychologie. Entstehung und Entwicklung eines in Vergessenheit geratenen, wissenschaftshistorisch relevanten Fachgebietes* (Bonn, 1990); B. Oelze, *Wilhelm Wundt: Die Konzeption der Völkerpsychologie* (Münster, 1991). The most recent contribution by G. Jüttemann, ed., *Wilhelm Wundts anderes Erbe. Ein Mißverständnis klärt sich auf* (Göttingen, 2006), does not add to the exisiting knowledge of Wundt's *Völkerpsychologie*.

16. See G. Lamberti, *Wilhelm Maximilian Wundt (1832–1920): Werk und Persönlichkeit in Bildern und Texten* (Bonn, 1995).

17. See S. Rebenich, *Theodor Mommsen: Eine Biographie* (Munich, 2002); F. Lenger, *Werner Sombart, 1863–1941: Eine Biographie* (Munich, 1994); C. Goschler, *Rudolf Virchow: Mediziner, Anthropologe, Politiker* (Cologne, 2002); J. Radkau, *Max Weber: Die Leidenschaft des Denkens* (Munich and Vienna, 2005).

18. See for instance W.D. Smith, *Politics and the Sciences of Culture in Germany, 1840–1920* (New York and Oxford, 1991), p. 127, who discusses Wundt in passing only.

19. K. Danziger, *Constructing the Subject: Historical Origins of Psychological Research* (Cambridge, MA, 1990); Cole, *Cultural Psychology*; R.W. Rieber, ed., *Wilhelm Wundt and the Making of a Scientific Psychology* (New York and London, 1980); J.D. Greenwood, 'Wundt, Völkerpsychologie, and Experimental Social Psychology', in *History of Psychology* 6 (2003), pp. 70–88.

20. Schneider, *Wundts Völkerpsychologie*, mentions Hellpach in passing. He is excluded from G. Eckardt, ed., *Völkerpsychologie: Versuch einer Neuentdeckung* (Weinheim, 1997).

21. H. Gundlach, 'Willy Hellpach; Attributionen', in C.F. Graumann, ed., *Psychologie im Dritten Reich* (Berlin, 1986), pp. 165–95; H. Gundlach, 'Willy Hellpachs Sozial- und Völkerpsychologie unter dem Aspekt der Auseinandersetzung mit der Rassenideologie', in C. Klingemann, ed., *Rassenmythos und Sozialwissenschaften in Deutschland: Ein verdrängtes Kapitel sozialwissenschaftlicher Wirkungsgeschichte* (Opladen, 1987), pp. 242–76. Gundlach's thesis is not convincing, as will be shown below. See also W. Stallmeister and H.E. Lück, 'Die Völkerpsychologie im Werk von Willy Hellpach', in Jüttemann, ed., *Wilhelm Wundts anderes Erbe*, pp. 116–27, and W.

Stallmeister and H.E. Lück, eds, *Willy Hellpach: Beiträge zu Werk und Biographie* (Frankfurt am Main, 1991), which contains a bibliography of Hellpach's works.

22. J. Radkau, *Das Zeitalter der Nervosität: Deutschland zwischen Bismarck und Hitler* (Darmstadt, 1998), pp. 15.

23. C. Jansen, 'Willy Hellpach. Ein antiliberaler Demokrat kommentiert den Niedergang der Weimarer Republik', in W. Schmitz and C. Vollnhals, eds, *Völkische Bewegung – Konservative Revolution – Nationalsozialismus: Aspekte einer politisierten Kultur* (Dresden, 2005), pp. 210–26, at pp. 210, 217; see C. Jansen, *Professoren und Politik: Politisches Denken und Handeln der Heidelberger Hochschullehrer, 1914–1935* (Göttingen, 1992); C.A. Kaune, *Willy Hellpach (1877–1955): Biographie eines liberalen Politikers der Weimarer Republik* (Frankfurt am Main, 2005). Tellingly, neither Jansen nor Kaune have studied Hellpach's folk psychology in detail.

24. R.J. Evans, *The Third Reich in Power, 1933–1939* (London, 2005).

CHAPTER I

Lazarus, Steinthal and the Invention of Folk Psychology

Moritz Lazarus and Heymann Steinthal are considered to be the founders of *Völkerpsychologie*. In 1851 Lazarus introduced the term into scholarly debates, and in 1859, together with Steinthal, he established the *Zeitschrift für Völkerpsychologie und Sprachwissenschaft* (*ZfVS*), subsequently published in twenty volumes until 1890, which gave the new discipline a platform and its most important forum.[1] Lazarus and Steinthal's folk psychology and the expectations and hopes they attached to this approach were closely linked to their position as emancipated, liberal Jews who identified strongly with Prussia and subsequently with the unified German empire. At the same time they kept their Jewish identity, refused to bow to the pressure to convert to Christianity, and became actively involved in the Jewish reform movement. They were typical products of the emancipation of the German Jews in the nineteenth century: strongly in favour of national unification under Prussian leadership and outspoken supporters of Jewish integration, they stopped short of full assimilation and proudly defended their Jewish heritage. To both Lazarus and Steinthal, their achievements as scholars and academics as well as their identity as educated citizens (*Bildungsbürger*) was the best proof of their integration into German society and made conversion to Christianity unnecessary, if not unhelpful.[2] Increasingly, their folk psychology reflected their socio-political position; while they started the journal as a decidedly scholarly venture, folk psychology turned more and more into a moral-political philosophy that comprised the ethics of reform-minded, liberal Jews in the German empire.[3]

As such, *Völkerpsychologie* became a life-long concern and project for both Lazarus and Steinthal; it summarized and contained their philosophical-scientific, political and religious-ethical convictions. The main purpose of the new discipline was to describe and understand the development of the folk spirit (*Volksgeist*), i.e., the progress of nations (or *Völker*), civilization and humanity, and by doing so to contribute to this very progress. Ultimately, folk psychology could not fulfil these high expectations. Indeed, several contemporary critics considered Lazarus and Steinthal's plans exaggerated and arrogant, if not naïve. The high hopes of establishing folk psychology as a super-discipline that would integrate, and at the same time tower over the humanities and the sciences, were disappointed, but this does not make Lazarus and Steinthal's folk psychology irrelevant. The approach was widely debated from the 1860s to the 1890s and found some followers. More importantly, it attracted a number of scholars who, by means of constructive criticism, appropriated main concepts of folk psychology, albeit in competing disciplines. Furthermore, Lazarus and Steinthal's folk psychology left visible marks not only on the German intellectual landscape, but also in France, and, to a lesser degree, in the U.S.A. and in Russia.

Biographical Background

The biographical backgrounds of Moritz Lazarus and Heymann Steinthal are important for an understanding of their concept of folk psychology. They both grew up in the German provinces.[4] Lazarus was born in the small town of Filehne (Wieleń) in the Prussian province of Posen in 1824. With hindsight he described his hometown as a typical Central European microcosm that was characterized by an ethnically and confessionally mixed population that invited reflections on the character of the different ethnic groups that lived side by side. Steinthal was born in the town of Gröbzig in Anhalt in 1823.[5] Both came from respected lower-middle class Jewish families with strong ties to the local Jewish communities, and both used the opportunities that opened up in higher education for Jews to leave the traditional milieu of their parents' generation behind. While attending the Gymnasium Lazarus experienced a short, but severe, crisis of identity when he broke with the orthodox Jewish faith of his family and became a secular, national-liberal Jewish German. According to Gershom Scholem, Lazarus was thus the epitome of the nineteenth-century assimilated German Jew, who completed the transition from purely Talmudic Judaism to a new German-Jewish identity in only five years.[6] Despite their secularism and harsh criticism of Jewish orthodoxy, neither Lazarus nor Steinthal considered abandoning Judaism and converting to Christianity. Instead, both scholars became active and outspoken representatives of the Jewish reform movement in Imperial Germany and fought for the recognition of the Jews' equal rights as German citizens.

At the University of Berlin, where they had met as students of the linguist Carl Heyse (1797–1855), both Lazarus and Steinthal abandoned plans to study theology and become rabbis, and immersed themselves instead in studying philosophy and the humanities.[7] As was common at the time, Lazarus studied a broad range of subjects in the old philosophical faculty, including history, linguistics, literature and languages; his main topic, however, was philosophy.[8] While attending the Gymnasium Martino-Katharineum in Braunschweig as a mature student between 1844 and 1846 – for lack of money, Lazarus had first taken up an apprenticeship – his teacher Friedrich Konrad Griepenkerl (1782–1849) introduced Lazarus to the works of the philosopher Johann Friedrich Herbart (1776–1841), the German philosopher who had succeeded Kant as the chair in philosophy at the University of Königsberg. Herbart was one of the first philosophers to define psychology as an empirical discipline that was to abandon all metaphysical speculation and cut its ties to theology. Instead, he proposed to study the mechanics of the human mind, taking the natural sciences and mathematics as role models.[9] Herbart's psychological philosophy made a lasting impression on Lazarus, who remained a follower of his psychology for all his life, and thus became a main representative of 'Herbartianism' in Germany.[10] Lazarus in turn introduced Steinthal to Herbart's works, and together they presented the critical assessment of his psychology as one of the reasons to embark on the project of *Völkerpsychologie*. Herbart, they claimed, had been close to 'finding *Völkerpsychologie*', but had stopped short of extending his psychological system to the study of groups and nations.[11]

Against the dominating trend at the University of Berlin in the 1840s, Lazarus did not join the Hegelians, but followed the philosopher Friedrich Eduard Beneke (1798–1854), who taught a mixture of critical empiricism and pragmatic philosophy that was similar to, but also competing with, Herbart's approach.[12] Despite Lazarus's critical, distanced view of Hegel, he was very familiar with his philosophical idealism. Indeed, he had already studied Hegel's *Aesthetics* while still a student at the Gymnasium in Braunschweig. This reading left an impression with Lazarus: as a young student at the University of Berlin he told one of his former teachers that he dreamed of one day integrating and reconciling Hegel's and Herbart's philosophy. While his concept of *Völkerpsychologie* drew on concepts from both thinkers, Lazarus's real role model was Herbart, whom he admired and referred to as the 'Newton of psychology' because of the precision and accuracy of his empirical analyses.[13]

After graduating with a doctorate in philosophy in 1849,[14] Lazarus became an independent scholar and was able to establish a literary and scholarly salon at his flat in Berlin. His now comfortable lifestyle was made possible by the financial support of the family of his wife Sarah Lebenheim, whom he married in 1850. Without any creative ambitions of his own, he became increasingly interested in the arts and literature, searched out contacts with artists and poets and, amongst other activities, became a member of the Prussian capital's most eminent literary club, the Tunnel under the Spree. This association, founded in 1827, dominated literary life in Berlin until the end of the nineteenth century and gave Lazarus the opportunity to mingle with personalities such as the writers Theodor Storm (1817–88) and Theodor Fontane (1819–98), and the painter Adolph Menzel (1815–1905).[15] Not surprisingly, Lazarus's closest friends, to whom he dedicated extended sections of his autobiography, were writers and novelists, not academics. Amongst them he counted Paul Heyse (1830–1914), Heinrich Rückert (1823–75), Berthold Auerbach (1812–82) and Gottfried Keller (1819–90), who had all contributed to developing Lazarus's folk psychology without sharing his academic ambitions in this field.[16] Lazarus's interest in the arts and literature stood in contrast to the high expectations of an academic folk psychology, since one of the reasons to establish this discipline was to distinguish it clearly from the speculations for which travel writers and journalists were notorious. Lazarus seems to have been aware of this conflict, but ignored it.[17] To him, academic folk psychology was meant to help develop the German folk spirit in the same way as national literature. Already in 1859, on the occasion of the centenary of Friedrich Schiller's birthday, he had been instrumental in founding the German Schiller Association, a charitable organization devoted to fostering national literature und thus encouraging works that emanated from the folk soul and served the 'general spirit of the nation'.[18]

Lazarus's first independent publication was a political pamphlet composed shortly after the failed revolution of 1848–49 in which he argued in favour of Prussian leadership within Germany. This treatise introduced the main tenets of *Völkerpsychologie*, avant la lettre and in popular form, and showed Lazarus as a dedicated patriot who yearned for the national unification of Germany under Prussian auspices.[19] In 1859 he became professor at the University of Berne on the basis of two volumes entitled *The Life of the Soul*, an eclectic collection of his philosophical-psychological writings. It covered a wide range of topics such as 'Education and Science', 'Honour and Glory' and 'Humour', but did not include any studies on folk psychology.[20] At Berne Lazarus held the first chair in psychology and *Völkerpsychologie* at a German-speaking university and became a respected teacher and administrator, serving both as dean of the faculty of philosophy and rector of the university. Despite the success and recognition he received for his academic work in Switzerland, however, Lazarus gave up his secure position at the University of Berne and returned to Berlin when his wife inherited a large sum of money in 1866.[21]

Upon his return to Germany Lazarus hoped to be appointed to a chair in philosophy at a German university, but several attempts to install him at the

University of Kiel failed.[22] From 1868 to 1872 he taught philosophy at the Prussian War Academy in Berlin, and in 1873, after his teaching contract at the War Academy was cancelled, he was made honorary chair (*ordentlicher Honorarprofessor*) in philosophy at the University of Berlin, a position that kept him at arm's length from the tenured faculty, but recognized his former status as chair in philosophy.[23] Lazarus enjoyed continued success as a public speaker and teacher – his first lecture course on *Völkerpsychologie* at the University of Berlin in 1873–74 attracted more than 120 students and had to be moved to a larger lecture theatre – and the sales of his books made him one of the most popular and well-known philosophers of the late nineteenth century. Much of his success was due to his talent for popularizing academic philosophy for a wider audience and to his abilities as a public speaker – most of his publications originated from lectures and speeches. Lazarus was not an original thinker, though, and never published a major work that could have received the attention and respect of his colleagues in the Faculty of Philosophy.[24]

Even though Lazarus received official recognition for his work – both the University of Berne and the Hebrew Union College in Cincinnati, Ohio, awarded him honorary doctorates, and on his seventieth birthday, Emperor Wilhelm II made him a *Geheimer Regierungsrat* – he did not reach the highest rung of the academic ladder by becoming a full professor at a German university. He shared this snub with Steinthal, but in his case the reasons lie in a mixture of his personal underachievement and the structural anti-Semitism prevalent at German universities. Still, both Lazarus and Steinthal's biographies represent success stories of Jewish emancipation and assimilation in Prussia and Germany; they both reached the glass ceiling that separated German Jews from their Christian colleagues and made it extremely difficult for Jews to become full members of the academic establishment at German universities.[25]

Despite their differences in character and temperament – Lazarus was an excellent speaker who enjoyed public appearances, while Steinthal was a more private person mainly devoted to his academic work – they remained close friends during their lifetime and formed an almost symbiotic partnership, both in private and professionally.[26] Like Lazarus, Steinthal was the son of a Jewish merchant. He attended the Gymnasium in the residential town of Bernburg in Anhalt where he received his *Abitur* in 1842, and registered as a student at the University of Berlin the following year. Similar to Lazarus, he studied a wide range of subjects, from classics to philosophy to history, but excelled in the study of ancient and modern languages. Amongst Steinthal's teachers were the classicist August Boeckh (1785–1867) and the linguists Franz Bopp (1791–1867) Wilhelm Grimm (1786–1859), and Carl Heyse, the father of Paul Heyse, to whom Steinthal was particularly dedicated.[27] In

1847 Steinthal was awarded a Ph.D. at the University of Tübingen for a dissertation in linguistics.[28] Only two years later he completed his *Habilitation* at the University of Berlin with a study that compared Wilhelm von Humboldt's and Hegel's philosophy of language.[29] This 'second doctorate' had become a requirement for teaching at a German university because of the declining standards of doctoral dissertations, and made Steinthal a *Privatdozent* – an unsalaried lecturer and member of the faculty of philosophy.[30] An eminent and productive linguist, Steinthal subsequently published a series of monographs on historical and systematic linguistics.[31] In 1852, and again in 1854, he won the Prix Volney, a prestigious award of the Institut de France for his studies in comparative philology. This award and the stipend it carried enabled Steinthal to embark on an extended research trip to Paris from 1852 to 1856, where he concentrated on the study of Chinese languages. Steinthal never settled in the French capital, though, and eventually turned down a lucrative offer to work as an interpreter for the French Foreign Office in China. In 1856 he returned to Berlin where he became adjunct professor at the university in 1862.[32]

In his linguistic studies Steinthal followed and developed Wilhelm von Humboldt's theory and philosophy of language.[33] In 1884, at a time when he had moved away from linguistics and concentrated on ethics, he still edited Humboldt's collected works on the philosophy of language. Importantly, next to Herbart and Hegel, Humboldt's philosophy was the third major inspiration for Lazarus and Steinthal's *Völkerpsychologie*: the centrality of language for the study of folk psychology owed much to Humboldt's concept of language and its importance for national culture.[34] For Steinthal, studying language was the best way to understand the folk spirit or national mind, since language transmitted the 'appropriations of the past in condensed form into the present', as he explained, with reference to Lazarus.[35] Thus understood, linguistic studies were a way to study the folk spirit, and linguistics a form of applied *Völkerpsychologie*. Steinthal and Lazarus thus continued a long tradition of philosophical study of language that stretched back from Herder to Humboldt to the brothers Grimm. With their eminent predecessors, Lazarus and Steinthal agreed that language was the foremost expression of the folk spirit. Accordingly, linguistics and philology aimed at explaining the spirit of nations by studying their literatures and the grammatical structures of their languages, and were thus the most important areas of research for *Völkerpsychologie*. Appropriately, *Sprachwissenschaft* was included in the title of Lazarus and Steinthal's journal.

The Folk as Will and Representation

In 1851 Lazarus introduced the term *Völkerpsychologie* into scholarly debates in an article published in Robert Prutz's journal *Deutsches Museum*. This short sketch outlined the main aims and arguments for a new academic discipline and already contained all the essential ideas that were necessary to establish an independent discipline of folk psychology that would synthesize and crown the humanities. In 1859, together with Steinthal, he expanded this text into a manifesto of the *ZfVS*, followed by several programmatic articles that further explained central problems of folk psychology.[36] So far, Lazarus's main argument went, psychology had been restricted to the study of the individual and thus remained incomplete. Since individuals could never be understood in isolation, folk psychology was the logical and necessary extension of individual psychology. Folk psychology would be defined in analogy to individual psychology and was meant to study the folk spirit in all its complexity. To position the new discipline, Lazarus and Steinthal rejected other disciplines that had hitherto studied man as a social being as one-sided. They were particularly critical of anthropology and ethnology: The former aimed to explain the characteristics of nations solely as the result of geological and climatic influences and ignored all psychological factors, while the latter was equally insufficient because it treated man as an 'animal', a mere 'product of nature' and thus represented little more than a 'chapter of zoology'. The mental development of mankind was systematically ignored from such perspectives, Lazarus and Steinthal maintained.[37]

Völkerpsychologie, in contrast, would bridge the gap between the sciences (natural history) and the humanities (history of mankind).[38] Nature was strictly determined, they argued: it was ruled by the 'blind necessity' of mechanical processes and the cycles of organic life. History, in contrast, was defined by freedom and progress. The 'essence of the spirit' (*Wesen des Geistes*), however, was ambivalent: similar to nature, it developed with law-like necessity, but at the same time, the spirit produced 'historically progressive, new and free creations' which were impossible in the 'realm of nature'. The spirit developed according to psychological laws and thus created progress: 'The law-like permanent activity of the spirit equals development, and progress is so much part of the nature of spirit, that the spirit therefore is not part of nature anymore.'[39] This paradox called for the establishing of a new discipline that would study the folk spirit, the subject matter of the humanities, with the methods of the sciences. Worded rather awkwardly, Lazarus and Steinthal thus called for the establishing of a 'social science', a generation before establishing 'sociology' became the concern of Germany's most eminent economists. *Völkerpsychologie* would provide a 'third way' between the sciences and the humanities on account of its synthetic outlook.[40]

To Lazarus and Steinthal, the folk spirit (*Volksgeist*) was the *causa causans* of history and therefore formed the object of the study of *Völkerpsychologie*. The aim of the new discipline was to discover the 'laws' that governed the historical development of the folk spirit. Folk psychology would thus illuminate the creation, the development and the decline of nations.[41] In order to achieve this aim, Lazarus and Steinthal argued, it was necessary to rescue the term 'folk spirit' from journalists, travel writers and politicians, who had abused it and turned it into an empty phrase for ideological purposes. Hence they tried to strip the term of its idealistic and romantic connotations: to them, the folk spirit did not represent a metaphysical idea, but simply described the 'essence of all inner and higher activity' of a folk as expressed by its language, myths, religion, customs and habits. It was mandatory to study this 'inner and higher' activity systematically from all possible angles in order to understand the laws that governed the development of the folk spirit.[42]

Lazarus and Steinthal presented *Völkerpsychologie* as an attempt to synthesize the rapidly increasing scientific, philosophical and historical knowledge, and interpret the material that individual disciplines had amassed in a coherent way. The aims and objectives of the new discipline were universal, all-encompassing and without limits. A discipline that studied man as a social being was overdue, Lazarus and Steinthal argued: 'Man is by birth a member of a *Volk*, and is thus determined in his mental development in manifold ways. The individual cannot be completely comprehended without regard to the mental whole (*die geistige Gesamtheit*) in which it has been created and in which it lives.'[43] Man could only exist as part of a national community, and since the folk represented more than the sum of its parts, folk psychology was the necessary extension of individual psychology.[44] One of the main tasks of folk psychology then was to clarify the relationship between the individual and the community. Well before systematic efforts were made to establish sociology as an academic discipline, folk psychology was based on one of the fundamental questions of such a social science, namely the relation between the individual and the community – in their mind the 'people' (*Volk*). Lazarus and Steinthal described this relation as an interaction (*Wechselwirkung*), but an asymmetric one: each and every mental activity of an individual was rooted in the spirit of the folk. The community regularly took precedence over the individual. Individual achievements could only be understood and explained as products of the folk spirit, even though they could only be expressed by individuals. Language was the prime example to illustrate this point: it was never 'invented' or 'created' by an individual, but as a means of communication presupposed the existence of a folk community. For civilized nations (*Kulturvölker*), language was a natural and characteristic medium, but it was passed on from generation to generation and perfected in the process. Equally, the customs, works of art and general culture of a nation were products of a 'slow and incremental progressive development', not creations of an individual.[45] A further central concept of Lazarus's folk psychology, which was linked to his understanding of the interaction between community and individual, was *Verdichtung* (literally 'condensation' or 'thickening'). This described the learning processes of nations, or even the whole of mankind, over longer periods of time, which allowed for the progressive development of culture and civilization. *Verdichtung* occurred 'when concepts and series of concepts, which have been discovered in earlier times by the most talented individuals and could only be grasped and understood by few, become slowly appropriated by whole classes of peoples and ultimately by the entirety of the people'.[46] Hence, the folk as a whole stood 'on the shoulders of giants': it profited from the discoveries of outstanding individuals whose ideas it used and took for granted, thus elevating its standard of culture and civilization.

Both Lazarus and Steinthal agreed with Humboldt that linguistic differences represented, by and large, essential differences between nations: 'The logical forms of thinking are intricately linked to language, and everyone who understands the essence of language correctly will find out that completely different forms of speaking simply reflect completely different forms of thinking.'[47] Hence language was the most important object of 'folk psychology', and *Sprachwissenschaft* (linguistics) included in the title of their journal; for Steinthal, there were few differences between folk psychology and linguistics: most of his systematic and historical studies on language, he saw as contributions to folk psychology. Even though, by following Herbart, Lazarus and Steinthal consciously dissociated themselves from the Hegelianism that dominated the University of Berlin in the 1840s, they could not escape the spectre of Hegelian philosophy. The most obvious borrowing from Hegel was the concept of an 'objective spirit'. Lazarus and Steinthal used this term to describe the intellectual heritage of a nation that made up its mental peculiarities. The objective spirit or 'general spirit' (*Gesamtgeist*) of a nation thus contained the accumulated knowledge of generations, from the most basic technical knowledge to the most elaborate pieces of art and science, and was thus of vital importance for the constitution of any community. The objective spirit allowed for the preservation of knowledge in condensed form on which each new generation could build; it thus made development and progress possible.

Each nation thus developed its own objective spirit. This folk spirit turned the multitude of individuals into a coherent people, since it functioned as the 'bond, the principle, and the idea of a people' through which a nation acquired its unity and became a harmonic, organic entity.[48] Lazarus and Steinthal defined the most basic terms of their folk psychology – 'folk' (*Volk*) and 'folk spirit' (*Volksgeist*) – in a circular way. Despite their efforts to provide a coherent definition of these central terms, it remained unclear which came first: folk or folk spirit. Lazarus and Steinthal had thus reached the 'limits of the sayable', since they were only capable of apprehending man as belonging to a folk, and history as national history. Man never just belonged to humanity, they argued, but was by necessity part of a folk. On the other hand, all other communities besides the folk – the family, professional associations, regional communities, 'tribes' – depended on the folk. Lazarus and Steinthal thus presented the separation of humanity into *Völker*, or nations, as the natural form of existence. Differences between nations appeared not primarily as the cause for conflicts and confrontations, but as the precondition for the 'development of mankind'. The diversity and pluralism of nations, Lazarus and Steinthal maintained, needed to be welcomed and encouraged, since it allowed for the advancement of human culture. Following the Herderian tradition, they expected that folk psychology would show how the 'diversity of nations' contributed to the 'development of the human spirit'.[49]

Still, Lazarus and Steinthal proposed an idea that went beyond the conventional wisdom of middle-class intellectuals who yearned for a unified German nation state. Their definition of the 'folk' introduced a notion that came close to modern theories of nations and nationalism on account of its rejection of all objective definitions. Language was considered an important common trait of the folk as the representation of the folk spirit. However, Lazarus and Steinthal argued that defining the folk by language alone was insufficient, since there was no general agreement on what constituted a language. Moreover, different nations used the same language, and some nations, such as Switzerland, used more than one language. Similarly, 'common descent' could not define a nation, since all nations were ethnically mixed. As a solution, Lazarus and Steinthal introduced a voluntaristic definition of the nation: the folk was the product of the will of its members to form a folk, and hence the result of a conscious and deliberate decision. A *Volk* depended on the subjective view of its members of their equality and unity. Despite their subjective origins, nations were no imaginations, but realities, and could be found as facts throughout history. But the folk was a mental product of the individuals who belonged to it and was thus endlessly re-created. It was the 'first product of the folk spirit'.[50] The folk, then, did not possess a fixed and immutable character, but underwent constant changes. Normally, nations progressed and reached higher levels of perfection, but they could also decline and even disappear. Despite this voluntaristic view that stressed the openness and plasticity of the folk, and anticipated more recent theories of nations and nationalism, Lazarus and Steinthal repeated a central idea of historicist thinking when they compared the development of nations to that of individuals who, through education and experience, formed a specific character which constituted a closed 'totality'. The 'rise' of a nation's level of learning and education happened 'for particular reasons and according to specific laws'. It was these laws that folk psychology would study systematically.[51]

Lazarus and Steinthal insisted that folk psychology would leave the empty speculations of both philosophical metaphysics and political journalism behind and instead study the folk spirit empirically, with the methods of the sciences; but they also expected the new discipline to serve a practical purpose. Writing before the national unification of Germany, Lazarus and Steinthal advertised folk psychology as a means to help the Germans become more aware of their own folk spirit. So far, they argued, the Germans had been too ready to appropriate foreign ideas that could not be reconciled with their own folk spirit. A strictly psychological study of German national life and history would contribute considerably to strengthen the German folk spirit, Lazarus and Steinthal argued.[52] Moreover, they continued, the folk spirit was characterized by an ambivalent relationship to 'individual spirits' since it depended on individuals, but could also come into conflict with them. Too much individualism, i.e., too much focus on individual interests and peculiarities, created factions and inner conflicts within a nation that harmed its 'general spirit' and its unity.[53] Folk psychology, then, was meant to strengthen the national consciousness of the Germans by studying and reassuring them about their own folk spirit. Hence the study of the German folk spirit was the main task of folk psychology; the knowledge of other nations and their spirits would merely provide comparative knowledge that allowed them to better understand and strengthen the German folk spirit. These national-pedagogical functions of folk psychology revealed another circular argument that undermined and devalued the whole approach. The subject matter of the new discipline – the folk spirit – was not only meant to be studied in an objective, empirical way, but also to be developed and enhanced by the very same study. Alongside and contradicting their own 'voluntaristic' definition of the folk, Lazarus and Steinthal thus introduced a normative and essentialist idea of the (German) folk and its spirit. Folk psychology, then, was not just a disinterested science, but, with good intentions, repeated the impasses of the Herderian tradition it followed.

Even though Lazarus and Steinthal's folk psychology appears as a proto-social science, with its focus on the folk spirit and the dogma of the priority of the community over the individual, and even though it is often presented as a precursor of modern social psychology,[54] it remained firmly anchored in the terminology and horizon of early- to mid-nineteenth-century philosophy. Compared with other contemporary attempts to establish a social science, Lazarus and Steinthal's folk psychology was therefore limited: they stuck to the vocabulary of their teachers, which was to become dated by the end of the nineteenth century. Their attempt to orientate folk psychology towards the sciences worked only on the level of analogy and was largely mediated by the psychology of Herbart; there were no genuine attempts to establish a new methodology other than the insistence on discovering historical 'laws of development'. And despite the subjective definition of the folk, or nation, Lazarus and Steinthal believed too much in the idea of the nation as the natural form of existence to allow for a critical analysis of it. A related structural problem of folk psychology was the Eurocentric, even Germancentric bias on which the whole approach rested. Echoing Hegel, for Lazarus and Steinthal 'history' started with the ancient Greeks and was limited to European nations. Only the European nations contributed to culture and civilization, and hence only they were of interest to folk psychology. Lazarus and Steinthal were not capable, or willing, to include non-European nations or even prehistoric, 'primitive' people into their studies. Their folk psychology thus differed from later approaches to cultural and social anthropology whose cultural relativism opened perspectives that were unattainable for the philosophers Lazarus and Steinthal.[55] Their concept of psychology was related to folklore, literary history and the philosophy of history – all disciplines that depended on the idea of the nation and rose in parallel with the national movement – but had little in common with early sociology or anthropology. In this respect the takeover of their journal by the Association of Folklore Studies (Verein für Volkskunde) in 1890, after the publication of twenty volumes, was a logical conclusion, since Lazarus and Steinthal's journal had overlapped more with folklore than with social anthropology.

Völkerpsychologie, Anti-Semitism and the Ethics of Judaism

After his return from Switzerland to Prussia, in 1866, Lazarus was increasingly involved in Jewish organizations and associations and became one of the most prominent representatives of the Reform movement in Judaism in Germany. His charitable work for the Jewish community increasingly absorbed his time, which had a negative impact on his academic work. While still nominally an editor of the journal, he did not contribute anymore to the *ZfVS* after his return to Berlin, leaving the day-to-day job of editing the journal to Steinthal. Instead, Lazarus became more and more immersed in public life and accepted a number of public offices. Most notably, he became a member of the board of the German-Israelite Community Association (Mitglied des Präsidiums des Deutsch-Israelitischen Gemeindebundes) and in 1869, and again in 1872, he presided over the Israelite synods in Leipzig and Augsburg.[56] One of the results of the meeting in Leipzig was the founding of the College for the Study of Judaism (Hochschule, from 1883 the Lehranstalt für die Wissenschaft vom Judentum) in Berlin, an initiative that owed much to Lazarus's efforts. He subsequently became chairman of the board of this central institution which trained reform-orientated rabbis and conducted independent research. Steinthal taught languages and linguistics at the Hochschule from 1872.[57] In his role as a leading representative of the Jewish community in Berlin, Lazarus was drawn into the public debate about anti-Semitism in the German Empire that developed in the 1870s. The degree and depth of anti-Semitism after the economic crash in 1873 had taken Lazarus, the stalwart Prussian and German nationalist, by surprise,[58] and when the court preacher Adolf Stoecker (1835–1909) and the historian Heinrich von Treitschke (1834–96) introduced anti-Semitism into respectable, 'educated' circles, Lazarus publicly defended the German Jews against their discrimination as a 'foreign nation' within Germany.[59]

The debate about anti-Semitism in Berlin, triggered by the publication of Treitschke's essay 'Unsere Aussichten' in 1879, marked a turning point not only for the history of German Jews, but also for Lazarus and Steinthal's folk psychology. Treitschke had argued that 'the German Jewish question' (*deutsche Judenfrage*) was not an empty phrase, but a pressing problem. Every year, Treitschke wrote, one could see numbers of 'ambitious trouser-selling youngsters' entering Germany from 'the inexhaustible Polish cradle' whose children and grandchildren were supposed to one day 'dominate Germany's stock exchanges and her newspapers'.[60] Accusing the German Jews of a lack of national solidarity, he urged his 'Israelite compatriots' to 'become Germans and to feel as Germans' instead of cultivating a separate German-Jewish identity. He had detected 'a spirit of presumption' (*Geist der Überhebung*) amongst the Jews and chastised their 'hollow, insulting overestimation' of themselves (*hohle, beleidigende Selbstüberschätzung*). The German Jews, Treitschke continued, tried to prove that the 'nation of Kant' had only become 'educated for humanity' by Jews, and that the language of Lessing and Goethe had only become receptive to beauty, spirit and wit by the efforts of the Jewish writers Ludwig Börne (1786–1837) and Heinrich Heine (1797–1856).[61] The Germans were still a young nation; they were therefore lacking a 'national style' and an 'instinctive pride' and were 'defenceless' against foreign intrusions – a point with which Lazarus and Steinthal agreed. It was not only lowly anti-Semitic rabble-rousers who shared these concerns, according to Treitschke. Because of the preposterous attitude of the German Jews, he wrote, even the most educated Germans – those not known for 'confessional' or national arrogance – were saying in unison: 'the Jews are our misfortune'.[62]

These accusations caused a wave of responses, in the first instance almost exclusively from German Jews. Lazarus replied in a public speech in front of members of the Jewish Community in Berlin on 1 November 1879, which was subsequently published as a pamphlet. In this lecture Lazarus drew on a cornerstone of folk psychology: the definition of the nation he had given in the first issue of the *ZfVS* almost twenty years earlier. Again Lazarus rejected attempts to define nationality by objective criteria such as descent, language, customs, a common territory or religion. In reality, nationality was the subjective choice of individuals: 'The real nature and true essence of nationality can only be understood out of its spirit.' The concept of the 'people' or 'nation' – Lazarus used both terms as synonyms – rested on the 'subjective view of the members of the people themselves about their equality and shared identity (*Zusammengehörigkeit*)'.[63] This definition left no doubts about the answer to the title question of his speech, and was a direct response to Treitschke's invective: the German Jews were already 'Germans, nothing but Germans; when the concept of nationality is concerned, we belong to only one nation, that is the German nation'.[64] Their religion did not turn the Jews into a nation of their own. Rather, Lazarus argued, they were one of the *Stämme* ('tribes') that made up the German nation; as a religion, Judaism had to be viewed as one of several confessions that coexisted within the German nation.[65]

While Lazarus openly opposed Jewish orthodoxy, he denied the need for the Jews to give up their religion and convert to Christianity as a way of solving the 'Jewish question'. Already 'complete, highly able and productive Germans', the Jews had to remain Jews in Germany. As such, the peculiarities and special traits of the Jewish 'tribe' would contribute to 'fulfilling the highest ideal of German nationality'. In trying to defend the German Jews and their honour as German citizens, Lazarus came close to the 'presumptuous' attitude that had infuriated his opponent Treitschke in the first place: according to Lazarus, the Jews had a special role to fulfil as part of the German people. They were obliged to preserve their heritage and 'put it into the service of the German folk spirit'.[66] The Jews were characterized by a specific communal spirit that was rooted in their religious traditions and had developed into a unique set of ethical ideals. In Lazarus's view, the Jews appeared as special Germans whose secular ethics had made them the foremost bearers of humanitarian progress.[67]

In contrast to the programmatic article that had launched the *ZfVS*, Lazarus was now strongly in favour of pluralism within a nation; indeed, he declared the great diversity (*Mannigfaltigkeit*) of a nation as a prerequisite for the progress of the folk spirit. 'Diversity' encapsulated 'true culture'; accordingly, 'each nationhood (*Volkstum*) which is to reach a high level of development has to be equipped with a great diversity of talents and ambitions'.[68] Thus Lazarus made a small, but important change to his original argument. Whereas in the earlier texts on *Völkerpsychologie* the nation had appeared as an harmonious, uniform entity that was created by the folk spirit, he now presented the nation as a diverse unity that benefited from internal pluralism, that is, from the variety of *Stämme*, confessions and classes it was made up of.

For this reason the Jews had to preserve their intellectual and ethical heritage and contribute it to the greater good of the German nation.

Lazarus's arguments succinctly summarized the self-image of liberal, reform-minded Jews in the German Empire as well as its problems, and as such he was rejected by both Heinrich von Treitschke and the philosopher Hermann Cohen (1842–1918), a former student of Lazarus and Steinthal. Treitschke declared that whereas Christianity was woven into the German people with all its fibres, Judaism was the national religion of an 'originally alien tribe' (*eines ursprünglich fremden Stammes*). He accused Lazarus of ignoring the difference between a religion and a confession, and insisted that the coexistence of several religions within one nation could only be seen as a transitional stage. Instead of the tolerant, productive and harmonious cooperation of several confessions for the higher good that Lazarus had in mind, Treitschke saw the only solution to the 'Jewish question' as the conversion of the Jews.[69] Personally more disappointing than Treitschke's response was Hermann Cohen's reply to his speech.[70] Cohen agreed with Treitschke on most points and attacked Lazarus's reformist agenda. He denied that the Jews had a special moral-intellectual role to play in Germany, and accordingly opined that Jews could not contribute anything specific to the German folk spirit. Like Treitschke, Cohen urged the Jews to assimilate completely into the German nation, not only in an intellectual-cultural way, but also in their look and physiognomy. The Jews had to show that they were eager and able to get rid of their 'peculiarities' and not to cultivate these, since this would indeed constitute a 'nation within a nation', which had to be avoided by all means: 'A dual national allegiance is not only immoral, but impossible.'[71]

The debate about anti-Semitism between 1879 and 1881 changed the meaning of folk psychology for Lazarus as it increasingly became a way of describing the Jewish spirit and justifying it against anti-Semitic accusations.[72] These formed the main reason for his decision to embark upon a major book project, a comprehensive study of the *Ethics of Judaism* that would occupy him for the rest of his life. In the wake of the debate over anti-Semitism, a meeting of representatives of reformist Jewish communities from Paris, London, Berlin and Vienna decided to commission a working group, chaired by Lazarus, to produce a reliable work on Jewish ethics to document the positive Jewish traditions and their contribution to civilization. After difficulties with the financing of the project had arisen – donations from wealthy Jewish citizens did not materialize and thus the necessary number of researchers could not be employed – Lazarus decided to write the *Ethics* on his own. During his lifetime Lazarus managed only to finish the first volume of this comprehensive study, which was published in 1898, with English and French translations following soon afterwards.[73] Reflecting his political-social consciousness as a liberal reformist German Jew, Lazarus tried to synthesize Kant and Judaism and presented the *Ethics of Judaism* as embodying universal values. He wanted to show that the continuous Jewish tradition was the real origin of modern humanism.[74] With this claim he represented the dilemma and the inner contradictions of Reform Judaism, for he reserved a privileged position for the unique Jewish spirit, but at the same time conceived the Jewish spirit as universal and progressive.[75] Similar to non-Jewish liberals, he presented his own political-social and moral values as universal and generally valid. In addition, and not unlike his anti-Semitic opponents, he essentialized the Jewish spirit, although he did not associate it with negative, but positive, connotations, since it embodied a general ideal of mankind.[76]

For his part, Steinthal responded to this dilemma of Reform Judaism in much the same way as Lazarus. Even though less exposed in public life than his colleague and brother-in-law, he was involved in several Jewish organizations, published regularly in the *Zeitschrift des Judentums* and responded to anti-Semitic accusations with the same vigour and conviction. To Steinthal, Judaism equalled moral-intellectual progress and was thus a vital part of the national spirit: 'Judaism equals humanity; and since humanism can be reconciled with any nationality, if the nation really aspires to it, so Judaism can be reconciled with any nationality.'[77] Steinthal repeated an argument that represented the pride of German Jews in their achievements and enraged the anti-Semites: he claimed that their 'double heritage' had turned the German Jews into better Germans because they combined German culture and *Bildung* with Jewish ethics.

Both Lazarus and Steinthal saw no conflict between folk psychology and their interest in ethics; on the contrary, they presented them as closely related, even complementary fields of study. After all, 'morals' and 'customs' of the folk and their historical development had always been understood as one of the products of the folk spirit. Lazarus now presented folk psychology as a discipline created on the 'basis of Judaism' whose ideas 'originated from the deepest sources of Judaism'. His studies on folk psychology had reconfirmed his identification with the Jewish faith and its ethical principles.[78] With hindsight, he saw his childhood experiences in the trilingual town of Filehne in the province of Posen as a reason for his life-long interest in *Völkerpsychologie*.[79] Appropriately, Lazarus's last public speech, delivered in Vienna in 1897 to much acclaim, was dedicated to a 'folk-psychological study of Judaism', thus combining the topics that had dominated his academic work and his activities as a public intellectual.[80] To Steinthal, too, ethics and *Völkerpsychologie* were intricately connected. Ethics did not start with the individual, he argued, but with the national community. The 'spirit' of the individual was rooted in the community, which was therefore the starting point both of folk psychology and of any kind of ethics.[81] In 1885 Steinthal published a comprehensive study entitled *General Ethics*, which underscored this point.[82] His ethics concluded once again by defining the folk as a 'general individual' and thus the highest moral institution. In this study Steinthal defined the 'objective spirit' in a way that was dangerously close to the 'metaphysical speculations' that folk psychology had intended to overcome. To Steinthal, the objective spirit represented the 'sum and the system of objects of all subjective spirits that have ever lived'. The objective spirit was the 'realm of the intelligible', of 'ideas and truth, beauty and the good'; it was the 'empirically highest concept, the definition of all conceivable perfection, the perfect object'.[83]

Reception and Impact of *Völkerpsychologie*

Despite its conceptual problems, Lazarus and Steinthal's folk psychology did find followers and supporters. Their journal became a respected forum for aspiring and established scholars alike. Not surprisingly, the journal proved most popular with linguists and historians of language, a stronghold of German academia in the nineteenth century and one of the focal points of folk psychology. Lazarus and Steinthal were able to publish a number of articles from eminent representatives of this well-established discipline: next to the Swiss philologist Ludwig Tobler (1827–95), who became a regular contributor to the journal,[84] the linguist Berthold Delbrück (1842–1922), professor at the University of Jena and an expert on Sanskrit, published on the origins of Indo-Germanic mythology and on the relationship between religion and psychology.[85] Adolf Tobler (1835–1910), professor of Romance language and literature at the University of Berlin, contributed an article on the French popular epos,[86] and Georg von der Gabelentz (1840–93) published a programmatic article on the comparative study of syntax.[87] Richard Boeckh (1824–1907), the son of Lazarus and Steinthal's teacher August Boeckh, and himself the pre-eminent German statistician of the late nineteenth century, published on the importance of language for nationality.[88] The ethnographer Adolf Bastian (1826–1905), whose approach to anthropology had much in common with Lazarus and Steinthal's folk psychology, but focused on extra-European civilizations, published a programmatic article on 'comparative psychology'.[89]

At the same time Lazarus and Steinthal generously opened their journal to young scholars. Amongst the contributors to the *ZfVS* was the philosopher Wilhelm Windelband (1848–1915), a student of the philosopher Hermann Lotze (1817–81), who would become a main representative of 'Southern German' Neo-Kantianism at the universities of Freiburg and Heidelberg. At the beginning of his career he published an article on 'epistemology from the perspective of folk psychology'.[90] Another early contributor was the philosopher Hermann Cohen, who would later become, together with Paul Natorp

(1854–1924), the main representative of the Marburg school of Neo-Kantianism. Before Cohen discovered Kant he had been a convinced follower of Herbartian psychological philosophy, to which he had been introduced by Steinthal at the University of Berlin.[91] Cohen followed the programme of folk psychology only partly; he was even more committed to Herbart's idea of a 'mechanics of the mind' than Lazarus or Steinthal. In 1869 he published an article in the *ZfVS* in which he tried to prove that all poetry had developed out of myths, an argument in line with the ideas of folk psychology. Cohen shared not only his admiration for Herbart with Lazarus and Steinthal, but also his biographical background: he came from a lower-middle class Jewish family in Coswig in Anhalt, was meant to become a Rabbi, but dropped the study of theology in favour of philosophy. After the first 'Berlin' debate about anti-Semitism, in 1879, Cohen became a major opponent of Lazarus and Steinthal's position and thus destroyed the friendship with his erstwhile teachers; Lazarus in particular never forgave Cohen his verbal attacks on his position.[92]

The philosopher Wilhelm Dilthey (1833–1911), a close friend of Lazarus in the 1850s, however, objected to the idea of folk psychology and, to the disappointment of the editors, decided not to contribute to the first volumes of the *ZfVS*. Dilthey saw the main flaw of folk psychology in the attempt to emulate the methodology of the sciences and thus surpass the established humanities, in particular philosophy and history. He objected to the plan of relegating history and philosophy to the status of auxiliary disciplines and criticized the attempt to establish historical 'laws of development'. Instead, and in accordance with Neo-Kantian ideas, he insisted on the essential difference between the humanities and the sciences and developed a theory of the *Geisteswissenschaften* that defended their independence from the sciences. According to Dilthey, psychology had to remain part of the humanities; it could not be practised by copying experimental methods of the sciences, but only with a qualitative, hermeneutic approach.[93] Still, and despite Dilthey's serious reservations about folk psychology, Steinthal could persuade him in 1878 to publish an article on the 'faculty at imagination of poets' in their journal.[94]

Judged by the high expectations of Lazarus and Steinthal, the reception of folk psychology by the academic community must have been disappointing. From its inception, their *Völkerpsychologie* received mixed reviews, with some commentators agreeing completely with their aims and welcoming the idea of a new, comprehensive discipline that would summarize and interpret the results of the humanities systematically. The philosopher Ludwig Noack (1819–85), himself a follower of Herbart's psychology, welcomed the idea of a folk psychology wholeheartedly and expected the project to become a sweeping success.[95] Ludwig Tobler, even though he contributed regularly to the *ZfVS*, published an extended review of the first volume of the journal that was much more sceptical of the whole approach. He missed an adequate definition of the crucial term *Volksgeist* and doubted that the 'spirit' could be exclusively understood as the product of society.[96] The Kantian philosopher Eduard von Hartmann (1842–1906), author of the *Philosophy of the Unconscious*, raised similar points. He argued that the legitimacy of folk psychology depended on the existence of a 'general spirit' (*Gesamtgeist*) or folk spirit, which had not been successfully proven. He also doubted that the 'general spirit' would always take precedence over the individual spirit, as Lazarus and Steinthal had claimed.[97] Writing in 1897, Paul Barth (1858–1922), a philosopher who was heavily influenced by Herbert Spencer's *Principles of Sociology* and sympathized with the idea of a 'social science', acknowledged Lazarus and Steinthal's role as pioneers in this field. However, he regretted the lack of positive results of folk psychology; so far, he claimed, the causal analysis of the development of the folk spirit that Lazarus and Steinthal had promised had not been accomplished.[98]

Other reviewers were even more critical. The philosopher Adolf Lasson (1832–1917), a colleague of Lazarus and Steinthal at the University of Berlin, could not hide his sarcasm and poked fun at their overambitious plans. He criticized the idea of a folk soul without which there could not be a folk psychology, even though Lazarus and Steinthal avoided the idea of a collective soul because of its metaphysical connotations and instead used the term 'folk spirit'. Lazarus and Steinthal had failed to give a precise definition of the 'folk', the main object of the new psychology, Lasson complained. Folk psychology did not meet the requirements of a scientific discipline since it had neither an object of study nor a distinct method. Unsurprisingly, the first issues of the new journal lacked coherence and presented a hotchpotch of unrelated articles. What Lazarus and Steinthal had in mind, Lasson continued, was old hat and existed already under the label 'cultural history': the fashionable term *Völkerpsychologie* merely pretended to be innovative. Lasson represented a major line of criticism of folk psychology: he neither rejected the legitimacy of studying the peculiarities of nations as expressed by their 'spirit', nor pointed the finger at the inconsistencies of their programme, but mainly objected to the way in which Lazarus and Steinthal had presented and advertised it.[99] The philosopher Julius Frauenstädt (1813–79), the editor of Schopenhauer's works, made similar objections: *Völkerpsychologie* was not a new academic discipline, but merely a branch of history and ethnography. Since there was no fundamental difference between individual and folk psychology, the latter was a pretentious label for the study of the different characters of nations.[100]

The novelist and philosopher of language Fritz Mauthner (1849–1923) continued this line of argument over forty years after the publication of the first issue of the *ZfVS*. With a similarly sarcastic tone, he saw the need for folk psychology as typical for a secular, modern age that required a postreligious 'identity'. He characterized Lazarus and Steinthal as 'directors' of an enterprise that could not precisely define its main object of study, the folk spirit, and thus bordered on the occult. Still, Mauthner had learned from Steinthal when he defined language as a human activity and social phenomenon, not an entity.[101] The cultural critic and Zionist activist Max Nordau (1849–1923), who in his earlier writings had speculated about the character of Germanic and Romance peoples, called folk psychology – together with mass psychology – a 'great mistake'. In his study on *The Meaning of History* Nordau argued that nations showed only superficial differences in character. The idea that each nation constituted a specific individuality was equally flawed; this was nothing more than a popular prejudice. However, Nordau accepted racial theories that had become increasingly popular in the early twentieth century, and used them to argue against Lazarus and Steinthal's folk psychology: 'None of the great European nations studied by *Völkerpsychologie* is of unified blood', therefore, Nordau continued, homogenous national characters did not exist.[102] Language was no sign for a folk soul, either. Nordau's verdict on folk psychology was devastating: the concept of a 'collective organism' was a misguided and mystical idea; the 'whole' (*die Gesamtheit*) an abstraction, hence fictional. 'Life' and 'reality' could only be grasped by studying individuals, not groups or even whole nations.[103]

One of the harshest critics of Lazarus and Steinthal was the linguist Hermann Paul (1846–1921), a onetime student of Steinthal and follower of Herbart's psychology. The introduction to his influential textbook on *Principles of the History of Language* opened with a damning critique of their folk psychology.[104] Paul disagreed with the analogy Lazarus and Steinthal had drawn between individual and folk psychology. True to Herbart, he rejected the very idea of a folk spirit with its own essence and agency: 'All psychological processes are conducted within the individual spirits, and nowhere else. Neither a folk spirit nor elements of the folk spirit, such as art, religion etc., exist for real, hence nothing can happen within or between them. Away with these abstractions!'[105] While Paul agreed that the humanities (*Kulturwissenschaft*) had to be based on psychology – though not on psychology alone, since human culture equally depended on nature – psychology could only be individual psychology, since only individual 'souls' existed and interacted with each other. Therefore, Paul argued, the concept of a 'folk psychology' made no sense. Lazarus and Steinthal had failed to address the interaction between individuals and instead speculated about a folk spirit that did not exist.[106]

Provoked by Paul's critique, Wilhelm Wundt stepped in to defend the general idea of *Völkerpsychologie*. Long before he started publishing his own ten-volume opus magnum from 1900 onwards, Wundt had been an attentive reader of Lazarus and Steinthal's journal.[107] In 1886 he published a riposte to Paul's invective which included a critical assessment of Lazarus and Steinthal's approach.[108] Wundt agreed with Lazarus and Steinthal that psychology should not be restricted to the individual but had to include human society as an object of study. The nation, or the folk, was therefore a natural object of study.[109] He did not agree, however, with the idea of establishing *Völkerpsychologie* as a kind of super-discipline that would reduce the entirety of the established arts and humanities to a secondary status. Instead, it should form an integral part of a future, comprehensive psychology that would be divided into two parts: individual psychology and *Völkerpsychologie*. Psychology would not make the established humanities redundant, however. Wundt doubted that it was possible to find 'historical laws' that were as accurate as laws of nature, but if so, historians would hardly leave it to folk psychologists to establish these laws. He mainly objected to Lazarus and Steinthal's combination of Herbartian psychology with Hegelian philosophy, a mixture that in his view had caused the conceptual problems of their approach. The real target of Wundt's article, however, was Hermann Paul's strictly individualist and truly Herbartian approach. Wundt argued that Lazarus and Steinthal had committed tactical errors which had diminished the chances of achieving their aims, but he agreed with the main assumptions of their folk psychology, namely that the psychological study of the folk was necessary, and developed his own concept of folk psychology along the lines sketched by Lazarus and Steinthal.[110]

The debate between Hermann Paul and Wilhelm Wundt over the legitimacy and possibility of folk psychology provoked a response from Steinthal, who by then had practically become the sole editor of the journal.[111] Against Wundt, he defended the claim that folk psychologists would be necessary to discover 'historical laws'; the historians were not equipped for this task. With a few exceptions – Steinthal mentioned Johann Gustav Droysen (1808–84), Georg Gottfried Gervinus (1805–71) and his idol Wilhelm von Humboldt – historians had not produced results that could pass as folk psychology, and the vast majority of them did not provide 'causal explanations'.[112] Steinthal was delighted that Wundt accepted folk psychology as a legitimate approach and agreed that its task was to formulate psychological laws of development. The study of existing 'folk spirits', which he now referred to as 'psychological ethnology', could be left to disciplines other than folk psychology. Steinthal claimed that it had never been Lazarus and his aim to 'delineate' a new discipline, but only to characterize a 'complex of tasks' and a 'mode of scientific study' (*eine Weise wissenschaftlicher Betrachtung*).[113] In order to reject Paul's critique of folk psychology, Steinthal used two main arguments. First, he argued that Paul had misread and misunderstood the idea of an 'objective spirit', which showed that he had understood little about progress in history.

Moreover, Paul had simply reformulated the concept of folk psychology and given it the new name, *Principienlehre der Gesellschaftswissenschaft*. Steinthal saw little difference between the aims of the two approaches, and considered Paul's criticism a pseudo-attack that had used inappropriate and insulting language.

A number of reviewers of Lazarus and Steinthal's folk psychology, then, did not deny the need for a social science or social psychology, but were not happy with Lazarus and Steinthal's terminology and their attempt to apply the method of the sciences to the subject matter of the humanities. The debate about folk psychology was thus part of the early, tentative efforts to conceptualize a social science; it contributed to these efforts by stimulating competing approaches. Possibly the first ever attempt to present a coherent system of social psychology was not developed in the U.S.A., where the discipline would boom in the twentieth century, especially after the Second World War,[114] but in the Habsburg Empire, by the Austrian educationalist and philosopher Gustav Adolf Lindner (1828–87), in direct response to Lazarus and Steinthal's *Völkerpsychologie*. Mostly forgotten as an early social scientist, Lindner's influence as the author of textbooks for the secondary schools of the Habsburg Empire cannot be underestimated. His volumes on empirical psychology, logic and philosophy became the standard texts throughout the empire and introduced generations of students to these fields, and were still in print long after his death. Indeed, both the young Sigmund Freud (1856–1939) and Franz Kafka (1883–1924) studied Lindner's *Lehrbuch der empirischen Psychologie* in their final year at the Gymnasium.[115] Lindner was born in a bilingual family in Rosdalowitz in Bohemia and was a student of Franz Exner (1802–53) at the University of Prague in the 1840s. Through Exner, Lindner became a loyal follower of Herbart, and with his textbooks he contributed to making Herbartianism the 'official' philosophy of higher education in the Habsburg Empire. After a career as a school teacher and school inspector, he became professor for pedagogy, psychology and ethics at the University of Prague in 1878, and in 1882 decided to join the Czech university when it was divided along national lines, thus becoming a senior colleague of the young Tomáš Masaryk (1850–1937), the future president of the Czechoslovak Republic and himself a proto-social scientist.[116]

Next to his introductory textbooks, Lindner's major contribution to the scholarly literature was a general psychology, published in two volumes. The first one, with the quirky title *The Problem of Happiness*, was dedicated to individual psychology, while the second volume dealt with the 'psychology of society' and introduced the term 'social psychology'.[117] To Lindner, social psychology and economics together formed the two, 'inner' and 'outer' parts of a general social science. He agreed with Lazarus and Steinthal that man as a social being needed to be studied as part of a community. Through their interactions, individuals created and constituted 'society'. Lindner accordingly defined social psychology as the discipline that studied psychological interactions within society that produced law-like regularities in the human world. As he wrote, 'The task of social psychology is the description and explanation of phenomena which depend on the interaction of individuals and on which rests the whole mental life of society.' In contrast to Lazarus and Steinthal, however, and in accordance with the Herbart school, Lindner claimed that society did not exist independently of the individuals: the 'mental life' of society could only be found in the individual consciousness of its members. Hence, Lindner concluded, social psychology could borrow its principles from individual psychology.[118]

What, then, represented 'society'? Lindner identified two 'natural creations in the history of mankind' that could be the object of the study of social psychology: nations and states (*Völker und Staaten*). Both nations and states formed coherent entities, but for different reasons: nations were defined by the common descent and common language of their members, while states comprised a common territory and a common legal order. Indeed, 'nationhood' (*Volkstum*) appeared as the expression of the most intensive mental interaction of a majority of people.[119] But in contrast to Lazarus and Steinthal, who had never cast any doubt on the importance of the nation, Lindner argued that since nations changed during the course of history and were lumped together in polyglot states, the state was the original representation of society (*Urbild der Gesellschaft*) and thus the most appropriate object of enquiry in the social sciences. In competitive mode Lindner highlighted further differences between his social psychology and Lazarus and Steinthal's *Völkerpsychologie*. While he focused on 'real personalities and their interactions', folk psychology studied the 'abstract emanations of the national spirit', i.e., language, religion, mythology and art: 'In short, social psychology deals with the mental personality of society itself, while folk psychology deals with single mental utterances; the latter follows the course of history, while the former strictly adheres to the teachings of psychology, and relies on history only to test its hypotheses.'[120] Lindner thus turned the hierarchy of disciplines that Lazarus and Steinthal had suggested on its head and relegated folk psychology to a secondary status vis-à-vis social psychology. Despite his critical attitude towards folk psychology, Lindner believed that both disciplines could coexist. But in his view, folk psychology would provide the empirical-historical material that social psychology would interpret and explain.[121]

The differences between Lindner's social psychology and Lazarus and Steinthal's folk psychology directly reflected their different national backgrounds and experiences. Even though Lindner did not stick to his neat differentiation between state and nation in the course of his study, his preference for the state over the nation as representing 'society' suited the requirements of an 'official' social science for the multinational and multilingual Habsburg empire. By contrast, Lazarus and Steinthal's focus on the *Volk* and the nation mirrored their identification with Prussia and the Prussian-dominated German empire. The bilingual Lindner, who tried to mediate between German and Czech interests, played down the importance of nationality within the larger state. His social psychology was a product of the political outlook of the multinational Habsburg Empire and of its 'backward' political structures, although, with hindsight, these now appear more 'modern' than Lazarus and Steinthal's folk psychology and its romanticist terminology. Faithful to Herbart, Lindner dropped the notion that the folk represented 'more than the sum of its parts', and abandoned the idea of the *Volksgeist*, one of the main stumbling blocks of *Völkerpsychologie*. In his presentation society was constituted by the interaction of individuals through communication, and produced regularities that the social sciences had to study, preferably on the basis of statistical data. Hence, the peculiar political and national structures of the Habsburg Empire enabled Lindner to formulate an alternative to Lazarus and Steinthal's folk psychology, which, on account of its Herbartian anti-essentialism and individualism, foreshadowed the development of the social sciences in the twentieth century.

Most important for the legacy of Lazarus and Steinthal's folk psychology was the philosopher and sociologist Georg Simmel (1858–1918), who taught from 1890 as *Privatdozent* and adjunct professor at the University of Berlin. Simmel became one of the intellectual stars of the German capital during the *fin de siècle*, although his established academic colleagues viewed his success as a teacher and author with jealousy and suspicion. Today Simmel has become one of the canonized, 'classic' authors of sociology and is considered one of its founders, even though he saw himself mainly as a philosopher who engaged only occasionally in sociological studies. Over the course of his career he grew increasingly sceptical of the fashionable new discipline.[122] Simmel had studied philosophy, history and *Völkerpsychologie* at the University of Berlin, where his primary teachers had been Lazarus and Steinthal. They were instrumental in starting his academic career when they agreed to publish his first academic article in the *ZfVS* – a version of his rejected Ph.D. dissertation entitled 'Psychological and Ethnological Studies on Music', which was inspired by Steinthal's study on the 'Origin of Language'. In this article Simmel tried to disprove Darwin's thesis that language originated in a natural human ability for singing. Instead, following his teacher Steinthal, he argued that language was a precondition for song.[123]

In his more mature and independent works Simmel appropriated central concepts of Lazarus and Steinthal's folk psychology, in particular the notion of an 'objective spirit' in the way Lazarus had used it. In one of his most famous essays, on 'The Metropolis and Mental life', which summarized ideas from his magnum opus *The Philosophy of Money*, Simmel characterized modern culture by the 'preponderance' of the 'objective spirit' over the 'subjective spirit'.[124] Characteristically, he did not share the optimism towards progress that was so prominent in his teacher Lazarus. While Lazarus had held an unreservedly positive view of the objective spirit as the force that enabled and represented cultural progress, Simmel stressed the conflict between the objective and the subjective spirit, i.e., between society and the individual. According to Simmel the individual in modern society was overwhelmed by the rapid development of the objective spirit; a development with which the subjective spirit could not keep pace. The 'progress' of human culture represented by the objective spirit – 'the immense culture which for the last hundred years has been embodied in things and in knowledge, in institutions and in comforts' – was ambivalent at best since it had caused the alienation of modern man from society. In Simmel's view, then, the development of modern culture was not a 'success story', as a whole generation of liberal intellectuals had been convinced, but a highly ambivalent process with almost tragic outcomes.[125]

One reason for the 'tragedy of culture' was the division of labour which had brought about an unprecedented level of specialization.[126] The very process that Lazarus had used to illustrate his concept of *Verdichtung*, i.e., the condensation of knowledge which made progress possible and had led to the establishment of civilization in the first place, had also created overly specialized and one-sided individuals; it had thus caused one of the major problems of modern society, according to Simmel. Equally, political progress was a chimera to him. The 'repressive bonds' of the eighteenth century that modern society pretended to have broken had been replaced by more subtle, invisible constraints. The 'money economy', the quantification of social relations and the division of labour, all characteristics of urban modernity, had increased the political independence of the individual from the community, but only at the price of new restrictions and regulations.[127] Simmel's works thus provide a negative echo of the optimism and humanistic idealism represented by Lazarus, which was in turn typical of the ascending, liberal middle classes of nineteenth century Germany. Simmel adopted, but also reworked, central themes of Lazarus and Steinthal's folk psychology into a sceptical theory of modernity which stressed the ambivalence of 'progress' and pointed at the costs of social and political modernization. Further differences distinguished Simmel from his teachers: even though he excelled in the analysis of the psychological consequences of modern society, he rejected the idea of a social 'science' since strict psychological, sociological and historical 'laws' could not be established.[128] Instead, Simmel cultivated an essayistic, philosophical style and wasted little time on methodological questions. He rarely informed his readers about the sources of his knowledge, and trusted his intuition.

Furthermore, while one of his main interests lay in the psychological conditions and consequences of the formation of groups and communities, he did
not share Lazarus and Steinthal's belief in the primordial importance of the
Volk over other social groups. Hence he abandoned the cornerstone of folk
psychology, the idea of the nation as the be-all and end-all of human civilization. This decision was a purely academic one; it did not reflect Simmel's
attitude to the German nation or prevent him from nationalistic outbursts
during the First World War similar to those of other German academics and
intellectuals.[129] Still, despite these differences Simmel's sociological and philosophical works owed a lot to Lazarus and Steinthal's folk psychology. His
major works were based on a number of central concepts he had found in
their writings, such as the 'objective spirit' or 'interaction', which he reworked
and reformulated into a critical theory of modern society that stressed conflict
and crisis over progress and harmony. Simmel thus took a peculiar mixture of
ingredients from folk psychology, which were stripped of their optimism and
belief in science, and replaced by a pessimism stemming from the cultural
criticism of the turn of the century, represented by Friedrich Nietzsche
(1844–1900), Stefan George (1868–1933), and the *Rembrandtdeutscher* Julius
Langbehn (1851–1907). Thus altered and reinterpreted, concepts from
Lazarus and Steinthal's folk psychology have found entrance into the core
writings of one of the founders of modern sociology.[130]

Even though none of the works of Lazarus and Steinthal were translated,
they found an audience outside the German-speaking lands – not too surprising at a time when German universities were at the peak of their international
reputation and when knowledge of German was a standard requirement for
academics. In Russia and the early Soviet Union, Lazarus and Steinthal's folk
psychology ultimately attracted the attention of the philosopher Mikhail
Bakhtin (1895–1975). Mediated via the literary critic A.N. Veselovskij
(1838–1906), who had been a student of Steinthal in the 1860s, and the
linguist A.A. Potebnja (1835–91), Bakhtin learned about Lazarus and
Steinthal's work on the relationship between language and myth, as well as the
general concept of a folk spirit. In a theoretical work on the 'problems of types
of speech' Bakhtin explicitly referred to Lazarus and Steinthal's folk psychology as a way of conceptualizing collective consciousness.[131] Even though there
existed clear differences between folk psychology and Bakhtinian philosophy,
there was an overlap between the two approaches that originated in a similar
intellectual style (*Denkstil*) and, most importantly, a shared interest in the folk
spirit or collective mind.[132]

In the United States, the sociologist William Isaac Thomas (1863–1947)
of the 'Chicago School', a former student at the University of Berlin in
1888/89, was a follower of Lazarus and Steinthal's folk psychology. Similar to
Georg Simmel, Thomas was interested in those aspects of folk psychology that

allowed for the study of everyday life. He argued that 'further advances in certain lines of individual psychology and social philosophy' were dependent on 'reliable generalizations' from folk psychology.[133] Thomas referred to folk psychology in order to criticize the 'absurdities' of physical anthropology and race psychology, most prominently represented by the Italian criminologist Cesare Lombroso (1835–1909) who tried to identify and classify 'criminal types' by studying their physiognomy.[134] For Thomas, folk psychology provided the answer to the flawed attempts of anthropologists to classify human races according to their physical appearance.[135] German folk psychologists, he explained, 'have insisted on the identity of the human spirit in all zones – an identity underlying all external differences and local coloring'. The 'races of man' were 'identical in the principle of their growth'; the differences between nations that could still be observed were caused by 'the local, the incidental and eccentric' and could thus be considered non-essential.[136] Thomas thus overlooked the essentialist elements in Lazarus and Steinthal, and, arguing against theories of racial differences, stressed their critique of physical anthropology.

The most eminent student of *Völkerpsychologie* in the U.S.A. was the German-born cultural anthropologist Franz Boas (1858–1942). As a former student of the ethnologist Adolf Bastian at the University of Berlin, Boas was familiar with the works of Lazarus and Steinthal. He defined 'cultural anthropology' as an holistic discipline whose subject matter was 'partly a branch of biology, partly a branch of the mental science'.[137] In a famous essay on the history of anthropology which he presented to the International Congress of Arts and Sciences in St. Louis in 1904, he referred to 'folk psychology' as the major influence for linguistic-anthropological studies and specifically mentioned Steinthal's contributions.[138] In its comprehensive outlook Boas's anthropology overlapped with folk psychology since it studied all manifestations of the *Volksgeist* – language, myths, religion and art – alongside the physical and geographical conditions of human life. Boas thus rejected simplistic theories of scientific racism while acknowledging the biological dimension of anthropology.[139] In contrast to Lazarus and Steinthal, Boas abandoned the idea of a hierarchy of civilizations with its Eurocentric bias and replaced it with a pronounced relativistic view; no 'culture' was deemed more worthy than any other, and all cultures merited to be studied for their own sake. Boas's cultural anthropology was an empirical discipline attentive to methodological problems that could not be practised from the convenience of an armchair. As a true synthesis of the disciplines that studied 'man', Boas practised a combination of physical anthropology, ethnology, linguistics and psychology that went beyond the scope of Lazarus and Steinthal's folk psychology. Being a very successful teacher – Alfred Kroeber (1876–1960), Margaret Mead (1901–78) and Ruth Benedict (1887–1948) were among his many students – Boas thus planted essential ideas of *Völkerpsychologie* in American cultural anthropology, but turned it into a truly interdisciplinary field of study and widened its outlook significantly.[140]

While Lazarus and Steinthal mostly ignored French philosophy – Steinthal had studied Auguste Comte's works during his extended stay in Paris but dismissed him as superficial and long-winded, and complained about the fundamental 'lack of psychology' in his writings[141] – French scholars read their folk psychology with interest and sympathy. One of their earliest French readers was the philosopher and psychologist Théodule Ribot (1839–1916), a crucial but somewhat forgotten personality of French academia during the *fin de siècle*. Together with Hippolyte Taine (1828–93), Ribot was one of the main opponents of traditional philosophical spiritualism in France. Inspired by both English and German psychology, he was a champion of experimental psychology and instrumental in introducing 'scientific' methods to French philosophy. He admired and translated the works of Herbert Spencer (1820–1903), wrote a major study on 'psychological heredity' inspired by Charles Darwin (1809–82) and Francis Galton (1822–1911), but was best known for his studies on amnesia and the 'diseases of memory'.[142] A student and friend of Jean-Martin Charcot (1825–93), he founded the first psychological laboratory in Paris according to the model of Wilhelm Wundt at the University of Leipzig. Similar to Wundt, with whom he was in correspondence since the 1870s, he favoured a comprehensive psychology that would integrate experimental methods and concepts, but would not be restricted to these. In 1876 he founded the *Revue Philosophique* which he edited until his death in 1916; from 1885 to 1888 he taught at the Sorbonne, and then held the first chair in psychology at the Collège de France until 1901, which was created for Ribot due to the efforts of Ernest Renan (1823–92).[143]

Ribot's monograph on *Contemporary German Psychology*, published first in 1879, mainly served to introduce the new experimental psychology of Gustav Theodor Fechner (1801–87), Hermann Lotze and Wilhelm Wundt to a French audience. It also included a chapter on the 'Herbart school' in Germany, which focused on folk psychology as outlined by Lazarus and Steinthal.[144] Alongside the anthropologist Theodor Waitz (1821–64), Ribot presented Lazarus and Steinthal as the main representatives of this Herbart school in Germany and thus ignored Austria and the Habsburg Empire, where Herbartianism played a much more important role than in Imperial Germany.[145] Waitz, Ribot commented, had amassed facts without arriving at a clear concept of a psychology of races (*psychologie des races*). In contrast, Lazarus and Steinthal were the real founders of what he called 'ethnic psychology'. Ribot was not much impressed with their individual scholarly contributions: Steinthal's linguistic works were based on the assumption of an *Allgeist* or general spirit that functioned as the 'precondition and bond of every society and as the foundation of moral life'. This notion showed Steinthal's 'meta-physical tendencies', Ribot opined.[146] Lazarus's main academic work, his collected essays on the *Life of the Soul*, was more the work of a *moraliste* than of a psychologist, according to Ribot. It contained fine observations on humour as a psychological phenomenon, and on tact, honour and glory. But Lazarus resembled the poets and *romanciers* on which he had relied for his studies, and did not possess the 'rigorous scientific method' that was necessary to classify facts and establish scientific laws.[147]

Lazarus and Steinthal's 'project' of a future folk psychology, however, as laid down in the programmatic articles of their journal, found Ribot's support. He fully agreed with their view that the people represented more than the sum of its parts, and that a specialized psychological discipline was necessary to complement individual psychology: 'Next to general psychology, which studies the individual, there is space for another discipline devoted to the study of man as a social being, or more precisely, the many groups human beings belong to: this discipline is ethnological psychology.'[148] To make the case for such a discipline it was necessary to show that individual psychology was an insufficient approach. Adopting the core idea of mass psychology, Ribot argued that this task could easily be achieved: as soon as people became part of a crowd or large group, they changed their behaviour and developed habits that the individual did not possess. It did not matter where this change in behaviour came from, since it could be observed and thus established as fact. History showed clearly to what degree the character of a people could differ from that of the individuals it was made up of.[149] Irrespective of how this difference could be explained, since it existed as a fact, it provided folk psychology (*psychologie des peuples*) with an object of study.

Ribot accepted Lazarus and Steinthal's concept of a *Volksgeist*, (*cet esprit d'un peuple*), even though he criticized their definition of the 'objective spirit' of a people as a 'bit mystical' (*un peu mystique*). The example of language as the primary element of the *Volksgeist* convinced him, though. Ribot assumed that the *Volksgeist* represented the average population of a nation; therefore one had to ignore children, 'idiots' and 'retarded people' as well as outstanding geniuses, to study the objective spirit. The remaining average represented the objective spirit of a nation.[150] Lazarus and Steinthal had clearly defined the elements which constituted the *Volksgeist* and would form the object of study of the new discipline: next to language they listed myths, religion, customs, poetry, writing, art, but also practical life, mores, professions, family life, and the many reciprocal relations between these manifestations of the objective spirit. They had thus outlined a proper scientific history which followed the model of the natural sciences and promised to elevate the study of history to the rank of a proper scientific discipline: 'The laws of biography, i.e., the development of individual spirits, have to be established by the psychology of the individual; in the same way, the laws of history, which could be called the biography of nations, have to be established by comparative psychology, which will thus constitute a truly scientific history.'[151] Still, Ribot was well aware of the shortcomings of Lazarus and Steinthal's grandiose plans. Despite outlining a neat programme of study, and despite the twenty years of its existence, their journal had not fulfilled its promises. It had provided a useful material basis for future research, but no precise results and no general conclusions. In this respect Lazarus and Steinthal had been even more empirically minded than John Stuart Mill. Most of the contributions were of a literary, not scientific, character. Most importantly, Lazarus and Steinthal had not provided a clear methodology for their new discipline; therefore, except for collecting interesting material, they had not yet achieved anything, in contrast to British anthropologists such as Edward Tylor (1832–1917), John Lubbock (1834–1913) and John McLennan (1827–81), whose research had been ignored by the German folk psychologists.[152]

The sociologist Celestin Bouglé (1870–1940), who had been a visiting student at the University of Berlin, then worked with Emile Durkheim (1858–1917) and became professor at the Sorbonne in 1908, presented Lazarus to French readers as the founder of 'social psychology' in Germany. In a study on the contemporary social sciences in Germany, he introduced him alongside Georg Simmel, the economist Adolph Wagner (1835–1917) and the philosopher of law Rudolf von Jhering (1818–92), thus slightly overestimating the standing and influence of his former teacher.[153] Bouglé summarized the main ideas of Lazarus and Steinthal accurately and without any criticism. The remaining problems and conceptual weaknesses of their 'social psychology' were not relevant, Bouglé argued, considering the advantages the new approach offered. Lazarus had shown the way not only for psychologists, but for all social scientists eager to overcome the deficits of traditional philosophy, which remained centred on the individual.[154] Emile Durkheim was equally familiar with Lazarus and Steinthal's folk psychology, which he considered 'interesting', but was more reserved in his comments than Bouglé. Agreeing with Ribot, he complained about the lack of positive results of folk psychology. So far it was little more than a fashionable term for general linguistics and comparative philology.[155] The philosopher Henri Berr (1863–1954), the founder of the *Revue de Synthèse*, incorporated Lazarus's concept of *Verdichtung* in history in his early study on *The Future of Philosophy*: 'The mind is the product of history; history is thinking in epitome.'[156] In his major work on the 'Historical Synthesis' he was more reserved towards Lazarus and Steinthal. Echoing Ribot's judgement, Berr praised the 'intriguing intuitions' on which folk psychology rested, but complained that it consisted of disparate elements that could not be reconciled in a genuine synthesis. Equally, he considered Wundt's approach legitimate, but asked for a more 'positive' method.[157]

The social philosopher Alfred Fouillée (1838–1912) became the most famous contemporary representative of a genuine French *psychologie des peuples* around the turn of the century. Originally a specialist on Greek philosophy, he turned to the philosophy of history and the study of contemporary society, and introduced a theory of *idées-forces* as the motor of historical development and the 'glue' of society.[158] In 1898 he published a *Psychology of the French People* which made ample use of Lazarus and Steinthal's folk psychology and adopted their definition of the folk spirit, which he rendered as *l'esprit national*. According to Fouillée, the national spirit was not only an effect, but also a cause, and it was not only defined by individuals, but defined them as well.[159] Like Ribot before him, Fouillée also referred to the results of mass psychology as an aid to folk psychology. Gabriel Tarde (1843–1904), Scipio Sighele (1868–1913) and Gustave Le Bon (1841–1931) had shown, he argued, that as part of a group the individual changed its character; hence large groups, and certainly nations, could not simply be treated as an addition of individuals. Every nation, Fouillée maintained, had its own unique consciousness and its own will, but the reigning individualism in the study of politics, economics, psychology and ethics had obscured this simple fact. Just as every individual was characterized and driven by a set of *idées-forces*, every nation had a similar set of guiding ideas.[160]

Fouillée's main target, however, were not the 'individualists' who had ignored the importance of society and the nation, but the craniologists and phrenologists who tried to explain the differences between nations by studying the average form of skulls or the weight of brains.[161] Fouillée referred to the jurist and sociologist Ludwig Gumplowicz (1838–1909) and Gustave Le Bon as representatives of such an approach; his main opponent, however, was the count Georges Vacher de Lapouge (1854–1936), an outspoken racialist anti-Semite and follower of the 'Aryan myth'. To counter such ideas, which had become increasingly popular by the end of the nineteenth century, Fouillée employed a paraphrase of Lazarus's definition of the nation: that a nation could never be defined exclusively by physiological, ethnographic or economic factors; rather, 'national individuality' manifested itself through psychological forces, namely language, religion, literature and art, buildings, and the image a nation held of itself and of others. On the whole, Fouillée pleaded for a middling position in the debate about nature and nurture: He conceded that biological factors played a part in constituting a nation, but could never exhaustively explain its peculiarities. As the three 'major causes' that formed a nation, he identified its 'constitution', 'temperament' and 'mental character'.[162] In contrast to Lazarus and Steinthal, then, Fouillée put more emphasis on biological factors in defining a nation, but he ultimately and emphatically agreed with their 'voluntaristic' definition of the folk spirit.[163] Despite Fouillée's effort in outlining a balanced approach to folk psychology that would meet academic standards, his study of the mind of the French people as well as a sketch of a comparative study of the character of European nations, published in 1903, did not live up to his own methodological and epistemological principles since it offered little more than a catalogue of common national stereotypes. As such, and despite the popularity of his books, Fouillée was not able to persuade critics of the merits of folk psychology.[164]

Ernest Renan (1823–92), author of the *Life of Jesus* and an even more famous, controversial and influential French scholar, had adopted the same cornerstone of Lazarus and Steinthal's folk psychology as Fouillée, i.e., their voluntaristic and subjective definition of the nation, albeit for different reasons and in a different context. Steinthal had known Renan personally since his time in Paris, and had published a very critical review of his study on the *General Character of the Semitic Peoples* in the first volume of the *ZfVS*. Lazarus had met Renan occasionally, too.[165] In his autobiography, Lazarus claimed that Renan had copied the central points of his famous lecture 'Qu'est-ce qu'une nation?', delivered in 1882 at the Sorbonne, which soon became a work of reference for scholars of nationalism, directly from his speech 'Was heißt national?', in which Lazarus had employed ideas from folk psychology to defend the German Jews against anti-Semitic accusations.[166] One of Lazarus's students, the teacher Alfred Leicht (b. 1861), who was in charge of editing his autobiographical writings and tried to preserve the image of his teacher for posterity, even accused Renan of plagiarism because he had not referenced Lazarus's text.[167] It is certainly possible that Renan, a scholar who was very familiar with German philosophy, arts and letters, found much inspiration in Lazarus's text. But regardless of questions of intellectual property, the similarities between both texts are striking: like Lazarus, Renan rejected 'objective' definitions of the nation, from language to territory and race, as insufficient. These objective factors all played a part in the formation of nations and had to be considered by historians and philosophers, but they could not alone explain the peculiarities of a nation. In contrast to Lazarus, Renan argued that the 'national spirit' depended as much on common memory as on forgetting, an argument that recalls Nietzsche's concept of 'monumental history', developed in his essay on the uses and abuses of history. To create a strong and powerful national spirit, Renan claimed, it was not only necessary to accumulate knowledge, but also to cast aside national defeats, and expunge the memory of negative national experiences. Moreover, a nation was not a given, but had to be re-enacted constantly, a mechanism for which Renan coined the term 'daily plebiscite'. In complete agreement with Lazarus, Renan argued that the existence of a nation ultimately rested on the will of its members to form it. In addition, Lazarus's and Renan's texts were directed against the same opponents, namely German-Prussian nationalists, such as Heinrich von Treitschke, who tried to 'complete' the political unification of Germany by targeting the alleged enemies of the nation: Catholics, Socialists, Jews and national minorities. But whereas Lazarus employed his definition of the nation to defend the rights of the German Jews as German citizens, Renan used the same idea to argue against German claims to the annexed regions of Alsace and Lorraine as 'naturally' German provinces.[168]

The popularity and knowledge of Lazarus and Steinthal's folk psychology in France is striking, given their own self-centred outlook and their general ignorance of everything French. Even Steinthal, who had lived in Paris for four years and gained insight into the intellectual and academic world of the French capital, could never shake off his typically German prejudices against French philosophy and culture, which he considered shallow and formalistic. Also, there was no lack of homegrown French attempts at formulating a social psychology in the guise of mass or crowd psychology, considered alongside folk psychology as one of the precursors of modern social psychology. Mass psychology, most successfully represented by Gustave Le Bon, was based on an elitist, anti-democratic outlook that was suspicious of the 'crowd'. Le Bon compared the behaviour of the crowd to that of women, savages and children, who were all incapable of rational thinking. Mass psychology, then, was a defence of the rational, male individual against the dangers of the democratic age, and as such had little in common with the generally positive view of the folk or the nation as put forward by *Völkerpsychologie*. On a general level, French interest in German folk psychology reflected the 'German crisis of French thinking' which led to a wave of cultural transfers across the Rhine; in the case of folk psychology this exchange remained a one-sided affair.[169] The defeat in the Franco-Prussian war in 1870–71 had caused a period of intensive soul-searching on the French part, and convinced many that the military defeat was due to the superior system of higher education in Germany, especially in Prussia.[170] Hence, a number of French scholars and academics went on pilgrimages to German universities to study and learn from their alleged superiority. Amongst the French students of German academia were Emile Durkheim and Célestin Bouglé, who brought back ideas of folk psychology with them. Secondly, and in contrast to English-speaking countries, French academics and intellectuals had fewer problems translating the peculiar German terms of Lazarus and Steinthal's *Völkerpsychologie*, which helped the transfer of German ideas to France considerably. The term *Völkerpsychologie* could be rendered accurately as *psychologie des peuples* – keeping the plural of *Völker*, in contrast to the English translation 'folk psychology' – even though only Fouillée used this option. Ribot translated *Völkerpsychologie* variously as *psychologie des races* or *psychologie ethnologique*, and Bouglé preferred to speak of *psychologie sociale*. Similarly, the awkward, but crucial term *Volksgeist* could be translated into French as *esprit national*, or, more liberally, as *esprit public*. The French reception and appropriation of Lazarus and Steinthal's *Völkerpsychologie*, then, was helped by a generally positive prejudice towards German science and scholarship after the defeat of 1871, which kept the attention of French scholars focused on the other side of the Rhine, and ensured the entanglement of French and German academic cultures.[171]

A Liberal Social Science

Lazarus and Steinthal's *Völkerpsychologie* epitomized the mentality of nine-teenth-century liberals with its belief in science, progress, and the nation; these convictions were re-enforced by their experience of Jewish emancipa-tion. Folk psychology was not an early form of scientific racism, but, quite to the contrary, an attempt to define the essence of a folk or a nation without reference to reductionist biological theories.[172] Lazarus and Steinthal had always argued against simplistic racial-anthropological ideas – even though the refutation of racial theories was not their main concern – and some of their sympathetic readers, such as Alfred Fouillée or W.I. Thomas, explicitly employed folk psychology to reject such scientific racism. More importantly, Lazarus and Steinthal's folk psychology contributed to the formation of the social sciences in the late nineteenth century, even though they were not able to establish their new discipline in any institutionalized form. Still, *Völkerpsychologie* had an important, but more inconspicuous impact on the emerging social sciences. Central aspects of the works of Georg Simmel and Franz Boas, for instance, both instrumental in establishing sociology and cultural anthropology respectively, were inspired by their reading of folk psy-chology. Lazarus and Steinthal's folk psychology was part of a larger debate surrounding the study of man as a social being that underscored the emer-gence of the social sciences. One of the first attempts at formulating a coher-ent social psychology, by the Austrian educationalist Gustav Lindner, was itself a critical reply to Lazarus and Steinthal's *Völkerpsychologie*; none of the more famous pioneers of the social sciences, from Simmel to Durkheim to Max Weber, could afford to ignore folk psychology. Moreover, Lazarus and Steinthal themselves, while sketching the programme for a future folk psy-chology, suggested a definition of the nation that might have inspired Ernest Renan's famous text on the same subject, pre-dating by more than a century the constructivist idea of nations as 'imagined communities' or 'invented traditions', as popularized in the 1980s.[173]

Lazarus and Steinthal's folk psychology thus provided a link between the philosophy of Herbart, Humboldt and Hegel and the pioneers of the social sciences in the early twentieth century. It was started as an attempt to provide an alternative to both historicism and philosophical idealism, but kept much of the Romantic terminology of the early nineteenth century – most importantly the concept of the *Volksgeist* – as well as an uncritical belief in the Volk as the source of everything that was good, true, and beautiful. Hence Lazarus and Steinthal contributed to 'cultural sociology' or 'cultural philosophy' only in an indirect way; their writings pre-dated the inflationary use of the term 'culture' by several decades.[174] Even though they dismissed much of what had been written on nations and their characters as philosophical speculation, political journalism and metaphysics, and prided themselves on their allegedly scientific approach to the study of the *Volksgeist*, their *Völkerpsychologie* was value-laden and partisan. This did not strike Lazarus and Steinthal as problematic since they never doubted the moral value of the folk or nation, and indeed celebrated it as the prerequisite of all culture and civilization. Their belief in universal progress was as strong as their admiration of the success of sciences. Folk psychology did not only study the folk spirit, but was intended to contribute to its progress. Thus, in the view of its founders, the repackaging of the central ideas of folk psychology to counter anti-Semitism did not pose a problem, but simply reconfirmed the usefulness and legitimacy of their approach. Neither was Lazarus's work on the *Ethics of Judaism*, in his view, a distraction from *Völkerpsychologie*; rather, it was a study of the essence of the Jewish spirit and as such his major contribution to folk psychology. With this reformulation of the basic idea of folk psychology, however, Lazarus and Steinthal ran into trouble, since they denied that the Jews constituted a nation of their own while at the same time they stressed the importance of the Jewish folk spirit.

Notes

1. M. Lazarus, 'Über den Begriff und die Möglichkeit einer Völkerpsychologie', in *Deutsches Museum. Zeitschrift für Literatur, Kunst und öffentliches Leben* 1(1851), pp. 112–26; M. Lazarus and H. Steinthal, 'Einleitende Gedanken über Völkerpsychologie, als Einladung zu einer Zeitschrift für Völkerpsychologie und Sprachwissenschaft', in *ZfVS* 1(1860), pp. 1–73.
2. See in particular U. Jensen, *Gebildete Doppelgänger: Bürgerliche Juden und Protestanten im 19. Jahrhundert* (Göttingen, 2005).
3. On Lazarus and Steinthal see I. Belke, ed., *Moritz Lazarus und Heymann Steinthal: Die Begründer der Völkerpsychologie in ihren Briefen*, 3 vols (Tübingen, 1971–1986); M. Bunzl, '*Völkerpsychologie* and German-Jewish emancipation', in H.G. Penny and M. Bunzl, eds, *Worldly Provincialism: German Anthropology in the Age of Empire* (Ann Arbor, MI, 2003), pp. 47–85; G. von Graevenitz, '"Verdichtung". Das Kulturmodell der "Zeitschrift für Völkerpsychologie und

Sprachwissenschaft"', in A. Assmann, ed. *Positionen der Kulturanthropologie* (Frankfurt am Main, 1994), pp. 148–71; I. Kalmar, 'The Volkerpsychologie of Lazarus and Steinthal and the Modern Concept of Culture', in *Journal of the History of Ideas* 48(1987), pp. 671–90; C. Köhnke, 'Der Kulturbegriff von Moritz Lazarus – oder: die wissenschaftliche Aneignung des Alltäglichen', in A. Höschen and L. Schneider, eds, *Herbarts Kultursystem: Perspektiven der Transdisziplinarität im 19. Jahrhundert* (Würzburg, 2001), pp. 39–67; C. Köhnke, 'Einleitung' in M. Lazarus, *Grundzüge der Völkerpsychologie und Kulturwissenschaft*, ed. C. Köhnke (Hamburg, 2003), pp. ix–xlii; C. Mehr, *Kultur als Naturgeschichte: Opposition oder Komplementarität zur politischen Geschichtsschreibung?* (Berlin, 2009), pp. 88–97; C. Trautmann-Waller, *Aux origines d'une science allemande de la culture: linguistique et psychologie des peuples chez Heymann Steinthal* (Paris, 2006).

4.   They both Germanized their first names: Lazarus from Moses to Moritz, Steinthal from Chajim to Heymann, sometimes also Heinemann, Hermann or Heinrich. On publications, Lazarus never spelled out his first name.

5.   Belke, 'Einleitung', in Belke, ed., *Lazarus*, vol. 1, pp. xiv–xv, lxxxii. On Lazarus's biography see N. Lazarus and A. Leicht, eds, *Moritz Lazarus' Lebenserinnerungen* (Berlin, 1906); M. Lazarus, *Aus meiner Jugend*, ed. N. Lazarus (Frankfurt am Main, 1913); N. Lazarus, *Ein deutscher Professor in der Schweiz. Mit Briefen und Dokumenten im Nachlaß ihres Gatten* (Berlin, n.d.); Jensen, *Gebildete Doppelgänger*.

6.   G. Scholem, 'Juden und Deutsche', in Scholem, Judaica II (Frankfurt am Main, 1970), pp. 20–46, at p. 32; Belke, 'Einleitung', in Belke, ed., *Lazarus*, vol. 1, p. xxvii.

7.   Ibid., p. xxiii.

8.   See Lazarus's letter to his brother Leiser, 13 May 1847, in Belke, ed., *Lazarus*, vol. 1, pp. 25–31.

9.   Belke, 'Einleitung', in Belke, ed., Lazarus, vol. 1, pp. xvi–xv; See J.F. Herbart, *Psychologie als Wissenschaft, neu gegründet auf Erfahrung, Metaphysik und Mathematik*, 2 vols (Königsberg, 1824–25); J.F. Herbart, *Lehrbuch zur Einleitung in die Philosophie*, third edition (Königsberg, 1834). Neither Lazarus nor Steinthal had studied with Herbart, who never taught at the University of Berlin, cf. S. Shamdasani, *Jung and the Making of Modern Psychology: The Dream of a Science* (Cambridge, 2003), p. 279.

10. On the school of Herbartianism and its impact see A. Hoeschen and L. Schneider, eds, *Herbarts Kultursystem: Perspektiven der Transdisziplinarität im 19. Jahrhundert* (Würzburg, 2001); A. Hoeschen and L. Schneider, 'Herbartianismus im 19. Jahrhundert: Umriß einer intellektuellen Konfiguration', in L. Raphael, ed., *Ideen als gesellschaftliche Gestaltungskraft im Europa der Neuzeit: Beiträge für eine erneuerte Geistesgeschichte* (Munich, 2006), pp. 447–77; C.G. Allesch, 'Johann Friedrich Herbart als Wegbereiter der Kulturpsychologie', in Hoeschen and Schneider, eds, *Herbarts Kultursystem*, pp. 51–67; G. Jahoda, 'Johann Friedrich Herbart: *Urvater* of Social Psychology', in *History of the Human Sciences* 19(2006), pp. 19–38; C. Sganzini, *Die Fortschritte der Völkerpsychologie von Lazarus bis Wundt* (Berne, 1913), p. 30.

11. Lazarus and Steinthal, 'Einleitende Gedanken', p. 7; Belke, 'Einleitung', in Belke, ed., *Lazarus*, vol. 1, pp. l–li.

12. Ibid., p. xix; F.E. Beneke, *Lehrbuch der Psychologie als Naturwissenschaft* (Berlin 1833). On Beneke see V. Gerhardt, R. Mehring and J. Rindert, *Berliner Geist: Eine Geschichte der Berliner Universitätsphilosophie* (Berlin, 1999), pp. 62–63, 160–61.

13. See Belke, 'Einleitung', in Belke, ed., *Lazarus*, vol. 1, p. xx; Lazarus to Krüger, 14 Dec. 1846, in Belke, ed., *Lazarus*, vol. 1, p. 23; M. Lazarus, 'Mathematische Psychologie', in *Cottas Morgenblatt für gebildete Leser*, 1855, pp. 481–86, 513–19.

14. M. Lazarus, *De educatione aesthetica*, Ph.D. dissertation (Halle, 1849). Lazarus took his exam at the University of Halle because it charged lower fees than the University of Berlin.

15. See T. Fontane, *Von Zwanzig bis Dreißig. Autobiographisches* [1898] (Munich, 1973), pp. 149–60; see A. Rössig, *Juden und andere Tunnelianer: Gesellschaft und Literatur im Berliner Sonntags-Verein* (Heidelberg, 2008).

16. Lazarus and Leicht, *Moritz Lazarus' Lebenserinnerungen*, pp. 1–104.

17. Lazarus told his friend Paul Heyse, who had become a celebrated writer, winning the Nobel Prize in Literature in 1910, that he had used two excerpts from his novel *In Paradise* (*Im Paradiese*) in a lecture on folk psychology: 'My colleagues would be genuinely surprised if they could hear how I feed the future masters of future knowledge with wisdom from the well of dubious novels.' Lazarus to Paul Heyse, 18 November 1875, in Belke, ed., *Lazarus*, vol. 1, p. 135.

18. Lazarus and Leicht, *Moritz Lazarus' Lebenserinnerungen*, p. 179.

19. M. Lazarus, *Die sittliche Berechtigung Preußens in Deutschland* (Berlin, 1850). See A. Leicht, *Lazarus, der Begründer der Völkerpsychologie* (Leipzig, 1911), p. 8; J. Toury, *Die politischen Orientierungen der Juden in Deutschland: von Jena bis Weimar* (Tübingen, 1966), p. 78.

20. M. Lazarus, *Das Leben der Seele in Monographien über seine Erscheinungen und Gesetze*, 2 vols (Berlin, 1856–57). Even an extended study on 'Geist und Sprache', which made up most of the second volume of *Das Leben der Seele* (pp. 3–258), did not deal with folk psychology, as Lazarus reminded his readers; see ibid., vol. 2, p. 22.

21. Belke, 'Einleitung', in Belke, ed., *Lazarus*, vol. 1, pp. xxvi–xxvii; N. Lazarus, *Ein deutscher Professor*.

22. Lazarus to Otto Ribbeck, 27 June 1871, in Belke, ed., *Lazarus*, vol. 1, p. 120.

23. Gerhardt, Mehring and Rindert, *Berliner Geist*, pp. 139–40.

24. Belke, 'Einleitung', in Belke, ed., *Lazarus*, vol. 1, p. xl; Lazarus to Eduard Rese, 20 May 1873, in Belke, ed., *Lazarus*, vol. 1, p. 124; Lazarus to Paul Heyse, 9 November 1873, in ibid., pp. 127–28; Lazarus to Eduard Rese, 7 December 1873, in ibid., p. 128.

25. Belke, 'Einleitung', in Belke, ed., *Lazarus*, vol. 1, p. xl; U. Sieg, 'Der Preis des Bildungsstrebens. Jüdische Geisteswissenschaftler im Kaiserreich', in A. Gotzmann, R. Liedtke and T. van Rahden, eds, *Juden, Bürger, Deutsche: Zur*

Geschichte von Vielfalt und Differenz 1800–1933 (Tübingen, 2001), pp. 67–96, at p. 74.

26. Steinthal had married Lazarus's younger sister Jeanette in 1859; Lazarus had treated Steinthal well before this date like a family member, and had supported him financially. Belke, 'Einleitung', in Belke, ed., *Lazarus*, vol. 1, pp. xxiii–xxv.

27. Belke, 'Einleitung', in Belke, *Lazarus*, vol. 2.2, pp. xvi–xvii. In 1856 Steinthal edited and published posthumously Heyse's 'System of Linguistics', see C.W.L. Heyse, *System der Sprachwissenschaft. Nach dessen Tod herausgegeben von H. Steinthal*, ed. H. Steinthal (Berlin, 1856).

28. H. Steinthal, *De pronomine relativo commentatio philosophico-philologica, cum excursu de nominativi particula*, Ph.D. dissertation (Tübingen, 1847). Similar to Lazarus, Steinthal chose the University of Tübingen because of the lower examination fees. He was actually awarded the Ph.D. in absentia.

29. H. Steinthal, *Die Sprachwissenschaft Wilhelm von Humboldts und die Hegel'sche Philosophie* (Berlin, 1848).

30. Trautmann-Waller, *Aux origines*, p. 8–17, passim; Belke, 'Einleitung', in Belke, ed., *Lazarus*, vol. 1, pp. lxxxv–lxxxvii; W. Bumann, *Die Sprachtheorie Heymann Steinthals: Dargestellt im Zusammenhang mit seiner Theorie der Geisteswissenschaft* (Meisenheim am Glan, 1966).

31. H. Steinthal, *Die Classification der Sprachen, dargestellt als die Entwickelung der Sprachidee* (Berlin, 1850); H. Steinthal, *Der Ursprung der Sprache, im Zusammenhange mit den letzten Fragen alles Wissens. Eine Darstellung der Ansicht Wilhelm von Humboldts, verglichen mit denen Herders und Hamanns* (Berlin, 1851); H. Steinthal, *Die Wurzeln der verschiedenen chinesischen Dialekte* (Berlin, 1854); H. Steinthal, *Grammatik, Logik und Psychologie, ihre Prinzipien und ihr Verhältnis zueinander* (Berlin, 1855); H. Steinthal, *Geschichte der Sprachwissenschaft bei den Griechen und Römern mit besonderer Rücksicht auf die Logik*, 2 vols (Berlin, 1863); H. Steinthal, *Die Mande-Neger-Sprachen. Psychologisch und phonetisch betrachtet* (Berlin, 1867).

32. Belke, 'Einleitung', in Belke, ed., *Lazarus*, vol. 1, pp. xcv–xcviii; see Lazarus to Steinthal, 21 December 1855, in Belke, ed., *Lazarus*, vol. 1, p. 93; Steinthal to Lazarus, 11 December 1855, in Belke, ed., *Lazarus*, vol. 1, p. 286.

33. H. Steinthal, *Die Entwicklung der Schrift, nebst einem offenen Sendschreiben an Herrn Professor Pott* (Berlin 1852), pp. 3–5; see Belke, 'Einleitung', in Belke, ed., *Lazarus*, vol. 2.2, p. xlii.

34. Steinthal, *Der Ursprung der Sprache*, pp. 61–84; Steinthal, *Grammatik, Logik und Psychologie*, pp. 387–91; H. Steinthal, ed., *Die sprachphilosophischen Werke Wilhelm von Humboldts* (Berlin, 1884).

35. H. Steinthal, *Philologie, Geschichte und Psychologie in ihren gegenseitigen Beziehungen. Ein Vortrag gehalten in der Versammlung der Philologen zu Meissen 1863* (Berlin, 1864), p. 45; see M. Lazarus, 'Verdichtung des Denkens in der Geschichte. Ein Fragment', in *ZfVS* 2(1862), pp. 54–62, at p. 57.

36. Lazarus, 'Verdichtung des Denkens in der Geschichte'; M. Lazarus, 'Über das Verhältniß des Einzelnen zur Gesammtheit', in *ZfVS* 2(1862), pp. 393–453; M. Lazarus, 'Einige synthetische Gedanken zur Völkerpsychologie', in *ZfVS* 3(1865), pp. 1–94.

37. Lazarus and Steinthal, 'Einleitende Gedanken', pp. 11–13.
38. Ibid., p. 15.
39. Ibid., pp. 17–18: 'Die gesetzmäßig gleichbleibende Thätigkeit des Geistes also ist Entwickelung, und der Fortschritt gehört so sehr zur Natur des Geistes, daß eben deshalb der Geist nicht zur Natur gehört.'
40. Ibid., p. 16.
41. Lazarus, 'Über den Begriff und die Möglichkeit', p. 121; see Sganzini, *Fortschritte*, pp. 33–34.
42. Lazarus, 'Über den Begriff und die Möglichkeit', pp. 121–22: 'Der Geist, im höheren und wahren Sinne des Wortes ist eben: die gesetzmäßige Bewegung und Entwicklung der inneren Tätigkeit.' See H.B. Schmid, '"Volksgeist." Individuum und Kollektiv bei Moritz Lazarus (1824–1903)' in *Dialektik. Zeitschrift für Kulturphilosophie* 16(2005), pp. 157–70.
43. H. Steinthal, *Grammatik, Logik, und Psychologie: Ihre Principien und ihr Verhältnis zu einander* (Berlin, 1855), p. 388.
44. Lazarus and Steinthal, 'Einleitende Gedanken', pp. 27–28.
45. Ibid., p. 31; Lazarus, 'Verdichtung des Denkens in der Geschichte', p. 57; Lazarus, 'Verhältniß des Einzelnen zur Gesammtheit'; see B. Weiler, *Die Ordnung des Fortschritts: Zum Aufstieg und Fall der Fortschrittsidee der 'jungen' Anthropologie* (Bielefeld, 2006), pp. 183–90.
46. Lazarus, 'Verdichtung des Denkens in der Geschichte', p. 54: 'sie geschieht, indem Begriffe und Begriffsreihen, welche in früheren Zeiten von den begabtesten Geistern entdeckt, von wenigen kaum erfaßt und verstanden, doch allmählich zum ganz gewöhnlichen Gemeingut ganzer Classen, ja der gesamten Masse des Volkes werden können.'
47. Lazarus and Steinthal, 'Einleitende Gedanken', p. 30: 'Mit der Sprache hängen dann die logischen Formen des Denken aufs Innigste zusammen, und Jeder, dem das Wesen der Sprache im wahren Lichte erscheint, wird erkennen, daß grundverschiedene Redeformen nur die Erscheinung grundverschiedener Denkformen sind.' For a follower of this widely held idea see F. Stehlich, *Die Sprache in ihrer Beziehung zum Nationalcharakter* (Berlin, 1882).
48. Lazarus and Steinthal, 'Einleitende Gedanken', pp. 28–29.
49. Ibid, pp. 5–6.
50. Ibid., pp. 32–36.
51. Ibid., pp. 63, 65–66.
52. Ibid., p. 66: 'Diese Zeit herbeizuführen wird eine wissenschaftlich strenge psychologische Betrachtung des deutschen Nationallebens und seiner Geschichte gewiß nicht wenig beitragen.'
53. Ibid., pp. 67–68.
54. See for instance G. Jahoda, *A History of Social Psychology from the Eighteenth-Century Enlightenment to the End of the Second World War* (Cambridge, 2007), pp. 121–37.
55. For a folk psychologist, Steinthal was surprisingly ignorant of Chinese history and culture: 'Was zunächst den Inhalt der Literatur betrifft, so ist dieser für die allgemeine Geschichte von geringem Interesse. Was gehen uns die Chinesen an? Und sie sind zu wenig mit den geschichtlichen Völkern in Berührung gekom-

men, als daß wir von ihnen viel anderes lernen als chinesische Geschichte.' Steinthal to Lazarus, 11 December 1855, in Belke, ed., Lazarus, vol. 1, p. 288. See Bunzl, '*Völkerpsychologie* and German-Jewish Emancipation', p. 79.

56. Lazarus's speeches at the synods are reprinted in M. Lazarus, *Treu und Frei, Gesammelte Reden und Vorträge über Juden und Judenthum* (Leipzig, 1887), pp. 1–53.

57. M.A. Meyer, *Response to Modernity: A History of the Reform Movement in Judaism* (Detroit, MI, 1995), pp. 189–91.

58. Lazarus to Paul Heyse, 23 December 1879, in Belke, ed. *Lazarus*, vol. 1, p. 151.

59. M. Lazarus, 'Was heißt national? [1880]', in Lazarus, *Treu und Frei*. pp. 53–113.

60. H. von Treitschke, 'Unsere Aussichten [1879]', in W. Boehlich, ed., *Der Berliner Antisemitismusstreit* (Frankfurt am Main, 1965), pp. 5–12.

61. Ibid., pp. 8–9.

62. Ibid., p. 11.

63. Lazarus, 'Was heißt national?', pp. 64–65; see Lazarus and Steinthal, 'Einleitende Gedanken', pp. 34–35.

64. Lazarus, 'Was heißt national?', p. 70.

65. On the concept of *Stamm* in the context of the debate about anti-semitism see T. von Rahden, 'Germans of the Jewish *Stamm*: Visions of Community between Nationalism and Particularism, 1850 to 1933', in N. Gregor, N. Roemer and M. Roseman, eds, *German History from the Margins* (Bloomington, IN, 2006), pp. 27–48; Jensen, *Gebildete Doppelgänger*, pp. 232–33.

66. Lazarus, 'Was heißt national?', pp. 90–91.

67. Ibid., p. 95.

68. Ibid., pp. 91, 93.

69. H. von Treitschke, 'Noch einige Bemerkungen zur Judenfrage [1880]', in Boehlich, ed., *Der Berliner Antisemitismusstreit*, pp. 77–90, at pp. 86–87.

70. U. Sieg, *Aufstieg und Niedergang des Marburger Neukantianismus. Die Geschichte einer philosophischen Schulgemeinschaft* (Würzburg, 1994), pp. 108–10; C. Köhnke, '"Unser junger Freund" – Hermann Cohen und die Völkerpsychologie', in W. Marx and E.W. Orth, eds, *Hermann Cohen und die Erkenntnistheorie* (Würzburg, 2001), pp. 62–77; U. Sieg, 'Der frühe Hermann Cohen und die Völkerpsychologie', in *Aschkenas* 13(2003), pp. 461–83.

71. H. Cohen, 'Ein Bekenntnis in der Judenfrage [1880]', in Boehlich, ed., *Berliner Antisemitismusstreit*, pp. 124–49, at pp. 136–37, 139: 'Ein nationales Doppelgefühl ist nicht nur ein unsittlich Ding, sondern ein Unding.'

72. See also M. Lazarus, 'Unser Standpunkt. Zwei Reden an seine Religionsgenossen am 1. und 16. Dezember 1880', in M. Lazarus, *Treu und Frei*, pp. 115–55.

73. M. Lazarus, *Die Ethik des Judenthums*, vol. 1 (Frankfurt am Main, 1898).

74. P.E. Rosenblüth, 'Die geistigen und religiösen Strömungen in der deutschen Judenheit', in W.E. Mosse and A. Paucker, eds, *Juden im Wilhelminischen Deutschland, 1890–1914*, second edition (Tübingen, 1998), pp. 549–98, at pp. 569–72; D. Baumgardt, 'The Ethics of Lazarus and Steinthal', in *Yearbook of the Leo Baeck Institute* 2(1957), pp. 205–17.

75. Rosenblüth, 'Die geistigen und religiösen Strömungen', p. 573.

76. Jensen, *Gebildete Doppelgänger*, p. 88. Hermann Cohen was among the outspoken critics of Lazarus's *Ethik des Judentums*; his discussion of this book destroyed their relationship beyond repair. See H. Cohen, 'Das Problem der jüdischen Sittenlehre: Eine Kritik von Lazarus' Ethik des Judentums [1899]', in H. Cohen, *Jüdische Schriften*, vol. 3 (Berlin, 1924), pp. 1–35.

77. H. Steinthal, 'Judentum und Patriotismus [1892]', in H. Steinthal, *Über Juden und Judentum. Vorträge und Aufsätze*, ed. G. Karpeles (Berlin, 1906), pp. 67–70, at p. 69.

78. Lazarus to the faculty of the Hebrew Union College, Cincinnati, 7 May 1895, in Belke, ed., *Lazarus*, vol. 1, p. 205.

79. Lazarus, *Aus meiner Jugend*, p. 32; see Köhnke, 'Einleitung', p. xxiii.

80. Belke, ed., *Lazarus*, vol. 1, p. 227.

81. H. Steinthal, 'Herrn Prof. Dr. M. Lazarus zu seinem fünfundzwanzigjährigem Doktorjubiläum am 30. November 1874', in H. Steinthal, *Über Juden und Judentum*, pp. 238–42, at p. 239.

82. H. Steinthal, *Allgemeine Ethik* (Berlin, 1885).

83. Ibid., p. 424.

84. L. Tobler, 'Ueber die dichterische Behandlung der Thiere', in *ZfVS* 2(1862), pp. 211–24; L. Tobler, 'Uebergang zwischen Tempus und Modus', in *ZfVS* 2(1862), pp. 29–53; L. Tobler, 'Das Wort in der Geschichte der Religion', in *ZfVS* 3(1865), pp. 257–66; L. Tobler, 'Ueber die psychologische Bedeutung der Wortzusammensetzung, mit Bezug auf nationale Charakteristik der Sprachen', in *ZfVS* 5(1868), pp. 205–31.

85. B. Delbrück, 'Die Entstehung des Mythos bei den indogermanischen Völkern', in *ZfVS* 3(1865), pp. 266–99; B. Delbrück, 'Über das Verhältnis zwischen Religion und Mythologie', in *ZfVS* 3 (1865), pp. 487–97.

86. A. Tobler, 'Ueber das volkthümliche Epos der Franzosen', in *ZfVS* 4(1866), pp. 139–210.

87. G. von der Gabelentz, 'Ideen zu einer vergleichenden Syntax', in *ZfVS* 6(1869), pp. 376–84.

88. R. Boeckh, 'Die statistische Bedeutung der Volkssprache als Kennzeichen der Nationalität', in *ZfVS* 4(1866), pp. 259–402. See S. Weichlein, '"Qu'est-ce qu'une Nation?" Stationen der deutschen statistischen Debatte um Nation und Nationalität in der Reichsgründungszeit' in W. von Kieseritzky and K.P. Sick, eds, *Demokratie in Deutschland: Chancen und Gefährdungen im 19. und 20. Jahrhundert. Historische Essays* (Munich, 1999), pp. 71–90.

89. A. Bastian, 'Zur vergleichenden Psychologie', in *ZfVS* 5(1868), pp. 153–80; A. Bastian, 'Der Baum in vergleichender Ethnologie', in *ZfVS* 5(1868), pp. 287–316. See M. Fischer, P. Bolz and S. Kamel, eds, *Adolf Bastian and his Universal Archive of Humanity. The Origins of German Anthropology* (Hildesheim and New York, 2007). Sgnazini, *Fortschritte*, p. 69, counted Bastian amongst the 'folk psychologists'.

90. W. Windelband, 'Die Erkenntnislehre unter dem völkerpsychologischen Gesichtspunkte', in *ZfVS* 8(1875), pp. 166–78.

91. Sieg, *Aufstieg und Niedergang*, pp. 108–10; H. Liebeschütz, *Von Georg Simmel zu Franz Rosenzweig. Studien zum jüdischen Denken im deutschen Kulturbereich*

(Tübingen, 1970); H. Cohen, 'Die platonische Ideenlehre psychologisch entwickelt', in *ZfVS* 4(1866), pp. 403–64; H. Cohen, 'Mythologische Vorstellungen von Gott und Seele', in *ZfVS* 5(1868), pp. 396–434, and 6(1869), pp. 113–31; H. Cohen, 'Die dichterische Phantasie und der Mechanismus des Bewußtseins', in *ZfVS* 6(1869), pp. 171–263.

92. Köhnke, '"Unser junger Freund"'; Sieg, 'Der frühe Hermann Cohen'.

93. W. Dilthey, 'Zur Kritik der Völkerpsychologie von Lazarus und Steinthal', in Dilthey, *Psychologie als Erfahrungswissenschaft, zweiter Teil: Manuskripte zur Genese der deskriptiven Psychologie*, eds G. van Kerckhoven and H.-U. Lessing (Gesammelte Schriften 22) (Göttingen, 2005), pp. 1–6. This harsh review of Lazarus and Steinthal's folk psychology remained unfinished and unpublished. See Dilthey's letters to his father (1863) in C. Misch, ed., *Der junge Dilthey. Ein Lebensbild in Briefen und Tagebüchern, 1852–1870*, (Leipzig and Berlin, 1933), pp. 180–81.

94. W. Dilthey, 'Über die Einbildungskraft der Dichter, mit Rücksicht auf Herman Grimm, Goethe, Vorlesungen, 2 Bde., Berlin 1877', in *ZfVS* 10(1878), pp. 42–104.

95. L. Noack, 'Die Idee der Völkerpsychologie', in *Psyche. Zeitschrift für die Kenntnis des Seelen- und Geisteslebens* 2, 1(1859), pp. 161–65: 'Wo ein Unternehmen in solchem Geist begonnen wird, kann ein glücklicher Erfolg nicht fehlen.' See also Anon., 'Zur Völkerpsychologie und Sprachwissenschaft', in *Blätter für literarische Bildung* 1(1861), p. 355; L. Schweiger, *Philosophie der Geschichte, Völkerpsychologie und Soziologie in ihren gegenseitigen Wechselbeziehungen* (Bern, 1899), pp. 65–78.

96. L. Tobler, 'Zeitschrift for Völkerpsychologie und Sprachwissenschaft', in *Neue Jahrbücher für Philologie und Pädagogik* 83(1861), pp. 257–80, at pp. 260–61.

97. E. von Hartmann, 'Das Wesen des Gesammtgeistes. (Eine kritische Betrachtung des Grundbegriffes der Völkerpsychologie) [1869]', in E. von Hartmann, *Gesammelte Studien und Aufsätze gemeinverständlichen Inhalts* (Berlin, 1876), pp. 504–19.

98. P. Barth, *Die Philosophie der Geschichte als Sociologie. Erster Teil: Einleitung und kritische Übersicht* (Leipzig, 1897), pp. 276–78.

99. [A.] Lasson, 'Review of Zeitschrift für Völkerpsychologie und Sprachwissenschaft', in *Archiv für das Studium der Neueren Sprachen und Literaturen* 27(1860), pp. 209–16. On Lasson see Jensen, *Gebildete Doppelgänger*, pp. 292–94, 300–304.

100. J. Frauenstädt, *Blicke in die intellectuelle, physische und moralische Welt nebst Beiträgen zur Lebensphilosophie* (Leipzig, 1869), pp. 241–43.

101. A. Janik and S. Toulmin, *Wittgenstein's Vienna*, second edition (Chicago, 1996), pp. 126–27.

102. M. Nordau, *Der Sinn der Geschichte* (Berlin, 1909), p. 138. See P. Zudrell, *Der Schriftsteller und Kulturkritiker Max Nordau. Zwischen Zionismus, Deutschtum und Judentum* (Würzburg, 2003), p. 39.

103. Nordau, *Der Sinn der Geschichte*, pp. 140, 146.

104. H. Paul, *Prinzipien der Sprachgeschichte*, fourth edition (Halle an der Saale, 1909), pp. 8–15.

105. Ibid., p. 11: 'Alle psychischen Prozesse vollziehen sich in den Einzelgeistern und nirgends sonst. Weder Volksgeist noch Elemente des Volksgeistes wie Kunst, Religion etc. haben eine konkrete Existenz, und folglich kann auch nichts in ihnen oder zwischen ihnen vorgehen. Daher weg mit diesen Abstraktionen.'

106. Ibid., p. 13.

107. W. Wundt, *Erlebtes und Erkanntes* (Stuttgart, 1920), pp. 199–201.

108. W. Wundt, 'Ziele und Wege der Völkerpsychologie [1886]', in Wundt, *Probleme der Völkerpsychologie* (Leipzig, 1911), pp. 1–35.

109. Wundt, 'Ziele und Wege', p. 2–3.

110. On Wundt's folk psychology see the following chapter.

111. H. Steinthal, 'Begriff der Völkerpsychologie', in *ZfVS* 17(1887), pp. 223–64.

112. Ibid., pp. 242–43.

113. Ibid., p. 246.

114. See R.M. Farr, *The Roots of Modern Social Psychology, 1872–1954* (Oxford, 1992); G. Jahoda, *Crossroads between Culture and Mind: Continuities and Change in Theories of Human Nature* (Cambridge, MA, 1992); S. Moscovici and I. Marková, *The Making of Modern Social Psychology: The Hidden History of How an International Social Science was Created* (Cambridge, 2006).

115. See E. Jones, *The Life and Work of Sigmund Freud*, vol. 1 (London, 1953), p. 409–10; W.W. Hemecker, *Vor Freud. Philosophiegeschichtliche Voraussetzungen der Psychoanalyse* (Munich, 1991), pp. 108–28; P.-A. Alt, *Franz Kafka: Der ewige Sohn* (Munich, 2005), p. 79. For a contemporary, largely positive appreciation of both Lazarus and Steinthal's folk psychology and Lindner's social psychology see A. Bachmann, 'Einiges über die bisherige Entwicklung der Völkerpsychologie und deren Verhältnis zur Geschichte', in F. Dworzak, *Erster Jahresbericht des Staats-Unterrealgymnasiums in Arnau* (Arnau, 1873), pp. 5–34.

116. See the entry on Lindner in *Allgemeine Deutsche Biographie: Nachträge bis 1899*, vol. 51 (Berlin, 1906), pp. 738–39; G. Jahoda, *History of Social Psychology*, pp. 59–62; On Franz Exner see D. Coen, *Vienna in the Age of Uncertainty. Science, Liberalism and Private Life* (Chicago and London, 2007), pp. 33–63.

117. G. Lindner, *Das Problem des Glücks. Psychologische Untersuchungen über die menschliche Glückseligkeit* (Vienna, 1868); G. Lindner, *Ideen zur Psychologie der Gesellschaft als Grundlage der Sozialwissenschaft* (Vienna, 1871). See Jahoda, *History of Social Psychology*, pp. 59–61, and Allesch, 'Johann Friedrich Herbart', p. 62.

118. Lindner, *Ideen*, pp. 5, 8, 12–14.

119. Ibid., p. 15, 'Das Volksthum oder die Nationalität erscheint allerdings als Ausdruck der intensivsten Verdichtung der geistigen Wechselbeziehungen in einer Mehrheit von Menschen.'

120. Ibid., p. 22.

121. Ibid., p. 23.

122. W. Lepenies, *Die drei Kulturen: Soziologie zwischen Literatur und Wissenschaft* (Frankfurt am Main, 2002), pp. 290–95.

123. G. Simmel, 'Psychologische und ethnologische Studien über Musik', in *ZfVS* 13(1882), pp. 261–305. On Simmel's biography see C. Köhnke, *Der junge*

Simmel in Theoriebeziehungen und sozialen Bewegungen (Frankfurt am Main, 1996), pp. 30, 51–62.

124. G. Simmel, 'Die Großstädte und das Geistesleben [1903]', in G. Simmel, *Aufsätze und Abhandlungen 1901–1908*, vol. 1, eds R. Kramme, A. Rammstedt and O. Rammstedt (Frankfurt am Main, 1995), pp. 116–31.

125. Ibid., p. 129.

126. G. Simmel, 'Über sociale Differenzierung. Sociologische und psychologische Untersuchungen [1890]', in G. Simmel, *Aufsätze 1887 bis 1890. Über sociale Differenzierung. Die Probleme der Geschichtsphilosophie*, ed. H.-J. Dahme (Frankfurt am Main, 1989), pp. 109–295.

127. Simmel, 'Die Großstädte', pp. 129–30.

128. Simmel, 'Über sociale Differenzierung', p. 125.

129. G. Simmel, 'Der Krieg und die geistigen Entscheidungen. Reden und Aufsätze [1917]', in G. Simmel, *Der Krieg und die geistigen Entscheidungen. Grundfragen der Soziologie. Vom Wesen des historischen Verstehen. Der Konflikt der modernen Kultur. Lebensanschauung*, eds G. Fitzi and O. Rammstedt (Frankfurt-on-Main, 1999), pp. 7–58; P. Watier, 'The War Writings of Georg Simmel', in *Theory, Culture, Society* 8(1991), pp. 219–33.

130. D. Frisby, *Simmel and Since: Essays on Georg Simmel's Social Theory* (London and New York, 1992), pp. 28–29; H.-J. Dahme and O. Rammstedt, 'Einleitung', in G. Simmel, *Schriften zur Soziologie. Eine Auswahl*, eds H.-J. Dahme and O. Rammstedt (Frankfurt am Main, 1995), pp. 7–34. On 'cultural pessimism' of the German *fin de siècle* see F. Stern, *The Politics of Cultural Despair: A Study in the Rise of the Germanic Ideology* [1961] (Berkeley, Los Angeles and London, 1974).

131. M.M. Bakhtin, *Speech Genres and other late Essays*, eds. C. Emerson and M. Holquist (Austin, TX, 1986).

132. A. Hoeschen, 'Anamnesis als ästhetische Rekonfiguration. Zu Bachtins dialogischer Erinnnerungskultur', in G. Oesterle, ed., *Erinnerung, Gedächtnis, Wissen. Studien zur kulturwissenschaftlichen Gedächtnisforschung* (Göttingen, 2001), pp. 246–48; C. Brandist, 'The Rise of Soviet Sociolinguistics from the Ashes of *Völkerpsychologie*', in *Journal of the History of the Behavioral Sciences* 42(2006), pp. 261–77. Even in Japan, German *Völkerpsychologie* found its readers and followers: see R. Reitan, '*Völkerpsychologie* and the Appropriation of "Spirit" in Meiji Japan', in *Modern Intellectual History* 7(2010), pp. 495–522.

133. W.I. Thomas, 'The Scope and Method of Folk-Psychology', in *American Journal of Sociology* 1(1896), pp. 434–45, at p. 435.

134. Ibid., p. 438. On Lombroso's 'criminal anthropology' see P. Becker, *Verderbnis und Entartung. Eine Geschichte der Kriminologie des 19. Jahrhunderts als Diskurs und Praxis* (Göttingen, 2002), pp. 291–311.

135. Thomas, 'The Scope and Method of Folk-Psychology', p. 439.

136. Ibid., pp. 439–40; see W.I. Thomas, 'The Province of Social Psychology', in *American Journal of Sociology* 10(1905), pp. 445–55. On Thomas, see M. Bulmer, *The Chicago School of Sociology: Institutionalisation, Diversity, and the Rise of Sociological Research* (Chicago, 1984), p. 36.

137. F. Boas, 'The History of Anthropology', in *Science* 20(1904), pp. 513–24, at p. 513.

138. Ibid., p. 518. A number of famous German academics had made the long journey to the Congress of Arts and Sciences, which was held in St. Louis at the same time as the World Fair. Amongst them were Max Weber, Werner Sombart, Ernst Troeltsch, and Karl Lamprecht. On the occasion, Lamprecht, like many lesser known German participants, published a popular travel book that was full of 'folk-psychological' observations on the 'Yankees' and their national habits; see K. Lamprecht, *Americana* (Freiburg, 1906); see H. Rollmann, '"Meet Me in St. Louis": Troeltsch and Weber in America', in H. Lehmann and G. Roth, eds, *Weber's Protestant Ethic: Origins, Evidence, Contexts* (Cambridge and New York, 1993), pp. 357–83; L.A. Scaff, *Max Weber in America* (Princeton and Oxford, 2011), pp. 54–70.

139. Bunzl, '*Völkerpsychologie* and German-Jewish Emancipation', pp. 82–85.

140. See G.W. Stocking Jr., 'Franz Boas and the Culture Concept in Historical Perspective', in G.W. Stocking Jr., *Race, Culture and Evolution* (Chicago, 1982), pp. 195–233; G.W. Stocking Jr., ed., *Volksgeist as Method and Ethic: Essays on Boasian Ethnography and the German Anthropological Tradition* (Madison, WI, 1996); H.W. Schmuhl, ed., *Kulturrelativismus und Antirassismus: Der Anthropologe Franz Boas* (1858–1942) (Bielefeld, 2009).

141. Steinthal to Lazarus, 12 September 1852, in Belke, ed., *Lazarus*, vol. 1, p. 266.

142. Th. Ribot, *L'hérédité, étude psychologique: sur ses phénomènes, ses lois, ses causes, ses conséquences* (Paris, 1873), and Th. Ribot, *Les maladies de la mémoire* (Paris, 1881). On the reception of Darwin in France, see Y. Conry, *L'introduction du darwinisme en France au XIXe siècle* (Paris, 1974).

143. S. Nicolas and D.J. Murray, 'Théodule Ribot, 1839–1916, Founder of French Psychology: A Biographical Introduction', in *History of Psychology* 2(1999), pp. 277–301; S. Nicolas, *Théodule Ribot (1839–1916): philosophe breton, fondateur de la psychologie française* (Paris, 2005); R.A. Nye, *The Origins of Crowd Psychology: Gustave Le Bon and the Crisis of Mass Democracy in the Third Republic* (London and Beverly Hills, 1975), p. 13.

144. Th. Ribot, *La psychologie allemande contemporaine (Ecole expérimentale)* (Paris, 1879), pp. 49–57. To an English audience Ribot presented Hippolyte Taine as the 'chief representative in France of what the Germans call *Völkerpsychologie*'. See Th. Ribot, 'Philosophy in France', in *Mind* 2(1877), pp. 366–86, at p. 376.

145. Hoeschen and Schneider, 'Herbartianismus im 19. Jahrhundert'; Hoeschen and Schneider, eds, *Herbarts Kultursystem*.

146. Ribot, *La psychologie allemande contemporaine*, p. 49.

147. Ibid., p. 50.

148. Ibid., p. 51: 'A coté de la psychologie ordinaire, qui a pour objet l'homme individuel, il y a place pour une autre science consacrée à l'homme social ou plus exactement aux divers groupes humains: c'est la psychologie ethnologique.'

149. Ibid., p. 52.

150. Ibid., p. 53.

151. Ibid., p. 54: 'Les lois de la biographie, c'est-à-dire du développement des esprits individuels, doivent se résoudre dans la psychologie de l'esprit individuel; et de

même les lois de l'histoire, qu'on peut appeler la biographie des nations, doivent se résoudre en une psychologie comparée qui constituerait la vrai science de l'histoire.'

152. Ibid., p. 56.
153. C. Bouglé, *Les sciences sociales en Allemagne: les méthodes actuelles* (Paris, 1896), pp. 18–42.
154. Ibid., pp. 38, 42. See W.P. Vogt, 'Un durkheimien ambivalent: Célestin Bouglé 1870–1940', in *Revue Française de Sociologie* 20(1979), pp. 123–39.
155. E. Durkheim, 'Cours de science sociale: leçon d'ouverture [1888]', in E. Durkheim, *La science social et l'action* (Paris, 1970), as quoted in E. Apfelbaum, 'Origines de la psychologie sociale en France: développements souterraines et discipline méconnue', in *Revue Française de Sociologie* 22(1981), pp. 397–407, at p. 402: 'Si nous n'avons rien dit tout a l'heure des intéressants travaux de Lazarus et Steinthal, c'est que jusqu'ici ils n'ont pas donné de resultats. La Völkerpsychologie, telle qu'ils l'entendaient, n'est guère qu'un mot nouveau pour désigner la linguistique générale et la philologie comparée.'
156. H. Berr, *L'avenir de la philosophie. Esquisse d'une synthèse des connaissances fondée sur l'histoire* (Paris, 1899), p. 423: 'L'esprit est le produit de l'histoire; l'histoire est la "concretion" de la pensée.'
157. H. Berr, *La synthèse en histoire. Essai critique et théorique* (Paris, 1911), p. 108. On Berr see *Henri Berr et la culture du XXe siècle: histoire, science et philosophie*, eds A. Biard et al. (Paris, 1994), On Berr's views of Germany see P. Schöttler, 'Henri Berr et L'Allemagne', in ibid., pp. 189–203.
158. A. Fouillée, *L'évolutionisme des idées-forces (Paris, 1890);* A. Fouillée, *La psychologie des idées-forces*, 2 vols (Paris, 1893).
159. A. Fouillée, *Psychologie du peuple français* (Paris, 1898), p. 4.
160. Ibid., pp. 6, 11.
161. Ibid., pp. ii–iii. See J.M. Hecht, 'The Solvency of Metaphysics. The Debate over Racial Science and Moral Philosophy in France, 1890–1919', in *Isis* 90(1999), pp. 1–24.
162. Fouillée, *Psychologie du peuple français*, pp. 14–15, 22.
163. Ibid, p. 74: 'Sans aller jusqu'à soutenir, avec Lazarus, que l'être des peuples ne repose sur aucun rapport objectif et proprement naturel – identité de race ou communauté de langue, régime des biens, etc. – il faut accorder que les rapports subjectifs et les dépendances sociales vont sans croissant: un peuple est avant tout un ensemble d'hommes qui se regardent comme un peuple, "l'œuvre spirituelle de ceux qui le créent incessant" – son essence est dans la conscience.'
164. See A. Fouillée, *Esquisse psychologique des peuples européens* (Paris, 1903).
165. Belke, 'Einleitung', in Belke, ed., *Lazarus*, vol. 1, pp. icv–icvi; Jensen, *Gebildete Doppelgänger*, pp. 86–87. See H. Steinthal, 'Zur Charakteristik der semitischen Völker', in *ZfVS* 1(1860), pp. 328–45; E. Renan, *Nouvelles considérations sur le caractère général des peuples sémitiques, et en particulier leur tendance au monothéisme* (Paris, 1859).
166. E. Renan, *Qu'est-ce qu'une nation? Conférence faite en Sorbonne, le 11 mars 1882* (Paris, 1882); Lazarus, 'Was heißt national?'.
167. Leicht, *Lazarus*, p. 19. Renan's text, however, did not include any references.

168. On Renan see D.C.J. Lee, *Ernest Renan: In the Shadow of Faith* (London, 1996); F. Mercury, *Renan* (Paris, 1990).

169. M. Espagne and M. Werner, eds, *Transferts: les relations interculturelles dans l'espace franco-allemand* (Paris, 1988); M. Espagne, *Les transferts culturels franco-allemand* (Paris, 1999); J. Paulmann, 'Internationaler Vergleich und interkultureller Transfer: Zwei Forschungsansätze zur europäischen Geschichte des 18. bis 20. Jahrhunderts', in *Historische Zeitschrift* 267(1998), pp. 649–85.

170. C. Digeon, *La crise allemande de la pensée française, 1870–1914* (Paris, 1959).

171. M. Espagne, *En-deça du Rhin. L'Allemagne des philosophes français au XIXe siècle* (Paris, 2004).

172. Cf. M. Dierks, 'Thomas Mann und die "jüdische" Psychoanalyse. Über Freud, C.G. Jung, das "jüdische Unbewußte" und Manns Ambivalenz', in M. Dierks and R. Wimmer, eds, *Thomas Mann und das Judentum* (Frankfurt am Main, 2004), pp. 97–126, at p. 100; see A. Brock, 'Was Wundt a "Nazi"?', in *Theory and Psychology* 2(1992), pp. 205–23.

173. Renan, *Qu'est-ce qu'une nation?*; B. Anderson, *Imagined Communities: Reflections on the Origin and Spread of Nationalism*, revised edition (London, 1991); E. Hobsbawm and T. Ranger, eds, *The Invention of Tradition* (Cambridge, 1983).

174. Cf. Köhnke, 'Einleitung', I. Kalmar, 'The *Volkerpsychologie* of Lazarus and Steinthal and the Modern Concept of Culture', in *Journal of the History of Ideas* 48(1987), pp. 671–90; R. vom Bruch, F.W. Graf and G. Hübinger, eds, *Kultur und Kulturwissenschaften um 1900. Krise der Moderne und Glaube an die Wissenschaft* (Stuttgart, 1989).

CHAPTER 2

Wilhelm Wundt's Folk Psychology

Wilhelm Wundt, one of the founders of modern, scientific psychology, is the scholar most closely associated with the concept of *Völkerpsychologie*. He devoted the last twenty years of his long career to writing a general and comprehensive folk psychology, which was published in ten massive volumes from 1900 – a task that Lazarus and Steinthal had not even attempted. Wundt considered his *Völkerpsychologie*, in contrast to the majority of his peers and most of his numerous students, his finest achievement.[1] It formed an integral part of his concept of psychology, which consisted of two separate, but complementary, branches. According to Wundt, all psychological knowledge was based on individual psychology, which dealt with simple processes of the mind that could be studied with experimental methods. Wundt borrowed these methods from physiology and introduced them to psychological research. This scientific approach to psychology, practised in his soon famous psychological laboratory, established Wundt's fame and reputation and secured him his place in the annals of the discipline as the founder of scientific psychology.[2] These experimental, physiological methods were, however, of limited use for psychologists, Wundt argued. They could only be applied to the study of the most basic functions of the mind, such as reactions, perceptions and sensations. The more complex, higher products of the mind asked for a different approach, since they could not be re-created in the environment of a laboratory but only observed indirectly. This notion of the scope of academic psychology put Wundt in an awkward position in the context of the 'professionalization' of the discipline: 'The same Wundt whose laboratory functioned as the inspiration and model for numerous imitators was also the source for a mounting stream of restrictions on the use of the experimental method in psychology.'[3] On the most important question of folk psychology, i.e., the relation between the individual and the community, Wundt agreed with Lazarus and Steinthal: complex and 'composite' psychological phenomena were not creations of the individual, but of the community, of the folk. *Völkerpsychologie*, then, while based on individual psychology, was a separate field of enquiry and formed the necessary extension of individual psychology. For Wundt, individual psychology and folk psychology were clearly distinguished, in scope and method; at the same time, they formed integral parts of psychology as a whole that comprehensively explained the development of human life.[4]

A Liberal Mandarin

Wundt was born in 1832 in Neckarau, near Mannheim, and grew up in the small town of Heidelsheim in Baden. He came from a well-respected middle-class family of the German *Bildungsbürgertum*. While the family had produced a number of university professors and priests, his father, who only became a country vicar, was a kind of an underachiever in a well-established family. An average student at secondary school, Wundt attended the Gymnasium at Heidelberg and passed the *Abitur* in 1851. He went on to study medicine, first at the University of Tübingen, then at the University of Heidelberg, where he would stay on as lecturer and adjunct professor until he left for a professorship in philosophy at the University of Zurich in 1874.[5] At both Tübingen and Heidelberg his mentor and teacher was his maternal uncle Philipp Friedrich Arnold (1803–90), professor of anatomy and physiology.[6] Other teachers of Wundt included the chemist Robert Bunsen (1811–99) and the physicist Philipp von Jolly (1809–84). While still a student Wundt had his first paper on anatomy accepted for publication, in 1855. In 1856 he was awarded a doctorate in medicine and became research assistant to the pathologist Karl Ewald Hasse (1810–1902). In 1857 Wundt left Heidelberg for a semester to work with the renowned physiologists Johannes P. Müller (1801–58) and Emil Dubois-Reymond (1818–96) at the University of Berlin. Upon his return to Heidelberg he completed his *Habilitation* and became a *Privatdozent* in the faculty of medicine. His first book, published in 1858, received lukewarm reviews: according to Solomon Diamond it was a 'mediocre if not trivial contribution' to physiology.[7] In the same year Wundt suffered a haemorrhage that threatened his life; an incident to which he attached great importance in his autobiography for changing his outlook on life.[8] From 1858 until 1863 Wundt was employed as research assistant to the physiologist and physicist Hermann von Helmholtz (1821–94) and in 1864 he was awarded the title of an adjunct professor at the University of Heidelberg. From 1871 Wundt finally received a regular salary from the university when he became stand-in professor of Helmholtz, who had moved to the University of Berlin.

His hopes of succeeding Helmholtz to the full professorship at Heidelberg, however, were disappointed.[9]

Before he became full professor in Zurich, in 1874, Wundt had had an interest in politics. During his time in Heidelberg in the 1860s he had been politically active outside the classroom and the laboratory. Having been an eye-witness to the crushing of the revolution in Baden in 1849 by the Prussian army when he was seventeen, he adhered to liberal ideas throughout his life.[10] He became a member of the Workers' Educational League in Heidelberg, for which he gave lectures to general audiences and served as its chairman, and published several popularizing articles in journals such as *Unterhaltungen am häuslichen Herd* and *Die Gartenlaube*.[11] From 1866 to 1868 Wundt was elected as representative of Heidelberg to the state diet of Baden, affiliated with the liberal Progressive Party (Fortschrittspartei). In parliament he was responsible for education policies and served as a member of the Peace Commission after the Prussian–Austrian war in 1866. According to his own account, however, Wundt abandoned his political engagement when he 'realized that politics could not be an avocation but required a total commitment that was incompatible with his scientific work'.[12]

Already, as a young lecturer in physiology, Wundt found it hard to deal with professional criticism – a character trait that would become more pronounced in his later career. In his reply to a critical review of one of his early articles by the young physiologist Hermann Munk (1839–1912) in 1861, for instance, Wundt employed 'the sort of ambiguous shifts of meaning that were to exasperate his opponents in other controversies throughout his career'.[13] As a young scientist Wundt was a 'loner', not a networker: instead of working in a team of researchers, he preferred the solitude of his study. He made little use of his position as research assistant to Hermann von Helmholtz, one of the rising stars in the natural sciences in Germany. The relationship with Helmholtz remained cool, and in the 1860s Wundt further alienated his former boss when he claimed to have introduced the concept of 'unconscious inference', which Helmholtz had in fact developed before him.[14] Even though Wundt managed to get numerous research articles published and authored several textbooks, his reputation as a physiologist remained limited. While keeping an exaggerated self-image, he was engaged in frequent quarrels with reviewers and critics who raised doubts about the accuracy of his scientific work. Unsubstantiated claims to originality did not impress his peers, and revealed Wundt as a difficult character. His branching out into the new field of scientific psychology, then into philosophy, proved to be a clever and necessary move, given his uncertain reputation as physiologist. Wundt's *Grundzüge der physiologischen Psychologie*, his most famous and successful single publication, constantly reprinted and translated into several languages, made this change possible. In it he systematically applied the experimental methods developed by physiologists to the study of the mind, thus creating 'a new discipline of the sciences' by creative transfer.[15] It provided Wundt with the opportunity to become full professor through the back door by swiftly changing disciplines. In 1874 he accepted a call to a chair in 'inductive philosophy' at the University of Zurich, and the following year he moved on to the more prestigious chair in philosophy at the University of Leipzig. In 1879 he opened a laboratory for experimental psychology that soon made him one of the academic stars of the university, famous well beyond Imperial Germany.

When he was appointed full professor in 1874, Wundt retreated to his ivory tower and devoted all of his time and energy to his teaching, research and publishing. At the University of Leipzig however, while otherwise not famous for socializing, Wundt became the doyen of an informal group of like-minded professors from the university – the historian Karl Lamprecht (1856–1915), the geographer Friedrich Ratzel (1844–1905), the economist Karl Bücher (1847–1930) and the chemist Wilhelm Ostwald (1853–1932) – who met regularly at a local coffee house.[16] On account of their similar approaches, these scholars represented a sort of 'Leipzig school' and shared basic ideas. They all sympathized or even appropriated central concepts of Wundt's folk psychology in the context of their respective disciplines. Wilhelm Ostwald was one of the most renowned scientists of Imperial Germany. He was instrumental in establishing physical chemistry as an academic discipline, and in 1909 was awarded the Nobel Prize for his works on catalysis. In addition to his scientific work, Ostwald published widely on philosophical and artistic matters, notably on what he called the 'imperative of energetics'. A leading figure of the Monistenbund in Germany, together with the biologist Ernst Haeckel (1834–1919), he also became a controversial figure for his attempts to apply a scientific interpretation to society and civilization.[17] Friedrich Ratzel, who was as important for the development of geography in Germany as Wundt was for psychology, became famous for his studies on what he termed *Anthropogeographie*, a cultural-historical approach to geography that criticized the idea of a common origin of civilization. Instead, Ratzel argued, similarities in human behaviour, practice and thinking were the results of the diffusion of cultures. While focusing on the impact of the natural environment on the human mind, Ratzel also introduced the term *Lebensraum* into academic discourse, which was later to be further developed by his student Karl Haushofer (1869–1946) and abused by Nazi ideologists.[18]

After his long apprenticeship as research assistant, lecturer, and adjunct professor without a salaried position, Wundt eventually became a successful, popular and influential professor, one of the 'mandarins' of German universities with almost unlimited power within his department and considerable influence within his university. While his lecture courses, notably those on *Völkerpsychologie*, were very popular and attracted large audiences, it was his psychological 'laboratory' that became a magnet for research students from Germany and abroad. The majority of Wundt's doctoral students concentrated on individual psychology and applied experimental methods, which were easy to learn and follow. Notably Otto Klemm (1884–1939), one of many of Wundt's students who was to become professor of psychology in his own right, wrote a dissertation related to folk psychology.[19] Despite his success as teacher and scholar, Wundt remained a solitary figure. Except for his like-minded colleagues at Leipzig, he was not interested in socializing and networking, pursued the study of his monumental folk psychology in defiance of any objections to its methodology and its main concepts, and stubbornly defended his positions against various critics. He only retired from his chair in 1915, when he was succeeded by his former student Felix Krueger (1874–1948) at the age of eighty-two, even before he had completed the final volume of his *Völkerpsychologie*.

Völkerpsychologie as the Developmental History of Mankind

Even though the first volume of his *Völkerpsychologie* was published only in 1900, and the final tome of the monumental study shortly before his death in 1920, Wundt had held an interest in and published on the topic early in his career. As early as 1862 he offered lecture courses on psychology designed for medical students; these were published under the title *Lectures on the Human and the Animal Soul* in 1863.[20] This sweeping survey included, following an overview of the study of individual psychology, Wundt's first attempt at folk psychology, even though he mentioned the term only in passing.[21] At the time, Wundt was still convinced that experimental methods could be applied to all psychological phenomena, and was mainly interested in individual psychology. The *Lectures*, however, included reflections on the very themes and topics which would later form the core of his *Völkerpsychologie*: language, myths, religion, customs and habits. The study was rather unpolished, obviously put together in a hurry, and it lacked a clear structure that could organize the vast amount of relevant empirical material.

The main principle of the anthropological and historical parts of the *Lectures* was Wundt's firm belief in the development and progress of civilization from primitive to higher forms. Suggestions for an adequate methodology of folk psychology, the main concern of the critics, were missing, and the relevant chapters read like a summary of the prejudices of the educated classes: 'The moral faults and qualities of the Negros derive from the peculiarities of their temperament and their character, and from their kind of sociability. The Negro is highly apathetic. He finds the greatest pleasure in idleness. He does not know the persevering energy with which the European devotes himself to the work he has freely chosen.'[22] Wundt later dismissed the book as a 'youthful folly'; as he explained in his memoirs, the 'old idea of a comparative psychology of races and peoples' had enticed him to conclude his survey of psychology with a sketch of anthropology and folk psychology. At the time of its publication Wundt thought highly of this study and considered it his greatest achievement yet. Severe criticism, however, convinced him that he had overestimated his capabilities and had produced a premature work. The time had not yet come for a 'psychological history of the development of mankind'.[23] Even though the book was reprinted six times during Wundt's lifetime, with the last, revised edition published in 1919, he had the sections on folk psychology removed from the second edition, from 1893 onwards.[24]

After this early disappointment Wundt became more cautious, but did not abandon his interest in folk psychology. During his short stint at the University of Zürich he offered a lecture course on *Völkerpsychologie* in order to test his ideas in front of a student audience before publication. The topic became a standard option of his teaching portfolio and proved to be very popular; at the University of Leipzig he lectured regularly on folk psychology in front of large audiences. When Willy Hellpach came to the University of Leipzig in 1897/8, Wundt's lecture course on *Völkerpsychologie* was one of the major attractions of academic life and reached well beyond the confines of the university. He delivered his lectures on Wednesday and Saturday afternoons in front of an overcrowded auditorium which included a large number of non-regular *Gasthörer*, members of the general public who were allowed to follow the public lectures at the university.[25] So despite the deliberately academic outlook of Wundt's *Völkerpsychologie*, its reception was not restricted to an academic audience, but appealed to the wider public, too. Eventually, even the seemingly indigestible ten volumes sold well and were reprinted several times during his lifetime.

Similar to Lazarus and Steinthal, Wundt's interest in folk psychology was related to his interest in ethics, the traditional moral philosophy. Wundt, however, published his monograph on the 'study of the facts and laws of moral life' well before his *Völkerpsychologie*, i.e., in reverse order, since he agreed with Lazarus and Steinthal that any study of ethics had to be built on folk-psychological knowledge of communal life. He described folk psychology as the 'portico' (*Vorhalle*) of ethics.[26] Accordingly, Wundt's *Ethik* included a number of topics that would feature later in his folk psychology, namely the study of customs, habits, and the development of morality. He also used the occasion for a critique of 'English moral philosophy', most notably Jeremy Bentham's (1748–1832) 'individualism and utilitarianism'. Next to Herbart and his 'mechanical', individualistic psychology, Wundt saw Bentham as one of the main culprits of academic 'individualism' since he ignored the 'simple fact' that the community had precedence over the individual and that any form of moral philosophy or ethics depended on communal life.[27]

In the same year as the first edition of his *Ethics*, Wundt published his first methodological article on *Völkerpsychologie*, spurred by Hermann Paul's attack on Lazarus und Steinthal. This contribution defined and demarcated Wundt's approach to folk psychology, which remained largely unchanged for the rest of his life.[28] In this article, later included in a collection of his theoretical works on or related to folk psychology, Wundt pointed to some of the apparent weaknesses and inconsistencies of Lazarus and Steinthal's approach. Their ambitious plan to position *Völkerpsychologie* as an independent discipline on top of the hierarchy of academic disciplines sounded arrogant and naïve to him. With a realistic view, Wundt doubted that historians and philosophers would accept the kind of secondary status that Lazarus and Steinthal had envisioned for them. Causal explanations and 'psychological interpretations', Wundt continued, were common practice in the humanities and did not suffice to distinguish folk psychology from more established disciplines. Historians would not leave it to the psychologists to discover and formulate the 'laws of history', if this were ever possible, which Wundt doubted.[29] He thus rejected one of the principal aims of Lazarus and Steinthal's folk psychology, which was also one of the main weaknesses of their approach, i.e., to transfer 'scientific' methods to the study of history in order to discover the 'laws of development' of the 'folk spirit'. Lazarus and Steinthal only had a vague idea of what constituted a 'scientific method', and had spent little time in explaining how such methods could be applied to the study of the human mind. The trained scientist Wundt, in contrast, had by then convinced himself of the limited use of scientific, experimental methods for folk psychology, and insisted on the strict separation between experimental-scientific methods for individual psychology, and qualitative-hermeneutic ones for folk psychology. While restricted to observation, the latter were no less accurate or objective than experimental methods, Wundt explained. After all, a number of scientific disciplines, such as geology or botany, did not proceed differently. Wundt agreed with Lazarus and Steinthal that the task of *Völkerpsychologie* was to study those mental processes which formed the basis of the general development of human communities as evidenced by their mental products (*Erzeugnisse*). But their neat distinction between descriptive and analytical disciplines was simplistic, Wundt argued. It was already outdated and not even supported by serious scientists anymore.[30]

Still, Wundt kept his criticism of Lazarus and Steinthal to tactical errors committed by the pair in advertising the 'new discipline'. The main target of his critique was Hermann Paul's strictly 'individualist' understanding of psychology, which he considered an ill-advised continuation of Herbart's 'mechanical' approach. If correct, it would have indeed made any form of *Völkerpsychologie* impossible. Wundt, in contrast, agreed with Lazarus and Steinthal that psychology had to go beyond the study of the individual. Only the systematic study of the community, i.e., the *Volk*, as an object *sui generis* could explain the higher and more complex 'products' of the human mind, such as language, myths and morality. He emphatically embraced and defended the very contentious label of *Völkerpsychologie* against its many critics, and distanced himself from more limited and popular understandings of the term used to 'describe the mental character of the different civilized nations and their relations with each other'. Like Lazarus and Steinthal, Wundt stressed that it was not his aim to contribute to 'specialized folk psychology', i.e., the characterology of the mental peculiarities of individual races and nations, but to write a general folk psychology. Folk psychology was a purely academic and theoretical discipline that had nothing in common with the speculations of travel writers and journalists about national characters. Readers who expected enlightenment about the German, French, or English 'character' would have been disappointed by Wundt and had to look elsewhere.[31]

In accordance with Lazarus and Steinthal, Wundt insisted that the folk, or nation, was by far the most important community formed by human beings. Other groups such as families, clans, or regional, local and professional associations only ever existed within a nation and depended on it, hence the name *Völkerpsychologie* was appropriate. Wundt thus dismissed alternative labels that had been suggested as more suitable and accurate for the new discipline. 'Group psychology', he opined, implied a focus on other, less important human communities than the nation and was therefore misleading.[32] Similarly, he preferred *Völkerpsychologie* over 'social psychology' or 'sociology': these disciplines were too focused on contemporary society, he argued, lacked psychological insight and ignored the developmental, historical character of civilization.[33] Sociology as a discipline was an unfinished product and not yet properly established, according to Wundt. It was not a philosophical discipline, as evidenced by Auguste Comte's and Herbert Spencer's contributions, but merely a kind of philosophy of history in disguise.[34] Sociology could certainly not provide folk psychology with a solid foundation.[35] The doubt about the very name *Völkerpsychologie*, then, brought forward by many critics, was not merely a question of terminology, but reflected the attempt to position the new discipline within an increasingly crowded field. Even more so than Lazarus and Steinthal, Wundt had to defend folk psychology against other disciplines, both well-established and emerging ones: the humanities, including linguistics, mythology and the philosophy of history, and the increasingly popular and independent social sciences which, by and large, had the same object of study. Still, Wundt insisted that folk psychology was clearly distinct from these disciplines since it studied 'all those "mental products" (*geistige Erzeugnisse*) which emanate from the community of human life and thus cannot be explained by the characteristics of an individual consciousness since they presuppose the interaction of many individuals'. While 'all appearances which the humanities study' were indeed 'products of the folk community', philosophers, historians and literary critics typically focused on exceptional individuals, events and ideas.[36] Hence the history of literature, art and science was not part of folk psychology as it focused on the works of outstanding individuals.[37] Similarly, where critics of Lazarus and Steinthal had argued that their *Völkerpsychologie* was window-dressing, since it merely introduced a fashionable new term for traditional cultural history, one of the main rivals of Wundt's folk psychology was social anthropology (*Völkerkunde, Ethnologie*). Like many of his peers, from Durkheim to Freud, Wundt depended on the empirical knowledge provided by ethnologists and social anthropologists, but he insisted that folk psychology and social anthropology were different approaches that needed to be kept separate. *Völkerkunde* studied the genesis, characteristics and diffusion of peoples over the globe, but neglected psychological aspects of these processes. It constituted, he insisted, a different discipline with a different set of research questions and interests. Like history and philosophy for Lazarus and Steinthal, social anthropology provided Wundt with the raw data necessary to discover and formulate the 'laws of development' of peoples, but it lacked the tools to reach the level of insight his folk psychology would offer.

Wundt further agreed with Lazarus and Steinthal that folk psychology depended on an understanding of the relation between the individual and the community, and adopted Lazarus's term 'interaction' (*Wechselwirkung*) to describe this relationship.[38] Importantly, and in contrast to the dreaded 'individualists', Wundt subscribed to the idea that the 'whole', i.e., the nation, constituted more than the sum of its parts and thus constituted a distinct object of study. To describe the reciprocal relationship between the individual and the community, Wundt introduced the term 'creative synthesis' (*schöpferische Synthese*). The folk, as a compound entity, was a product of the creative synthesis of interacting individuals and represented a new entity with its own quality and characteristics. Analogous to the human organism and the human mind, which also represented more than the sum of its parts, Wundt conceptualized the folk as a complex entity that could not be reduced to its constituent parts, but needed to be analysed as a whole. In addition, the concept of a creative synthesis accounted for progress in history. Wundt used it not only to define the interaction between individual and folk, but also to account for the transformation of primitive forms of civilization to higher stages of development.[39]

Wundt took issue with Lazarus and Steinthal's preference for the term 'folk spirit', but, in contrast to most of their critics, mainly because of the Hegelian connotations of the term. Instead of 'folk spirit', Wundt preferred the term 'folk soul' (*Volksseele*), which proved to be even more contentious and caused multiple misunderstandings of his approach. As a scientist, Wundt insisted on the descriptive, non-metaphysical character of the term 'soul'. Its religious origins and the notion of a substance of the soul had to be overcome. To Wundt, 'soul' was a purely technical term that described the mental state of an individual and comprised a person's perceptions, feelings and volitions. Accordingly, Wundt saw no reason to avoid the term 'folk soul' since it simply referred to the collective perceptions, emotions and volitions of whole nations, or peoples. It described empirical, mental facts which formed the focus of any folk psychology, i.e., the 'mental products' of a folk community. Those critics, Wundt argued, who had claimed that folk psychology was an impossible discipline since a folk soul did not exist were themselves guilty of a hidden form of metaphysics, since they still believed in the material existence of the soul and did not understand its psychological character.[40] In addition, the concept 'soul' as used in modern psychology referred to the physiological foundations of psychological processes and was therefore more appropriate than 'mind' or 'spirit' (*Geist*) which excluded or neglected these.[41] For Wundt, then, the term 'folk soul' had the same status as contemporary concepts such as 'national identity' or 'mentality': It had no material substance, but was a 'mental fact' that could be and indeed needed to be studied in a scientific way.[42]

Originally, Wundt's *Völkerpsychologie* had a neat and clear tripartite structure that he had borrowed from Lazarus and Steinthal. Folk psychology studied the products of the folk soul, i.e., those emanations of the human mind that were constitutive parts of any folk and had not been created by an individual. The prime example for this kind of mental product was language; hence the starting point of folk psychology was the study of the origins and development of language. The second major part focused on myths, which included fairy tales, epics and all forms of religious thought. The third part, customs, was the most difficult to define, or rather to delineate: it included everything from table manners, mores, attitudes to gender and sexuality, to complex systems of law, economics, politics and the state. Not surprisingly, Wundt experienced major difficulties with his original three-fold structure of folk psychology, and was forced to widen and expand its scope into a truly universal anthropology of mankind.[43]

The clearest and most concise summary of Wundt's concept of *Völkerpsychologie* can be found in the introduction to the one-volume *Elements of Folk Psychology*, first published in 1912.[44] In contrast to the long, multi-volume version of *Völkerpsychologie*, which analysed the appearances of the folk soul independently and diachronically, the one-volume digest provided a chronologically organized history of mankind (or civilization). Wundt argued that such a comprehensive summary was the real aim of his *Völkerpsychologie*. 'Development' was the main organizing principle of his approach, and Wundt put forward a number of bold theses about the origins of language, social practices and institutions. Similar to the development of the individual from childhood to adolescence to adulthood, peoples developed in clearly defined stages, he argued. The first stage in this *Völkerentwicklung* was the primitive age, which formed the 'lowest level of culture'.[45] The primitive age was followed by the totemistic age, defined as a state of mind where, in contrast to modern times, the 'animal ruled over the human being'. The next step in the development of mankind was the age of heroes and gods, which was defined by the emergence and rule of individuals and the military (*kriegerische*) organization of the 'tribal community'. The age of heroes and gods witnessed the emergence of the state as the political organization of peoples, as well as national religions: epic tales now replaced the myths and fairy tales of earlier times. The fourth stage of the development of mankind was characterized by the predominance of the national state and national religions, which still dominated the present time. The future development of civilization, however, would overcome the existing national divisions and lead to 'humanity', a truly universal world civilization. The *Elements* focused on 'pre-historical', 'primitive' civilizations, mainly for pragmatic reasons: Wundt assumed that his readers knew less about these older forms of civilization than about the modern *Kulturnationen*.[46] Essentially, folk psychology had to be understood as developmental history since it studied the more or less regular, progressive changes of mankind from primitive to higher, more civilized stages of development.[47]

Ultimately, Wundt's folk psychology aimed at a strictly teleological philosophy of history which presented the development of mankind as a one-dimensional path to 'humanity'. Similar to Lazarus and Steinthal, Wundt thus represented the optimistic idea of progress that had underpinned traditional liberalism, but had increasingly come under attack from cultural pessimists since the 1890s. He also firmly believed in the 'unity of mankind', characteristic of Enlightenment thinking, and focused on those traits that were common to all nations while he neglected the differences between them. The main aim of Wundt's *Völkerpsychologie* was not very different from Lazarus and Steinthal's approach. Folk psychology would provide a synthesis of the results of specialized research in the humanities. It would replace neither history nor cultural history as empirical disciplines, but the speculative philosophy of history as represented by Hegel. More so than Lazarus and Steinthal, Wundt stressed the dependence of folk psychology on individual psychology. Throughout his life, he stuck to three fundamental points on the relationship between experimental psychology and folk psychology: 'First, that experimental psychology could never be more than a part of the science of psychology as a whole; second, that it needed to be supplemented by a branch of psychological studies that was devoted to the investigation of human mental processes in their social aspects; and third, that this latter type of study was able to make use of information that was no less objective than the data of experimental psychology.'[48] However, Wundt found it difficult to convince his critics of the unity of psychology and was at pains to demonstrate the causal relationship between individual, experimental psychology and folk psychology. Despite his criticism of authors who wanted to restrict psychology to the study of individuals, or those who used simple analogies between individuals and the community, his folk psychology was based on such an analogy. The three-part structure of Wundt's folk psychology was not only borrowed from Lazarus and Steinthal, but also mirrored his notion of the individual mind. In Wundt's description, the 'folk soul' was represented by language, myth (and religion) and customs, in the same way as the individual soul consisted of imagination, emotions and the will.[49] Similarly, Wundt's approach to history was characterized by a deep-seated belief in historicist ideas that treated each nation as a 'collective singular' and compared them to individuals. Folk psychology as the 'developmental history of mankind' took its underlying motives from the *Bildungsroman* when it presented the history of civilization as a continuous learning process that moved towards humanity.[50]

Surprisingly, and in contrast to Lazarus, Wundt provided no clear definition of the folk, or the nation, even though he always, and passionately, defended the label *Völkerpsychologie* against competing names that might have better described what he was actually doing, such as social psychology. Since he was interested in the universal development of mankind, he did not contribute to the study of individual nations, in which he deliberately showed no interest. For Wundt, the nation was just a stage in the development of mankind that would be overcome on the way towards humanity. He thus represented not only a 'psychology without the soul', as critics of his physiological and experimental studies had complained, but also 'folk psychology without the folk'. The largest part of Wundt's *Völkerpsychologie*, which could be practised from the comfort of an armchair, was lagging behind the methodological standards of contemporary social anthropology. Wundt had never done any fieldwork or empirical studies of his own and depended completely on the results of others. Not surprisingly, given the all-encompassing nature of folk psychology, Wundt could not stay abreast even of the state of research in relevant fields and often relied on outdated studies. As one of the last polymaths, he did not fit into an academic landscape that increasingly prized specialization over encyclopaedic knowledge. But while Wundt might have got away with a synthetic, popularizing world history, his insistence that his *Völkerpsychologie* was an original contribution to science and represented 'research' did not convince even his most sympathetic readers. Thus one of the main arguments that Wundt had used to criticize and distance himself from Lazarus and Steinthal's backfired. If it was possible to discover the 'laws of development' by way of analysing other scholars' research, why would historians, anthropologists or linguists leave this task to the psychologist Wundt, rather than do it themselves? Folk psychology, like all emerging social sciences, was caught in an awkward position: representatives of established disciplines denied that there was room for a discipline with such high aims that lacked a specific object of study and a distinct method. Eventually, Wundt managed to upset almost everyone with his folk psychology: while the majority of modern psychologists, intrigued by the perspective of turning psychology into a proper science by employing experimental methods, were disappointed by Wundt's traditional approach to *Völkerpsychologie*, and while the representatives of the established humanities treated Wundt as a dilettante who presented well-known specialized knowledge as 'research', the champions of alternative social sciences saw him as a dangerous competitor to their own efforts.

Reception and Appropriation of Wundt's *Völkerpsychologie*

The first volume of Wundt's *Völkerpsychologie*, published in two parts in 1900, was devoted to the psychological analysis of the origins and the development of language. This was not a surprising choice by Wundt; ever since Lazarus and Steinthal, the study of language had played a central role for folk psychology. Language was deemed the most obvious and striking example for the need of folk psychology: it was a product of the mind, yet not the creation of an individual, it showed clear 'laws of development', and it could be studied as a 'social fact'. Accordingly, the first volume of Wundt's *Völkerpsychologie* immediately caught the attention of German linguists. Berthold Delbrück (1842–1922), professor at the University of Jena and a representative of the school of neogrammarians (*Junggrammatiker*), was quick to publish a book-length review of it in 1901.[51] He found much praise for Wundt's efforts and presented him as part of a venerable tradition of philosophers and psychologists who had focused on the study of language, with Wilhelm von Humboldt, Heymann Steinthal and Hermann Paul as his predecessors. While Delbrück pointed out numerous errors in details, he was not overly critical of Wundt's psychology of language and predicted that it would become a useful resource for future scholars. Delbrück treated Wundt, however, as a non-specialist and outsider of comparative linguistics, and by listing his mistakes, he indicated that Wundt was not quite capable of making an original contribution to the field.[52] Wundt was irritated and offended by Delbrück's critique, and published his own reply immediately.[53] Ludwig Sütterlin (1863–1934), professor of German language and literature at the University of Heidelberg, assumed a similar attitude of damning Wundt with praise. He presented the first volume of *Völkerpsychologie* as an alternative to Hermann Paul's *Principien der*

Sprachgeschichte, one of Wundt's arch-enemies. In contrast to Delbrück, but agreeing with many other critics, Sütterlin considered the very term *Völkerpsychologie* misleading, since Wundt was not dealing with the folk soul, but with the minds of individuals insofar as they were influenced by and dependent on social interactions. Therefore, it would have been better to speak of mass psychology or *Volkspsychologie* (losing the plural of *Völker*). Despite pointing out several mistakes and premature generalizations, Sütterlin praised Wundt for having given equal attention to semantics, in contrast to most linguists who exclusively studied comparative grammar.[54] Ottmar Dittrich, a linguist on whose works Wundt had relied, was even more sympathetic towards the doyen of psychology. He did, to be sure, criticize Wundt's definition of a sentence, and complained that he had relied too heavily on written instead of spoken language, a grave mistake especially from a psychological point of view. On the whole, however, Dittrich admired the synthetic power of Wundt's folk psychology. For the first time, he argued, language and linguistic development had been analysed from a strictly psychological point of view. He had no doubt that linguists would have to rely on Wundt's psychology for the foreseeable future.[55]

In 1910 the linguist Hermann Paul repeated his plain rejection of any kind of folk psychology in a public lecture at the University of Munich. His attack was now directed personally at Wundt.[56] Again, Wundt reacted promptly and recycled his earlier, damning critique of Paul's position. Since Paul adhered to a Herbartian, strictly individualistic view of psychology, Wundt accused him of a 'hidden metaphysics', even worse than open metaphysics. Wundt denied that his notion of a folk soul was defined in analogy to the individual soul. The folk soul was a construction, not a metaphysical idea; it simply represented the mental products of human communities. Such products existed, hence individual psychology clearly needed to be extended and complemented by folk psychology.[57] Moreover, Paul's denial of the need for folk psychology depended on a misleading understanding of what constituted a scientific law: his attempt to substitute the concept of scientific laws with principles was unhelpful since it only covered up this misunderstanding and caused further confusion. Language, myth and customs, Wundt insisted, were creations of the community, not the individual.[58] The history of human society showed clearly that the community had priority over the individual.[59]

Generally speaking, representatives of the humanities were more sympathetic towards Wundt's *Völkerpsychologie* than psychologists, who were eager to distinguish themselves from the humanities, and from philosophy in particular. The young Martin Heidegger (1889–1976), whose Ph.D. dissertation had dealt with Wundt's *Logik*, provided a good example of this attitude when he wrote an appreciative, but neutral review of Wundt's *Probleme der Völkerpsychologie*. Folk psychology was a 'necessary extension of individual psychology', Heidegger agreed with Wundt.[60] Typically, philosophers and literary critics were less concerned with methodology and were more open-minded towards Wundt's folk psychology than those psychologists who were desperate to become 'proper' scientists. Wundt found himself in the awkward situation he had warned Lazarus and Steinthal of: folk psychology depended on the empirical research of the established humanities, whose representatives were not happy about being relegated to secondary status by a folk psychologist who assumed the role of supreme arbiter. Instead, mirroring Max Weber's verdict that a truly modern contribution to science had to be a specialist work,[61] Wundt was not taken completely seriously by linguists, folklorists, anthropologists and mythologists, whose works he had exploited for his folk psychology. None of these scholars had been waiting for the omniscient psychologist to produce a grandiose synthesis of the history of civilization that they had not been capable of.

Wundt's folk psychology was not, however, universally rejected. Scholars in the humanities found much praise for his efforts, especially for the synthetic power of his work. The social anthropologist Alfred Vierkandt (1867–1953) paid tribute to his former teacher Wundt, even though he did not follow his methodology or key concepts of his folk psychology.[62] Vierkandt called Wundt's *Elements of Folk Psychology* a 'social psychology' and was not alone in considering it a misnomer: it was not a psychological study, he argued, but a comparative cultural history. As such it did not build on experimental psychology, as Wundt had insisted. While Vierkandt agreed with Wundt's dismissive reply to Hermann Paul, he still felt the lack of a positive contribution to psychology. Since Wundt claimed that he was mainly studying interactions, most of his research belonged to sociology, not psychology.[63] The Viennese ethnologist Rudolf Trebitsch (1876–1918) praised Wundt's *Elements* for providing, for the first time, a 'precise definition of primitive man'. The book provided a 'good service' to ethnology. He remarked critically that Wundt might have used empirical data selectively so that it fit into his overall concept. The volume included some 'rationalistic speculations', but overall Trebitsch considered it an 'excellent piece of work'.[64]

The literary critic Friedrich Kauffmann (1863–1941), an expert on popular mythology and Germanic sagas, was full of praise for Wundt's folk psychology, in particular the second volume, which dealt with his own specialism. One had to go back to the French encyclopaedists of the eighteenth century, or to Auguste Comte and Herbert Spencer, to find a match for the achievements of Wundt, Kauffmann claimed. Finally, he reckoned, a German representative of the 'sociological method of research' had emerged who did not pale in comparison to his forerunners. Against the criticism of linguists, Kauffmann defended Wundt's folk psychology and commended it to anyone interested in sociology or folklore. Despite his praise, however, he did not use the term *Völkerpsychologie*, but rather referred to Wundt's work as a 'psychology of German intellectual history' (*deutsche Geistesgeschichte*). Kauffmann's subsequent review of the enlarged second edition of the same volume was less enthusiastic, but still appreciative of the energy needed for such a huge task.[65] The historian Ernst Bernheim (1850–1942), best known for a massive textbook on historical methods and the philosophy of history, included a sympathetic discussion of folk psychology in a chapter on 'social-psychological factors' within history. Bernheim agreed with the 'communitarian' stance of Wundt, Lazarus and Steinthal: groups developed a mind of their own and constituted more than the sum of their parts. With Wundt and against Lazarus, not surprisingly, he argued that folk psychology could and should not take over the historians' task and delegate them to a secondary status.[66] However, Bernheim questioned the assumption that the folk was by far the most important community: the family, clans, estates or professional guilds could exert a similar influence as the folk or the nation. Hence Bernheim suggested using the more inclusive term 'social psychology' instead of 'folk psychology'. He also warned against the hypostatization of collective concepts such as *Volksseele* or *Zeitgeist*. Karl Lamprecht and Ludwig Gumplowicz had provided bad examples of such a practice within academia.[67]

Of the regulars of the *Positivisten-Kränzchen* at Leipzig, the historian Karl Lamprecht owed most to Wundt's folk psychology. His controversial cultural history, the focus of the 'Lamprecht controversy' in which neo-Rankean historians such as Georg von Below (1858–1927) and Max Lenz (1850–1932) accused Lamprecht of 'materialism' and 'positivism', reconstructed the mental development of the German nation from the middle ages to modern times.[68] It was an exercise in 'special' folk psychology, a task that Wundt, more concerned with the universal features of the history of civilization, was happy to leave to historians. Lamprecht wrote a psychological history of the German nation which, he argued, had developed in clearly defined stages. He avoided the controversial term 'folk psychology' and preferred to speak instead of social psychology. Equally, where Wundt used the term 'folk soul', Lamprecht spoke of 'national consciousness'. Aside from the terminology, however, Lamprecht agreed with the main parameters of Wundt's folk psychology and borrowed heavily from it.[69] He agreed that the folk, or nation, – and not exceptional individuals, as the historicists argued – was the subject of history. History developed in clearly distinguishable stages, which represented stages of mental development – an idea that he shared with Wundt as much as with the economist Karl Bücher. Thus Lamprecht's highly controversial cultural history contributed to the bad reputation of folk psychology among academics, especially historians who blamed him for 'psychologizing'. At the same time he popularized the approach among a wider audience on account of the success of his multi-volume *German History*.[70]

Experimental psychologists were much less convinced by Wundt's approach than some philosophers, historians and linguists. Harsh criticism of Wundt's folk psychology came, ironically, from those psychologists who followed the research design of his 'physiological psychology' and practised psychology as a natural science. One of the centres for this kind of scientific psychology was the University of Würzburg, where Oswald Külpe (1862–1915), Narziß Ach (1871–1946), Karl Bühler (1879–1963) and Karl Marbe (1869–1953) had established a strictly experimental school that focused on the 'psychology of thought' (*Denkpsychologie*). The Würzburg School concentrated exclusively on experimental psychology in order to re-establish the discipline as a natural science, and, to the chagrin of Wundt, tried to study the human mind with these methods. Wilhelm Brönner (b. 1878), a student of Marbe, published a devastating critique of Wundt's folk psychology as part of a Ph.D. dissertation in which he evaluated different theories of collective psychological phenomena. Adhering to a strictly individualist position, Brönner's and the Würzburg School's arguments against *Völkerpsychologie* resembled those of Hermann Paul. He squarely dismissed Wundt's concept of a 'creative synthesis', i.e., the notion that the folk represented more than the sum of its parts and had to be studied as an entity of its own. Brönner also rejected the idea that the mind of the nation constituted a separate object of enquiry. Only individuals could be studied by psychologists, since phenomena such as a collective consciousness, a collective spirit or a collective soul did not really exist, either in physical or in a psychological form.[71] The alleged products of the folk soul – language, myth and customs – did not prove the existence of a folk soul either. Anticipating the behaviourist understanding of social psychology, Brönner and the Würzburg School thus defined social psychology as the study of individual behaviour under social conditions. This perspective would have indeed made any notion of group psychology, including folk psychology, redundant. Since it became the dominant trend of social psychology in the twentieth century, it partly explains the reluctance with which professional psychologists have looked at folk psychology.[72] Not surprisingly, Wundt strongly disagreed with the notion that experimental methods could be applied to any psychological problem, and wrote an angry reply directed at the Würzburg School. Establishing folk psychology was, after all, the consequence of his belief that only the most basic psychological processes could be assessed with experimental methods. His critique of the Würzburg School's attempts to study 'thinking' or 'consciousness' by means of interviews in an experimental set-up was equally as devastating as Brönner's assessment of his folk psychology.[73]

Wundt had started publishing his *Völkerpsychologie* at a time when the social sciences, and in particular sociology, were slowly emerging as distinct disciplines, after decades of latency. He had clearly distinguished folk psychology from sociology: one of the reasons he stuck to the much debated term *Völkerpsychologie* over 'social psychology' or 'sociology' was the 'presentist' outlook of the latter. The champions of sociology, in turn, could not ignore Wundt's folk psychology since it too obviously overlapped with their own efforts to study society systematically. Folk psychology found itself in competition with sociology to establish a true social science, positioned between the natural sciences and the humanities. Many sympathetic critics of Wundt argued that he had really created a 'social' psychology, and early sociologists appropriated major insights of his folk psychology in their own attempts to establish a new academic discipline. Emile Durkheim (1858–1917) for instance, the French 'founding father' of sociology, owed much to Wundt. Having spent the academic year 1885/6 in Leipzig in an effort to make himself familiar with the German 'moral sciences', he gained a first-hand experience of Wundt's psychology, and subsequently wrote two reports for the French Ministry of Education on the state of the 'positive sciences' and on 'moral philosophy' in Germany.[74] A former student of Théodule Ribot, who admired Wundt's experimental psychology,[75] Durkheim was particularly impressed by Wundt's anti-metaphysical approach to moral philosophy. His report on the state of moral philosophy in Germany was in fact an extended review of Wundt's *Ethics*, which he compared to the works of the 'socialists of the chair' (*Kathedersozialisten*), namely the economists Adolph Wagner (1835–1917) and Gustav Schmoller (1838–1917), as well as Albert Schäffle (1831–1903) and the philosopher of law Rudolf Jhering (1818–92). All these scholars, Durkheim explained, provided an alternative to the Manchester School of political economy and agreed that society was not simply a collection of individuals, but constituted an object of its own. In addition, they had demonstrated that morality and law were not intellectual abstractions, but empirical facts which had to be acknowledged and studied as such.[76] Durkheim confirmed that Wundt's method was 'purely empirical' (*nettement empirique*), and strongly agreed with him that 'collective phenomena' such as morality and religion had to be studied empirically. Social psychology (Durkheim's translation of *Völkerpsychologie*) would provide the relevant material to do so. It was a common mistake to view the individual as the 'principal motor' of social life, whereas 'collective facts' such as ethics and religion originated in other social facts.[77] According to Durkheim, Wundt's study was outstanding for mainly two reasons: first, it was rigorously based on facts and avoided abstract or normativist speculations, and second, it showed that morality had 'evolved' according to laws that science was to determine.[78]

In his later career Durkheim played down the inspiration he received from Wundt, not least because he was accused of depending too heavily on ideas that originated in Germany. In 1907 the Catholic writer Simon Deploige (1868–1927) attacked Durkheim directly and argued that his sociology was not of French origin, as Durkheim had proudly claimed, but nothing but a German import. All of Durkheim's 'main ideas were basically German in origin' and therefore alien to French thinking.[79] Deploige's attack was part of the polemic against Durkheim's school and the Nouvelle Sorbonne, and as such, according to Wolf Lepenies, a 'rear battle of the Dreyfus affair': the defamation of Durkheim's sociology as 'German' included a barely disguised anti-Semitic attack.[80] In his defence, while conceding that he had learned much from German philosophy and social science, Durkheim played down the importance of German academics for his sociology and insisted on the originality and 'Frenchness' of his approach. He still treated Wundt's works with respect and referred to him in all his major works.[81]

In 1913 Durkheim published a long review of Wundt's *Elemente der Völkerpsychologie* in his journal *L'année sociologique*, which showed him more sceptical and reserved than in his earlier comments on Wundt's *Ethics*.[82] Wundt's insistence on the name *Völkerpsychologie*, instead of 'social psychology' did not convince Durkheim since it revealed an odd understanding of sociology. So far, Durkheim explained, his own sociology had been criticized not for 'presentism', but for focusing too much on primitive forms of civilization.[83] Moreover, Durkheim was not convinced by Wundt's method of studying contemporary primitive civilizations in order to gain insight into historical forms or even the origins of civilization. Wundt's interpretation of the four 'ages' of mankind showed that he had not kept abreast of specialized research. He had misinterpreted totemism and ignored its religious and social character, and was not able to account for the sudden appearance of the individual during the age of heroes and gods. Most importantly, Wundt's argument rested on assumptions from the philosophy of history, which presupposed a steady, uni-linear development of mankind – Wundt also ignored national differences – towards a clear goal, 'humanity'. Instead of constructing the history of mankind as a single integrated process, as Wundt had done, the history of civilization had to be compared to a tree with many related, but different, branches. According to Durkheim, Wundt had been too ambitious in his attempt to write a comprehensive history of mankind, which had forced him to employ simplifying concepts. But despite these serious objections to Wundt's study, Durkheim still found much to praise in it. If it was impossible to answer all the questions that folk psychology raised, Wundt had done the best that was possible for an individual scholar; whatever the 'objective value' of his synthesis, it demanded the respect of the reader.[84] Marcel Mauss (1872–1950), Durkheim's nephew and close collaborator, reviewed the volumes of Wundt's *Völkerpsychologie* that were devoted to his own specialism, myth and religion, for Ribot's *Revue philosophique*, and came to similar conclusions: as 'one of the last encyclopaedic minds in Germany', Wundt's work showed 'the usual flaws of the philosopher – excessive systematization, hasty generalization, multiplied and complicated divisions'. But even specialists could profit from his work since he tried to clarify facts and define concepts that were frequently used, but often overlooked.[85] He found much to praise in Wundt's study on the development of art, especially his 'genetic classification of various arts' and his general distinction between 'plastic arts' and 'musics'. But Wundt, surprisingly, had not captured the social nature of art but tried to 'explain history by individual psychology, by the general faculties of human consciousness'. Wundt had ignored the creation and the enjoyment of art, therefore his study had 'no psychological life and no philosophical interest' because it was unrelated to 'sociological reality'.[86] Similarly, Wundt did not provide a clear understanding of myth because he had missed one of its essential elements, i.e., belief.

Similar to Georg Simmel's adaptation and appropriation of central parts of Lazarus's *Völkerpsychologie*, Durkheim had made good use of concepts he had found early on in his career in Wundt's philosophical writings. He did not simply borrow these concepts, but translated and changed them in the process. What Wundt called the 'folk soul', often misunderstood as a form of 'national character', came close to Durkheim's 'collective representations'. Similarly, Durkheim could not agree more with Wundt that the 'facts of moral life' had to be considered 'social facts': values, ideas and belief systems needed to be studied with the same rigorous methods as the material world. In contrast to Wundt, Durkheim did not try to write an all-encompassing, universal world history, but restricted himself to more limited topics and limited his universalist ambitions to the sociological method. He also avoided the temptation of an open teleology in the manner of Wundt. Wundt, then, seems to have served Durkheim as much as inspiration as foil in his effort to establish a truly scientific sociology.[87]

Durkheim's German counterpart, the economist Max Weber (1864–1920), who would be equally credited with establishing sociology as an independent discipline, had no patience with Wundt's folk psychology, and fired a broadside against him. Included in his assessment of the 'historical school' of economics, Weber attested to his reputation as a ruthless reviewer when he put forward a damning judgement on the methodology of Wundt's folk psychology.[88] According to Weber, the idea of a 'creative synthesis', which was meant to characterize the development of the folk soul and to account for the progress of civilization, was based on a barely disguised value judgement and thus misleading and untenable. Weber accused Wundt of presenting his psychology as an objective, empirical science, when it was in fact built on judgements about the progress and relative worth of civilizations which could never be proven 'empirically'. Wundt's psychology was full of value judgements dressed up as scientific statements, a practise that was anathema to Weber: 'There is simply no bridge that leads from the merely "empirical" analysis of a given reality on the basis of causal explanation to the assertion or denial of the "validity" of any kind of value judgement; Wundt's "creative synthesis", the "law" of the constant "increase of psychological energy" etc. contain value judgements of the purest kind.'[89] Weber reacted allergically to the very notion of historical laws of development on which Wundt's folk psychology was based. He was even more outspoken in his critique of Karl Lamprecht, Wundt's close colleague at the University of Leipzig, against whose 'cultural history' he held a grudge. He dismissed it categorically as a flawed approach, in a strange alliance with neo-Rankean political historians who defended the principle of historical individuality against Lamprecht's approach. Despite his outburst against Wundt and Lamprecht, however, Weber's own famous studies on the 'spirit' of capitalism came close to folk-psychological speculations of the kind he detested in other people's works: his search for the specific Western 'mentality' that had produced capitalism shared many similarities with studies of the folk soul and its products. However, Weber was well aware of the hazards of generalizing about collective spirits and national minds. This was one of the reasons why he put so much emphasis on the importance of the 'ideal type' as an 'exaggerated' construction of reality for the sake of analytical clarity.[90]

Werner Sombart (1863–1941), Weber's much more successful colleague and co-editor of the *Archiv für Sozialwissenschaften und Sozialpolitik*, had many fewer problems with the concept of folk psychology. In contrast to the more scrupulous Weber, Sombart was never afraid of sweeping generalizations, even though he was very much aware of the pitfalls of applied folk psychology based on judgements about national characters. In his study on *The Jews and Economic Life*, published in 1911 as a riposte to Weber's thesis of the pivotal role of Puritanism in the development of capitalism, he inserted a chapter on the Jewish 'mind', or 'character' (*jüdische Eigenart*), which dealt with the methodological problems of studying a national character.[91] In it, Sombart conceded that folk psychology had been abused by dilettantes, in particular anti-Semitic propagandists, which had led authors such as the Austrian economist Friedrich Hertz (1878–1964) and the French philosopher Jean Finot (1858–1922) to deny that any kind of 'collective-psychological judgement' was possible.[92] Sombart, however, was convinced that national characteristics existed, and that all social scientists relied on a folk-psychological hypothesis. To avoid premature generalizations about national characters, he suggested making use of statistical data to define the psyche of the Jews. But since this method required a large amount of empirical work, he preferred a more 'artistic' approach, which simply defined the Jewish type on the basis of everyday observations and judgements. This method produced little more than a catalogue of character traits of the Jews that repeated the common stereotypes it was based on. Sombart thus practised the kind of pseudo-science that he had complained about, and which contributed to the bad reputation of folk psychology, since he was mainly interested in studying individual national characters, and not, like Wundt, the unity of mankind.[93]

One of the most famous readers of Wundt's folk psychology was the founder of psychoanalysis, Sigmund Freud (1856–1939). When he published four essays taken from his journal *Imago* under the title *Totem and Taboo* in 1913, he presented them as a 'first attempt' to apply 'notions and results of psychoanalysis' to unresolved problems of *Völkerpsychologie*. The major inspiration for this attempt, Freud explained, had been Wundt's folk psychology and the studies of his former collaborator Carl Gustav Jung (1875–1961) of the Zürich School of psychoanalysis with whom he had recently split in typically acrimonious fashion. While Freud had relied on their results to master the vastly expanded ethnological, folkloristic and anthropological literature, his own works differed methodologically from these two approaches.[94] According to Freud, the origins of society, religion, ethics and art had to be explained through the Oedipus complex. In *Totem and Taboo*, Freud made the conscious effort to widen the scope of psychoanalysis and analyse collective phenomena with the help of the psychoanalytical toolbox and thus develop his theories into a universal psychological anthropology. As such, he was competing with Wundt's folk psychology.[95] The notion that Freud took over the idea of a 'racial soul' from the folk psychology of Lazarus, Steinthal and Wundt, is not correct, however. None of these authors used the term *Rassenseele*.[96] Freud's former crown prince, now one of his fiercest rivals, the Swiss psychologist Carl Gustav Jung, was equally familiar with the folk psychology of Lazarus, Steinthal and Wundt. Having abandoned Freud's pansexual theories – which caused his feud with Freud – he moved closer to the topics and themes of folk psychology and made use of Wundt's findings in his search for universal archetypes of the mind.[97]

Many of Wundt's books were translated into English, French and other European languages – the massive volumes of his *Völkerpsychologie* were the exception to the rule, but even these were regularly reviewed outside Germany. Some reviewers based their judgement on Wundt's folk psychology on their own notions about the national character of the Germans: to F.N. Hales's taste, writing for the British journal *Mind*, Wundt's study of language contained 'far too much theory, and too little fact'. The book disappointed, possibly because of the high expectations raised by Wundt's reputation, and it was not a pleasure to read: 'Nearly 1,300 pages of pale German ink on the most exasperating German paper – the physical discomfort of reading them might easily damp the most ardent enthusiasm!'[98] Others, such as the American anthropologist William Churchill (1859–1920), considered Wundt's study of language 'a monument of genius'.[99] The American linguist Leonard Bloomfield (1887–1947), in turn, was full of praise for Wundt's *Elemente der*

Völkerpsychologie. The author's 'vast learning, powerful psychological insight, vivid sense of history' and his 'stylistic ability to present states of flow and change' had produced 'a work of tremendous and awing effect', even though Wundt had not adequately discussed language in this volume, in contrast to the multi-volume *Völkerpsychologie*.[100]

The English translation of Wundt's *Elemente der Völkerpsychologie* was published in 1916, simultaneously in London and New York, in the middle of the First World War. The reviewer of the journal *Folklore*, R.R. Maret, complained mainly about the translation of the German term *Völkerpsychologie*. Wundt's method seemed legitimate to him, and he generally agreed with his theory of distinct 'ages' or 'stages' of historical development. He dismissed, however, the decision by the translator to introduce the 'neologism "Folk Psychology"'. Wundt was really doing social psychology, and 'to treat "folk" as equivalent to "society" or "community" seems an outrage on the English language'. Still, Wundt had produced 'a book which, even when it is least convincing, is always instinct with the suggestiveness of a powerful mind'.[101] Much more critical was the young T.S. Eliot (1888–1965) who reviewed the study for the *International Journal of Ethics*. Eliot saw it as 'a classic almost upon its appearance', which marked 'the end, rather than the beginning, of an epoch'. The book defined 'the limits of the Folk Psychology much more clearly than did its predecessor'. The main problem of Wundt's approach, according to Eliot, was the teleological philosophy of history which structured it and outdid even Hegel in its 'schematism'. Wundt's neat four 'stages' of the development of mankind confused stages of culture with periods of time, 'which tends to cast suspicion upon its scientific value; and further that the scheme involves a philosophic teleology'. There was no psychology in Wundt's *Völkerpsychologie*: 'The first part of the work is descriptive anthropology, the last part is philosophy of history.' 'Progress in this science', Eliot concluded, required 'a less ambitious synthesis', and would be 'closely dependent upon advance in individual psychology, such as that of psycho-analysis'.[102] George Herbert Mead (1863–1931), best known as a representative of the 'pragmatist' school of philosophy, raised similar doubts about Wundt's 'philosophy of history'. Some of Wundt's explanations of the origins of customs and beliefs did not convince, but overall, he found enough positive aspects in Wundt's study to judge it a good book.[103] Herman Haeberlin presented Wundt's Völkerpsychologie, in accord with its author, as the 'crowning achievement of his thought'. In an extended review for the *Psychological Review* he paid respect to the efforts of Wundt, but also raised serious doubts about his approach. Wundt's 'plea for folk psychology' was based on a 'well-balanced succession of premises and conclusions' which offered 'a good example of Wundt's argumentative brilliancy. The line of thought is enticing, and still the one decisive point in his argument for the reality of the folk soul is gained by a subtle *coup d'état.*' Haeberlin did not accept the idea of an 'immediate experience' of the 'overindividual' folk soul: 'But if there is no overindividual actuality, then there can be no folk soul. The one falls with the other.'[104]

Wundt's folk psychology, despite its scope and its critical reception, was a commercial success and found many readers outside academia. There is ample evidence of the popularization of Wundt's folk psychology, traces of which can be followed outside the works of academic psychologists, sociologists and historians. A prominent example is Harry Graf Kessler (1868–1938), the 'Red Count', who had studied folk psychology with Wundt at Leipzig. Kessler used folk psychology in his studies on the reception of art and aesthetics and employed Wundtian terminology to lend his writings an 'aura of scholarship' and to prevent being accused of 'uncontrolled subjectivity' in his discussions of modern art.[105] Furthermore, Kessler adopted ideas taken from Wundt's folk psychology in his travel writings, but also in theoretical contributions about the origins of national character and nationality.[106] Another former student of Wundt who would become a famous intellectual and scholar in his own right was Martin Buber (1878–1965).[107] After having studied philosophy, psychology and German literature at the universities of Berlin, Vienna and Leipzig – where he had been enrolled in Wundt's lectures on *Völkerpsychologie* – Buber worked as an editor for the publishing house Rütten & Loening in Frankfurt am Main. In this capacity, he initiated and edited a collection of social-psychological monographs, simply entitled *Die Gesellschaft*. As a whole, this series of short, popular books aimed to provide answers to questions that Wundt's folk psychology had raised, but then ignored and avoided; it constituted a comprehensive, multi-authored assessment of contemporary society. As such, it took clues from Wundt in stressing the psychological character of social relations, but applied this perspective to present-day society. Buber's collection, according to the publisher's marketing material, responded to the demand for an academic, yet accessible and well-presented study of the 'forms and appearances of social life'. The authors were asked to concentrate on a psychological study of society, in contrast to current sociology: instead of discussing the 'external structures of social life' ('der äußere Aufbau des Lebens der Gesellschaft'), the aim of the series was to show how the interaction of human beings, their emotions and volition, created 'the social' or society as such. The collection was an attempt to provide popular summaries of academic knowledge to a broader audience; taken together, the short books would provide a comprehensive survey of the 'psychology of society'.[108] Among the contributors were some of the best-known social scientists and philosophers of the early twentieth century, such as Georg Simmel on 'Religion', Werner Sombart on 'The Proletariat' and Fritz Mauthner on 'Language'.

The First World War and the Philosophy of Nations

The beginning of the First World War drew Wundt, by then an aging, but still active professor, back onto the public stage. With the beginning of the hostilities, Wundt, like many of his colleagues, turned into a 'political professor'.[109] He gave numerous public speeches to support the German war effort and boost public morale.[110] In 1914 he signed several public declarations by German academics and intellectuals, including the notorious 'Manifesto of the 93', published in English under the title 'To the Civilized World' (*An die Kulturwelt*), which defended the German conduct of war against French and British accusations. The manifesto justified the German invasion and occupation of neutral Belgium as an act of defence, denied that the German army had committed atrocities against civilians, and argued that the much-maligned Prussian 'militarism' was not the perversion, but the precondition, of German *Kultur*, which needed to be protected against the jealousy and revanchism of Germany's neighbours.[111] In public speeches Wundt followed the spirit of this declaration when he turned French and English reproaches against Germany on their head and accused England of ignoring international law because of the sea blockade of Germany, which extended the war to the civilian population. Employing the full pathos of early war-time propaganda, Wundt invoked the model of Johann Gottlieb Fichte (1762–1814) and his *Addresses to the German Nation* a hundred years earlier, when he claimed a universal mission for the German nation: civilization and culture as a whole depended on German ideas, and the Germans represented 'humanity'.[112]

During and after the First World War the demand for 'differential' folk psychology increased substantially as part of the war of words that intellectuals in all warring nations were busily conducting. German professors outdid each other in denigrating the national character of the enemy nations: especially during the first fifteen months of the war, hundreds of essays, brochures, pamphlets and monographs on the 'folk spirit' and 'national character' of the European nations were published in Germany. This literature tried to give meaning to the conflict, explain it to the general public and thus contribute to the war effort by stabilizing the home front. Because they were fighting the war on two fronts, German intellectuals found themselves in a more difficult position than their British and French counterparts: they had to justify their position simultaneously against the Western nations (France and Britain) and against the Russian empire. The main target of German scorn and hatred, however, was England. Famous and typical examples of German anti-English propaganda were the sociologist Werner Sombart's pamphlet *Händler und Helden* (1915), the historian Hermann Oncken's *Unsere Abrechnung mit England* (1914) and the philosopher Max Scheler's *Der Genius des Kriegs und der deutsche Krieg* (1915), which included a chapter on 'cant' as the defining trait of the English nation.[113] Many lesser known authors published similar pamphlets which decried English superficiality and hypocrisy.[114] Wundt's *Die Nationen und ihre Philosophie*, first published in 1915, fitted neatly into this kind of literature. It was reprinted several times during the war and in the 1920s, and was, not surprisingly, recycled during the Second World War. Although not the most radical example of its genre, Wundt's pamphlet was typical in the way it justified the German war effort, and served a double purpose by addressing both the German public and the enemy nations.[115]

Most of German war-time propaganda was very different in character from the kind of folk psychology that Lazarus, Steinthal and Wundt had propagated before 1914. While the then common understanding of the term, with its focus on 'national character', suggested that the discipline would instantly provide 'expert knowledge' in support of the German war effort, Wundt's universalist understanding of folk psychology was ill-suited for this purpose. He could not simply apply the methodology of *Völkerpsychologie* to Germany's war propaganda, since he had little to say about the individual characters of nations. His folk psychology was part of an older tradition of 'idealistic universalism' that was indebted to Enlightenment thinking, and attempted to explain the universal traits of nations and peoples, not their characteristics and differences. Wundt had not even provided a definition of the concept of the nation – as Lazarus had done – but simply took it for granted as the normal form of organization of human beings. To Wundt, the nation was just another stage in the development of mankind towards 'humanity', a truly universal and inclusive world culture.[116]

To contribute to the German war effort, then, Wundt had to produce a different kind of *Völkerpsychologie*. He fell back on exactly those reductionist ideas, usually employed by journalists and literati, that he had tried to avoid in his academic folk psychology, and argued that the character of a nation found its most perfect expression in the products of high culture: the arts, literature, and philosophy. These, Wundt maintained, provided an insight into the depths of the folk soul.[117] To prove this point, Wundt's study on *The Nations and their Philosophy* included a brief overview of modern European philosophy from the fifteenth century to the present day. Wundt believed that national philosophical traditions represented the 'spirit', or 'mind', of the nation, and thus mirrored the development of the character of the European nations and their relative positions vis-à-vis each other. The history of European philosophy, according to Wundt, was another story of progress: it had moved on from the Italian Renaissance to French rationalism, on to English empiricism and utilitarianism, and had culminated in German idealism. Over time, Wundt argued, the leading position in philosophy had been passed on from one nation to another. At present, the Germans represented the highest form of philosophical thinking, which in turn made them the leading nation in Europe. This Whiggish history of philosophy fitted in perfectly with German attempts to make sense of the war: many German intellectuals were convinced that France and England were old nations which had passed their prime and were therefore envious of the achievements of the German Empire, the ascending 'young nation' which had surpassed its western neighbours in all respects. England and France had lured Germany into a deadly conflict to preserve their status, hence she was justified to defend herself with all available means.

Wundt went on to characterize the European nations according to their 'philosophical styles', as represented by individual philosophers. Thus the 'mind' of the French was explained by Cartesian rationalism, while the English 'folk soul' was characterized by empiricism and utilitarianism. Wundt tried to give a fair and balanced account of non-German philosophers – David Hume's 'psychology of experience' fared especially well in his account – but there was a clear villain in his plot: Jeremy Bentham, whose 'individualism' he had already criticized in his *Ethik* in 1886. In the heated atmosphere of the First World War, Wundt identified 'utilitarianism' as the main character trait of the English and used the concept as shorthand for the flaws of their national character. Since utilitarianism was based on a strictly individualistic view of the world, it was selfish, egotistical and bereft of any ideals. Comfort, gain, success and material wealth were the only values the English recognized. To Wundt, a nation whose character was based on utilitarianism was seriously flawed, since it lacked the sense of duty and commitment to the higher good of the community which characterized the German nation.[118]

The concluding chapter of Wundt's study reflected on the 'spirit of the nations during war and peace'. The exceptional situation of the war, he argued, allowed deep insights into the soul of a nation, because during the conflict 'conventional lies of diplomatic discourse' had been dropped by diplomats and politicians.[119] At last, during the war, the leaders of the warring nations had revealed what they really thought of each other. For the folk psychologist, this opened an exceptional opportunity to study the real character of nations. Another way of gaining insight into the character of a nation, Wundt argued, was the study of national anthems and patriotic songs. This method resembled folklore studies with their focus on folk songs, fairy tales and other products of oral culture as authentic expressions of the soul of a nation.[120] The French 'Marseillaise', Wundt argued, showed that 'honour' and 'glory' were the most important values of the French nation.[121] In contrast to the national anthem 'God Save the King', he continued, the 'real', representative English national song was 'Rule Britannia', a piece in which the Briton invested the 'entire passion of his soul'. Its lyrics revealed 'power' and 'domination' as the highest values of the English nation that formed its character. The German equivalent of these songs was not the national anthem, either, but the 'Wacht am Rhein'. It showed 'steadfastness', 'loyalty' and 'duty' as German characteristics.[122] Wundt believed that he had thus found suitable empirical material both to study the 'mind of the nation' and to prove his main point, namely that England was a selfish and egotistical nation, as expressed by philosophical individualism and utilitarianism. Germany, in contrast, was characterized by its devotion to the community and the common good. The Germans worked, defended and fought for higher ideals, not for material gain. England represented superficial materialism and mere *Zivilisation*; Germany, on the other hand, stood for idealism, communal values and *Kultur*. This perspective was typical of German war propaganda and can be, to a degree, explained by the geopolitical situation of the war. German intellectuals had to defend their own nation simultaneously against Russian 'barbarism' and French and British 'civilization', hence the increasing popularity of the dichotomy between civilization and culture which celebrated German *Kultur* as profound and dismissed *Zivilisation* as shallow. This dichotomy had been known before the war, but was massively popularized during the conflict, most famously by Thomas Mann in his *Betrachtungen eines Unpolitischen*.[123] Since Germany was 'encircled' by a 'world of enemies', German professors and intellectuals presented themselves as defenders of universal *Kultur*, which still only they possessed, in much the same way as French intellectuals declared the war a crusade for civilization, both peculiarly French and universal at the same time.[124]

Wundt's short book betrayed the deliberations and restrictions of his *Völkerpsychologie*, and had little to do with his academic approach as a whole. Methodologically, he practised the very reductionism that he had tried to avoid in his *Völkerpsychologie*. Without hesitation he drew general conclusions from the contributions of individual philosophers to the character of whole nations. In the last volume of his *Völkerpsychologie* and his autobiography *Erlebtes und Erkanntes*, both published in 1920, shortly before his death, he repeated the main arguments of his wartime pamphlet and thus did much harm to his reputation as a scholar. These publications, widely distributed, contributed more to the bad reputation of folk psychology than any of Wundt's academic studies; the publications put forward exactly the kind of speculative stereotyping that became shorthand for any kind of *Völkerpsychologie* and confirmed the arguments of the critics of such an approach. Little did it matter that he had abstained from such pamphleteering in his academic work, where he was eager to show the universal structures and laws of development of the whole of mankind. In accordance with the majority of German academics and intellectuals who contributed to the 'war of words' during the First World War, Wundt identified England as the main enemy of the German Empire. As an old liberal, he showed the typical signs of a disappointed love affair with England that characterized many of his colleagues who had little to say about France, Germany's arch-enemy, and even less about Russia's 'barbarism', but were furious about England's 'betrayal' of her Germanic cousins. Wundt could not hide his disappointment about England, the country he had admired, but which he now held responsible for Germany's predicament during the war and ulti-mately for her defeat. An explanation for the behaviour of the English could be found in their collective soul, and the study of their philosophy as well as their folk culture provided the necessary insights.

Wundt's position was typical for the heightened nationalism of the German upper and middle classes during the First World War. He put forward a radical-nationalist point of view, but stayed away from racist-bio-logical arguments in his writing. Only in this way did his wartime propaganda stay true to his pre-war academic work: far from being a variety of racist thinking, *Völkerpsychologie* had been an alternative to racial theories which had enjoyed increasing popularity since the beginning of the twentieth century. The enormous effort Wundt put into reconstructing the development of the folk soul was made necessary by his rejection of reductionist racial-anthropo-logical theories. Wundt's nationalism was not *völkisch*, either: despite his eulogy of the German spirit and the idea of a German world mission, it rested on a cultural, not racial, understanding of the 'folk' or nation. For the same reason, any kind of anti-Semitism was absent from Wundt's wartime writings, as from most other anti-English pamphlets authored by German academics and intellectuals during the war. Despite the similarities between anti-Semitic propaganda and the German critique of English utilitarianism, hypocrisy and materialism, only in exceptional cases were anti-Semitic and anti-English arguments merged.[125] Wundt, then, remained true to his liberal roots, but became re-politicized and radicalized by the circumstances of the first 'total war'.

The Demise of Academic *Völkerpsychologie*

Wundt's wartime propaganda, but also a controversy with his own student and successor Felix Krueger about the appropriateness of the term *Völkerpsychologie*, announced the general attitude towards his folk psychology that would take hold after his death in 1920, when criticism of Wundt's folk psychology continued. The social anthropologist Richard Thurnwald (1869–1954), who clung on to the controversial term *Völkerpsychologie* when he established the *Zeitschrift für Soziologie und Völkerpsychologie* in 1925, dis-tanced himself from Wundt's approach and dismissed it as outdated. Thurnwald complained that Wundt's work was based on the incomplete nineteenth-century knowledge which had quickly been superseded in the meantime. Wundt had relied on second- and third-hand data provided by travellers and missionaries without critically scrutinizing his sources, a major flaw which made most of his speculations worthless, Thurnwald argued. Wundt's lax attitude towards methodology was all the more surprising since he was known as a diligent researcher when he introduced experimental methods to modern psychology. According to Thurnwald, *Völkerpsychologie* needed to be professionalized and thus turned into a 'normal science'. Instead of the armchair ethnology that could never fulfil the expectations it raised but resorted to largely unfounded und improvable speculations, he called for meticulous empirical research and fieldwork. According to Thurnwald, the way in which the concept *Völkerpsychologie* could be maintained was to abandon the idea of a comprehensive super-discipline that would integrate the humanities and the social sciences; instead, it had to be turned into a specialized field of the social sciences, in close cooperation with sociology and social anthropology, which Wundt had seen as competitors, but not as partners, for his discipline.[126]

Those of Wundt's students who had been sympathetic towards folk psychology but had voiced their concern about inconsistencies and idiosyncrasies of their teacher's approach – in particular Wundt's successor Felix Krueger, but also Hans Volkelt (1886–1964) and Otto Klemm (1884–1939) – continued their barely concealed criticism of *Völkerpsychologie*. In contrast to Wundt, Felix Krueger, who succeeded him on the prestigious chair of philosophy at the University of Leipzig, had argued during the First World War that 'group psychology' should focus on studying the differences between nations, not their similarities. Taking his clue from Wundt's *Elemente der Völkerpsychologie*, Krueger thought it was finally time to abandon the awkward term *Völkerpsychologie* and replace it with the more neutral 'developmental psychology'. After all, *Entwicklung* was the central term of Wundt's folk psychology, and 'developmental psychology' was the more comprehensive concept since it included child and animal psychology. Even though Krueger had presented his criticism in a polite way that paid tribute to the achievements of his teacher, he was met with a brash reply from Wundt, who plainly dismissed the suggestions of his former student.[127]

In a 1922 *Gedenkschrift* for Wundt, Krueger continued with his criticism of the concept of *Völkerpsychologie*, couched in general praise for his teacher and predecessor. He now presented Wundt as a quintessentially 'German thinker' who represented typical character traits of his nation. Wundt's 'profound objectivity' (*tiefgegründete Sachlichkeit*) was 'German'; he was a 'natural scholar' (*eine Gelehrtennatur*), which was rare to find outside Germany; 'like every true German' he enjoyed hiking; his political activities in the 1860s had shown him as a humble 'man of the people' who happily engaged with and helped men from all walks of life; while passionate in his patriotism, he always remained fair towards foreign nations. Above all, his 'methodical thinking', his profound learning and his meticulous and wide-ranging research clearly showed his 'Germanness'.[128] After this eulogy of the achievements of his teacher, Krueger went on to renew his criticism of the whole idea of *Völkerpsychologie* (he now used the term only in inverted commas). Wundt's wide-spanning studies on the 'development of culture' were not accurately labelled as 'folk psychology', Krueger maintained. Wundt had insisted on this name because of his belief in the historical and psychological importance of the *Volk*, with which Krueger agreed. But Wundt's 'historicizing' approach had corrupted the whole endeavour; already the original structure of folk psychology, with its exclusive focus on language, myth and customs, had been too limited, largely for pragmatic reasons since these topics had long been researched. Wundt had come close to 'positivism' – now clearly associated with the 'West' and considered detrimental because of its 'atomizing' perspective, which obscured insight into the 'whole' – and had too often shied away from clear judgements in order to avoid 'metaphysical speculations'. Still, Krueger opined, Wundt had avoided the pitfalls of fully fledged positivism because of his deep respect for everything that had grown organically, be it a living organism or the character of each *Volkstum*.

Krueger used the occasion of the *Gedenkschrift* to advertise once again his own 'developmental psychology' as the better alternative to Wundt's folk psychology. 'Development' (*Entwicklung*), Krueger was convinced, was a truly and originally German concept.[129] His long obituary was a remarkable attempt to appropriate Wundt into the German-nationalist right and present him as an anti-Western, *völkisch*, thinker. Despite the pronounced nationalist views Wundt published during the First World War, his *Völkerpsychologie* had little in common with *völkisch* ideology – in contrast to his son's publications. Max Wundt (1879–1963), a philosopher at the Universities of Jena and Tübingen, represented *völkisch* anti-Semitic ideology in an almost pure form and contributed to the forced reinterpretation of his father's work.[130] Wundt's indebtedness to the Jewish scholars Lazarus and Steinthal was not mentioned by Krueger. The 'repudiation' and forgetting of Wundt, then, was not only the work of experimental psychologists, mostly American scholars, who did their best to ignore folk psychology and play down its importance, but also that of his German students and followers. Moreover, by stressing the genuinely 'German' character of Wundt, Krueger used his example to prove the assumptions of 'differential' folk psychology. As an individual, Wundt now appeared as evidence of the unique traits of the German character.

In the same volume, Hans Volkelt, at the time *Privatdozent* at the University of Leipzig, assessed Wundt's folk psychology and contributed to its reinterpretation. Loyal to his teacher Krueger, he advertised 'developmental psychology': Wundt's folk psychology was really a 'genetic social psychology', Volkelt argued, and Wundt had been the 'most eminent psychologist of development'. According to Volkelt, one of the main principles of Wundt's folk psychology, the idea of a 'creative synthesis', would be more adequately termed 'principle of mental development'.[131] He applied Wundt's general principles of development, i.e., continuity, *Wertsteigerung*, 'creative synthesis' and the 'heterogony of purposes', to Wundt's own biography and showed how his works had developed organically, following a necessary logic.[132] Wundt's biggest achievement, Volkelt argued, was his integration of individual and folk psychology. In contrast to experimental psychologists, he had not lost sight of the 'whole' and had thus contributed to the emergence of *Ganzheitspsychologie*.[133] Still, the weakness of his folk-psychological works was his underestimation of the importance of individual psychology in the study of primitive peoples. Despite his generous appreciation of the achievements of Wundt, Volkelt insisted that his *Völkerpsychologie* was a misnomer; it would be better described as a combination of communal, social and cultural psychology. The concept that integrated these different parts, however, was 'development' as suggested by Krueger.[134]

The philosopher Willy Moog (1888–1935) summarized the general attitude towards folk psychology in the inter-war period in a textbook on contemporary philosophy that was published after Wundt's death. Like many critics before him, Moog was not happy with the name *Völkerpsychologie* and criticized the strict separation between individual and folk psychology. Wundt had paid too little attention to the interaction between the individual and the community, Moog complained, and encountered conceptual problems, since he had widened the scope of folk psychology constantly. The end result was an encyclopaedic and universal study of civilization that provided interesting and useful information, but failed to introduce a specific method for the study of folk psychology. Therefore, folk psychology did not constitute a scientific discipline.[135] Quite in contrast to Wundt's intentions, Moog dismissed his approach as a whole as an example of 'psychologism', since for Wundt, psychology formed the basis of history as well as of ethics, logic and metaphysics.[136]

The easy dismissal of folk psychology in the nationalistic post-war atmosphere of the Weimar Republic may come as a surprise, since 'differential' folk psychology was more popular than ever, not least because of the war of words during the World War to which German academics, including Wundt, had contributed.[137] As a consequence of the war, some academics called for an increase in the efforts to build up *Völkerpsychologie* as an academic discipline, because they saw Germany's defeat as a consequence of the naïve outlook of their political and military leaders. Due to the lack of 'political psychology' and knowledge of their enemies' characters, the argument went, Germany had lost the propaganda war against the Allied nations.[138] The kind of

Völkerpsychologie that these authors called for, however, had little in common with Wundt, Lazarus and Steinthal's approach, and resembled more the 'characterology of nations' that they all had wanted to replace by serious, reliable scholarship. Wundt's universalist outlook, however compromised by his war publications, did not meet the demands of the highly nationalized atmosphere of the 1920s. Instead, the works of the 'race psychologists' Hans F.K. Günther (1891–1968) and Ludwig Ferdinand Clauss (1892–1974), two outsiders to the academic community, filled the gap that folk psychology had left. Günther and Clauss were both active in the 'Nordic Movement', and, judged by the print-run of their books, became the most successful racial theorists in Germany in the inter-war period.[139] Their works provided simple answers to the question of national character: according to Günther and Clauss, the European nations were made up of six distinct racial groups, each of which displayed typical physical and mental traits. Indeed, physical traits were presented as signifiers for mental traits in their studies.[140] Although Günther claimed to work on a sound scientific basis and presented his writings as serious research, he relied entirely on secondary literature and the interpretation of arbitrarily chosen pictures, including paintings and drawings alongside photographs. The Nordic race constituted an ideal for him and served as the yardstick by which all other racial groups were to be judged: 'If one studies the talents of different races by looking at the number of creative individuals [they produced], then the Nordic race is exceptionally gifted.'[141] In contrast to the success and popularity of their writings, however, the academic influence of Günther and Clauss was ambiguous and limited. They did not succeed in establishing a 'school' of race psychology, despite the enormous success of their books, and the scientific community adopted an ambivalent and awkward, if not outright critical attitude towards their ideas. Only with the help of the National Socialists were they able to pursue academic careers in the 1930s. With backgrounds in the humanities – Günther had been a secondary school teacher of German language and literature, and Clauss was a philosopher by training and onetime research assistant of Edmund Husserl (1859–1938) at the University of Freiburg – they were usually looked upon by anthropologists and psychologists with unease and suspicion.[142] Nevertheless, Günther and Clauss offered an alternative approach to nineteenth-century folk psychology, apparently in tune with racial ideas, that offered simple answers to complex questions.

In 1932 Max Hildebert Boehm (1889–1968), one of the prominent intellectuals of the radical right in the Weimar Republic, published his study *Das eigenständige Volk*. In it, he attempted to establish a *Volkslehre* as an independent field of study and included a chapter on the 'essence of the folk' (*Volkswesenheit*), which explicitly criticized the tradition of folk psychology.[143] Boehm presented folk psychology as part of the legacy of the 'new enlightenment' that had followed the era of Hegel. Characterized by a belief in individualism and empiricism, this period had produced sociology, Wundt's 'psychology without soul' and a folk psychology that 'didn't know the folk'. All these approaches were based on a 'cult of causality' and had tried to 'explain' everything by applying mechanical or biological laws. Employing the language of the cultural pessimist, Boehm accused the nineteenth century as a whole of fragmentation (*Zersetzung*), *Weltzerdenkung*, and radical doubt (*Zweifelsucht*). The main target of his critique was modern sociology because it had not developed an adequate concept of the folk.[144] Boehm singled out Hermann Paul, one of the major critics of *Völkerpsychologie*, as a typical representative of the kind of exaggerated individualism and empiricism he loathed, but Wundt did not fare much better in his judgement. His folk psychology had remained a cross between psychology and sociology, based on developmental history.[145] Recent theoretical studies of the character of the folk had reached an impasse, Boehm concluded.[146] Common theories of race, however, did not find Boehm's approval, either, since they were based on even shakier ground than folk psychology. While Boehm was certainly a 'personality of the right', he did not subscribe to Günther's or Clauss's racial theories, nor to similarly simplistic concepts of the *Volk* and *Volkstum* which had become the cornerstone of the political ideology of the radical right in Germany. His solution to the conceptual dilemma of the 'social sciences' was to introduce a new term: *Volkheit* was meant to overcome the problems of defining the *Volk* or the nation conclusively. At the same time, Boehm drew the consequences from the problems of providing such a definition for academic purposes. *Volkheit*, he explained, was a political concept which should be exempt from analytical or academic scrutiny.

Wundt's Legacy

A major inspiration for Wundt's folk psychology had been Lazarus and Steinthal's *Zeitschrift für Völkerpsychologie und Sprachwissenschaft*, along with the first volume of Theodor Waitz's *Anthropology of Primitive Peoples* which was published in the same year as the first volume of the *ZfVS*. Waitz's study provided Wundt with much of the ethnographic material on which his folk psychology depended, which he later extended to the pioneering works of British social anthropologists.[147] Lazarus and Steinthal provided Wundt with the name for the second branch of psychology, and he stuck to it throughout his career, despite serious criticism. He also accepted and continued the general structure of folk-psychological studies they had suggested: folk psychology was the study of the developmental laws of language, myths and customs. Wundt's concept of folk psychology, then, owed more to the efforts of Lazarus and Steinthal than he was ready to admit. In his critical evaluations of their programmatic articles he stressed the differences between their approaches; at closer inspection, however, the similarities between the two versions of *Völkerpsychologie* outweigh the differences by far.[148]

Clear differences existed between Lazarus, Steinthal and Wundt in their biographical background and their professional standing. While Lazarus and Steinthal remained outsiders to the scientific community, mainly because of their Jewish background, which had prevented their promotion to full professorships, Wundt became one of the 'mandarins' of the German universities during the Kaiserreich. He was the scion of a well-established Protestant family of the *Bildungsbürgertum* and thus not affected by any extra-academic obstacles in pursuing his career; coincidentally, he profited from the expansion of the German universities after unification in 1871. When he was finally called to a full professorship in philosophy at the University of Leipzig in 1875, after a long period as research assistant and unsalaried *Privatdozent* at the University of Heidelberg, he had reached the highest level of academic achievement. As *Ordinarius*, i.e., chair in Philosophy, he occupied a powerful and influential position at one of Germany's foremost universities at a time when these were at the peak of their international fame and influence.[149] Wundt made full use of the opportunities this position offered to him: he published at a breathtaking rate; his output included popular introductions and textbooks, which he revised and which were translated several times, as well as research articles in journals. In addition, Wundt was a very popular and successful teacher. He supervised dozens of doctoral students, many of whom pursued academic careers as psychologists and copied Wundt's psychological 'laboratory'. Wundt did not establish a 'school', however. He was reluctant to travel and rarely took part in conferences or other academic meetings. Stanley Hall (1844–1924), one of Wundt's former American students, tried to bring him to the U.S.A. twice, in 1900 and in 1909, but was turned down each time.[150] Wundt was not part of a network outside of his own university, and, particularly as a folk psychologist, had 'many students but no genuine disciples'.[151]

Wundt's *Völkerpsychologie* remained eclectic. It was designed as an all-encompassing 'developmental history of mankind' that borrowed material, ideas and approaches from neighbouring fields as diverse as linguistics, anthropology, literature, philosophy and history. It competed with the fledgling social sciences, in particular with social anthropology and sociology. In this respect, too, Wundt added little to Lazarus and Steinthal's folk psychology, and attracted similar criticism. He was at pains to convince his critics of the need for folk psychology, in particular the advantage of a 'psychological' interpretation of history over the established humanities. Similar to his predecessors, Wundt practised folk psychology as an armchair scholar and used the empirical knowledge made available by social anthropologists and cultural historians to draw wide-ranging conclusions about the mental development of mankind from the origins of civilization to the present day. Wundt also became the nemesis of traditional *Völkerpsychologie*. Increasingly cantankerous and dogmatic, he ignored serious and even sympathetic criticism of his studies and stuck to idiosyncratic concepts and definitions that had not convinced his peers. The Wundtian concept of *Völkerpsychologie* did not find many followers after his death in 1920 and was rapidly forgotten, even though speculations about the spirit and character of nations attracted much interest during and after the First World War. Both academics and the general public turned increasingly to theories of race to explain the differences between nations, while folk psychology as an academic discipline was soon obliterated.

Notes

1. W. Wundt, *Völkerpsychologie: Eine Untersuchung der Entwicklungsgesetze von Sprache, Mythus und Sitte*, 10 vols (Leipzig, 1900–1920); see C.M. Schneider, *Wilhelm Wundts Völkerpsychologie: Entstehung und Entwicklung eines in Vergessenheit geratenen, wissenschaftshistorisch relevanten Fachgebietes* (Bonn, 1990); G. Eckardt, 'Einleitung in die historischen Texte', in Eckardt, ed., *Völkerpsychologie: Versuch einer Neuentdeckung* (Weinheim, 1997), pp. 78–112. Despite its promising title, G. Jüttemann, ed., *Wilhelm Wundts anderes Erbe: Ein Missverständnis löst sich auf* (Göttingen, 2006), does not provide new insights into Wundt's *Völkerpsychologie*.
2. See W. Wundt, *Grundzüge der physiologischen Psychologie* (Leipzig, 1873). This introductory text was Wundt's most successful and influential work; it was translated into several languages and remained in print until long after his death. Wundt's role as founder of scientific psychology was canonized by E.B. Titchener (1867–1927), a former English student of Wundt who became professor of psychology at Cornell University, and by Titchener's student E.G. Boring (1886–1968), author of the influential study *A History of Experimental Psychology* [1929], second edition (New York, 1950). For recent histories of psychology that by and large follow this tradition see for instance B.R. Hergenhahn, *An Introduction to the History of Psychology*, sixth edition (Belmont, 2009), pp. 265–71; C.J. Goodwin, *A History of Modern Psychology*, third edition (New York, 2008), pp. 98–120.
3. K. Danziger, *Constructing the Subject: Historical Origins of Psychological Research* (Cambridge, MA, 1990), p. 36. See M.G. Ash, 'Academic Politics in the History of Science: Experimental Psychology in Germany 1871–1941', in *Central European History* 13(1980), pp. 255–86.
4. See W. Wundt, *Erlebtes und Erkanntes* (Stuttgart, 1920), p. 218: 'Beide, Individualpsychologie und Psychologie der Gemeinschaft, gehören zusammen, und das Denken in seiner die komplexen Vorgänge des Seelenlebens umfas-

senden Bedeutung läßt sich ebensowenig aus den Eigenschaften des individuellen Bewußtseins allein ableiten, wie sich etwa der Staat als eine rein individuelle Erfindung begreifen läßt.'

5. The most thorough study of early Wundt can be found in S. Diamond, 'Wundt before Leipzig', in R.W. Rieber, ed., *Wilhelm Wundt and the Making of a Scientific Psychology* (New York and London, 1980), pp. 3–70. See also W.G. Bringmann, W.D.G. Balance and R.B. Evans, 'Wilhelm Wundt 1832–1920: A Brief Biographical Sketch', in *Journal of the History of the Behavioural Sciences* 1(1975), pp. 287–97; G. Lamberti, *Wilhelm Maximilian Wundt (1832–1920): Leben, Werk und Persönlichkeit in Bildern und Texten* (Bonn, 1995).

6. Among Arnold's students at Heidelberg were Sigmund Exner (1846–1926) and Richard von Krafft-Ebing (1840–1902). See Diamond, 'Wundt before Leipzig', p. 18.

7. W. Wundt, *Untersuchungen über das Verhalten der Nerven in entzündeten und degenerirten Organen*, Ph.D. dissertation (Heidelberg, 1856); W. Wundt, *Die Lehre von der Muskelbewegung, nach eigenen Untersuchungen* (Braunschweig, 1858). See Diamond, 'Wundt before Leipzig', p. 26.

8. Wundt, *Erlebtes und Erkanntes*, pp. 115–18.

9. Diamond, 'Wundt before Leipzig', p. 58.

10. Wundt, *Erlebtes und Erkanntes*, pp. 13–29.

11. Diamond, 'Wundt before Leipzig', p. 40. See W. Wundt, 'Der Blick. Eine physiognomische Studie', in *Unterhaltungen am häuslichen Herd*, 1863, pp. 1028–33; W. Wundt, 'Der Mund. Physiognomische Studie', in *Unterhaltungen am häuslichen Herd*, 1862, pp. 503–10; W. Wundt, 'Die Geschwindigkeit des Gedankens', in *Die Gartenlaube*, 1862, pp. 263–65.

12. Diamond, 'Wundt before Leipzig', pp. 41–42; Wundt, *Erlebtes und Erkanntes*, p. 29.

13. Diamond, 'Wundt before Leipzig', pp. 27–28.

14. Ibid., p. 32.

15. Wundt, *Grundzüge der physiologischen Psychologie*, p. iii.

16. W. Ostwald, *Lebenslinien: Eine Selbstbiographie*, 3 vols (Berlin, 1926–27), p. 81, on Wundt see pp. 88–91; W. Hellpach, *Wirken in Wirren: Lebenserinnerungen. Eine Rechenschaft über Wert und Glück, Schuld und Sturz meiner Generation*, 2 vols (Hamburg, 1948), vol. 1, p. 169; R. Chickering, 'Das Leipziger "Positivisten-Kränzchen" um die Jahrhundertwende', in G. Hübinger, R. vom Bruch and F.W. Graf, eds, *Kultur und Kulturwissenschaften um 1900, II: Idealismus und Positivismus* (Stuttgart, 1997) pp. 227–45.

17. W. Ostwald, Der energetische Imperativ (Leipzig, 1912). See B. Görs, N. Psarros and P. Ziche eds, *Wilhelm Ostwald at the Crossroads between Chemistry, Philosophy and Media Culture* (Leipzig, 2006).

18. On Ratzel, see G. Buttmann, *Friedrich Ratzel: Leben und Werk eines deutschen Geographen* (Stuttgart, 1977); D. Steinmetzler, *Die Anthropogeographie Friedrich Ratzels und ihre ideengeschichtlichen Wurzeln* (Bonn, 1956); M. Bunzl, 'Franz Boas and the Humboldtian Tradition: From Volksgeist and Nationalcharakter to an Anthropological Concept of Culture', in G.W. Stocking Jr., ed., *Volksgeist as Method and Ethic: Essays on Boasian Ethnography and the German Anthropological*

Tradition (Madison, WN, 1996) , pp. 17–78, here pp. 41–44; A. Zimmerman, *Anthropology and Antihumanism in Imperial Germany* (Chicago and London), 2001, pp. 202–7.

19. O. Klemm, *G.B. Vico als Geschichtsphilosoph und Völkerpsycholog* (Leipzig, 1906). Even Klemm devoted only a short paragraph on folk psychology as a branch of 'comparative psychology' in his *History of Psychology*, published in German in 1911, in which he criticized Lazarus and Steinthal for their adherence to Herbart, but remained conspicuously silent on Wundt's folk psychology. See O. Klemm, *A History of Psychology* (New York, 1914), pp. 111–12.

20. W. Wundt, *Vorlesungen über die Menschen- und Thierseele*, 2 vols (Leipzig, 1863).

21. Wundt, *Vorlesungen*, vol. 2, pp. 449–51.

22. See in particular ibid., pp. 118–39, at p. 137: 'Die sittlichen Fehler und Vorzüge der Neger entspringen aus ihren Temperaments- und Charaktereigenthümlichkeiten und aus ihren geselligen Zuständen. Der Neger ist in hohem Grade apathisch. Träges Nichtstun ist ihm der höchste Genuß. Die ausdauernde Energie, mit der sich der Europäer einer frei gewählten Arbeit widmet, kennt er nicht.'

23. Wundt, *Erlebtes und Erkanntes*, p. 205. See the review by the leading Herbartian philosopher in Germany, M.W. Drobisch, 'Über den neuesten Versuch, die Psychologie naturwissenschaftlich zu begründen', in *Zeitschrift für exacte Philosophie* 4(1864), pp. 313–48. Despite this critical assessment of Wundt's early work, Drobisch was later instrumental in hiring Wundt at the University of Leipzig. See also Anon., 'Review of Wundt, Vorlesungen über die Menschen- und Thieseele, II', in *Literarisches Centralblatt für Deutschland* 15(1864), pp. 964–66; Diamond, 'Wundt before Leipzig', pp. 44–46.Wundt, *Erlebtes und Erkanntes*, pp. 199–209.

24. W. Wundt, *Vorlesungen über die Menschen- und Thierseele*, second edition (Hamburg and Leipzig, 1892).

25. Hellpach, *Wirken in Wirren*, pp. 170–71.

26. W. Wundt, *Ethik: Eine Untersuchung der Tatsachen und Gesetze des sittlichen Lebens* (Stuttgart, 1886), p. iii: 'Als die Vorhalle zur Ethik betrachte ich die Völkerpsychologie, der neben anderen Aufgaben insbesondere auch die zukommt, die Geschichte der Sitte und der sittlichen Vorstellungen unter psychologischen Gersichtspunkten zu behandeln.' This study was reprinted and enlarged several times during Wundt's lifetime.

27. Ibid., pp. 336–49.

28. W. Wundt, 'Ziele und Wege der Völkerpsychologie' in W. Wundt, *Probleme der Völkerpsychologie* (Leipzig, 1911), pp. 1–35. Other contributions by Wundt on the theory and methodology of *Völkerpsychologie* can be found in the introductory chapters of his books on folk psychology; see in particular W. Wundt, *Völkerpsychologie, vol. 1: Die Sprache*, second edition (Leipzig, 1904), pp. 1–33; W. Wundt, *Elemente der Völkerpsychologie: Grundlinien einer psychologischen Entwicklungsgeschichte der Menschheit* (Leipzig, 1912), pp. 1–11.

29. Wundt, 'Ziele und Wege der Völkerpsychologie', p. 5.

30. Ibid.

31. Wundt, *Elemente der Völkerpsychologie*, p. 1. Wundt referred to Karl Hillebrand, *Zeiten, Völker und Menschen*, 6 vols (Berlin, 1873–86), for an example of 'specialized' folk psychology. Typically, Hillebrand (1829–1884), who had emigrated to Strasbourg and Paris after the failed revolution of 1848–49 and became Heinrich Heine's private secretary, was not an academic, but a popular political writer who showed little interest in methodological or theoretical questions.

32. Wundt, *Elemente der Völkerpsychologie*, pp. 4–5: 'In der Gesamtentwicklung des geistigen Lebens aber – das ist das Entscheidende – ist das Volk der Haupteinheitsbegriff, an den sich alle anderen angliedern.'

33. Wundt, *Völkerpsychologie*, vol. 1, p. 2.

34. This argument, which had its merits, backfired; see A.L. Kroeber, 'The Possibility of Social Psychology', in *American Journal of Social Psychology* 23(1918), pp. 633–50, at p. 645, who saw 'no great difference between the sociologists [i.e., Comte and Spencer] and Wundt'.

35. Wundt, *Völkerpsychologie*, vol. 1, pp. 4–6.

36. Wundt, *Elemente der Völkerpsychologie*, pp. 1–3.

37. Wundt, *Völkerpsychologie*, vol. 1, p. 3.

38. W. Wundt, 'Über das Verhältnis des Einzelnen zur Gemeinschaft', in *Deutsche Rundschau* 18(1891), pp. 190–206.

39. Ibid.

40. Wundt, *Völkerpsychologie*, vol. 1, p. 9.

41. Ibid., p. 7: 'Vom Geist und von geistigen Vorgängen reden wir überall da, wo an irgendwelche Beziehungen zur körperlichen Natur nicht gedacht, oder wo geflissentlich von ihnen abgesehn wird. Bei der Seele und den seelischen Vorgängen sind uns dagegen stets zugleich die Beziehungen zum physischen Leben gegenwärtig.'

42. W. Wundt, 'Ziele und Wege der Völkerpsychologie', p. 13.

43. Wundt, *Völkerpsychologie*, vols 6–10.

44. Wundt, *Elemente der Völkerpsychologie*, pp. 1–11. This book was the only one to be translated into English as *Elements of Folk Psychology: Outlines of a Psychological History of the Development of Mankind* (London, 1916), hence most British and American commentators' knowledge of Wundt's folk psychology was restricted to this volume.

45. Wundt, *Elemente der Völkerpsychologie*, pp. 7–8.

46. Ibid., p. iv.

47. Following Helmuth Plessner, Wolfgang Eßbach has argued that 'development' served as the 'redemptive word' (*erlösendes Wort*) of the nineteenth century and as such must be considered as one of the key concepts of debates about modernity. According to Eßbach, speaking of 'development' enabled intellectuals to make sense of their experience of the dissolution of traditional forms of social organization. See W. Eßbach, 'Vernunft, Entwicklung, Leben. Schlüsselbegriffe der Moderne', in W. Eßbach, *Die Gesellschaft der Dinge, Menschen, Götter* (Wiesbaden, 2011), pp. 131–40; H. Plessner, *Die Stufen des Organischen und der Mensch: Einleitung in die philosophische Anthropologie* (Berlin and Leipzig, 1928).

48. Danziger, *Constructing the Subject*, p. 37.

49. Sganzini, *Fortschritte der Völkerpsychologie*, pp. 120–21.

50. Wundt, *Elemente der Völkerpsychologie*, p. 7: 'Wie die Kindheit, das Jugend-, das Mannesalter stetig ineinander übergehen, so verhält es sich aber nicht anders bei den Stufen der Völkerentwicklung.'

51. B. Delbrück, *Grundfragen der Sprachforschung: Mit Rücksicht auf W. Wundts Sprachpsychologie erörtert* (Straßburg, 1901). See A. Gardt, *Geschichte der Sprachwissenschaft in Deutschland vom Mittelalter bis zum 20. Jahrhundert* (Berlin, 1999), p. 278.

52. Delbrück, *Grundfragen*, pp. 5, 175–76.

53. W. Wundt, *Sprachgeschichte und Sprachpsychologie: Mit Rücksicht auf B. Delbrücks 'Grundfragen der Sprachforschung' erörtert* (Leipzig, 1901).

54. L. Sütterlin, *Das Wesen der sprachlichen Gebilde: Kritische Bemerkungen zu Wilhelm Wundts Sprachpsychologie* (Heidelberg, 1902).

55. O. Dittrich, 'Review of Wundt, *Völkerpsychologie*, Band 1: Die Sprache, Leipzig 1900', in *Zeitschrift für Romanische Philologie* 27(1903), pp. 198–210. The fairly positive view of Wundt's psychology of language was confirmed at a much later time when his folk psychology as a whole had long been neglected and forgotten. See A.L. Blumenthal, 'A Reappraisal of Wilhelm Wundt', in *American Psychologist*, November 1975, pp. 1081–88.

56. H. Paul, 'Über Völkerpsychologie. Rektoratsrede', in *Süddeutsche Monatshefte* 7(1910), pp. 363–73.

57. W. Wundt, 'Sprachwissenschaft und Völkerpsychologie', in *Indogermanische Forschungen. Zeitschrift für indogermanische Sprach- und Altertumskunde* 28(1911), pp. 205–19, at pp. 206–7.

58. Ibid., p. 213.

59. Ibid., p. 218.

60. M. Heidegger, 'Probleme der Völkerpsychologie. Von Wilhelm Wundt [1915]', in M. Heidegger, *Gesamtausgabe, 1. Abteilung: Veröffentlichte Schriften 1910–1976*, vol. 36 (Frankfurt am Main, 2000), pp. 33–35. See W. Wundt, *Logik: Eine Untersuchung der Prinzipien der Erkenntnis und der Methoden wissenschaftlicher Forschung*, third edition, 3 vols (Stuttgart, 1906).

61. M. Weber, 'Wissenschaft als Beruf [1917]' in M. Weber, *Gesammelte Aufsätze zur Wissenschaftslehre* (Tübingen, 1988), pp. 582–613, at p. 588.

62. A. Vierkandt, *Naturvölker und Kulturvölker: Ein Beitrag zur Sozialpsychologie* (Leipzig, 1896).

63. A. Vierkandt, 'Review of W. Wundt, *Elemente der Völkerpsychologie* and *Probleme der Völkerpsychologie*', in *Zeitschrift für Psychologie und Physiologie der Sinnesorgane*, 1. Abteilung 72(1915), pp. 428–29. On Vierkandt see Gerhardt, Mehring and Rindert, *Berliner Geist*, pp. 243–46.

64. R. Trebitsch, 'Wilhelm Wundts "Elemente der Völkerpsychologie" und die moderne Ethnologie', in *Zeitschrift für angewandte Psychologie* 8(1914), pp. 275–309, at p. 309. On Trebitsch see B. Hurch, 'Zum Verständnis und Unverständnis von Rudolf Trebitsch: Der Beitrag eines Ethnologen zur Baskologie', in *Österreichische Zeitschrift für Volkskunde* 62 (2009), pp. 3–69; See also the neutral review by E. Meumann, 'Review of W. Wundt, *Völkerpsychologie*,

Band 3: Die Kunst, 2. Auflage, Leipzig 1908', in *Archiv für die gesamte Psychologie* 14 (1909), pp. 46–48.

65. F. Kauffmann, 'Review of Wundt, *Völkerpsychologie*, Band 2: Mythus und Religion, 1. Teil, Leipzig 1905', in *Zeitschrift für deutsche Philologie* 38 (1906), pp. 558–68, at p. 558.; F. Kauffmann, 'Review of Wundt, *Völkerpsychologie*, 2. Band: Mythus und Religion, 2. Auflage, Leipzig 1906–1909', in *Zeitschrift für deutsche Philologie* 41 (1909), pp. 361–72.

66. E. Bernheim, *Lehrbuch der historischen Methode und Geschichtsphilosophie: Mit Nachweis der wichtigsten Quellen und Hilfsmittel zum Studium der Geschichte*, third and fourth edition (Leipzig, 1903), pp. 605–29, at pp. 605–6.

67. Ibid., p. 620.

68. See M. Lenz, 'Lamprechts Deutsche Geschichte, 5. Band', in *Historische Zeitschrift* 77(1896), pp. 385–447; G. von Below, 'Review of *Deutsche Geschichte*, von Karl Lamprecht', in *Historische Zeitschrift* 7 (1893), pp. 465–98; K. Lamprecht, *Die kulturhistorische Methode* (Berlin, 1900); K. Lamprecht, *Die historische Methode des Herrn von Below: eine Kritik* (Berlin, 1899).

69. K. Lamprecht, *Was ist Kulturgeschichte? Beitrag zu einer empirischen Historik* (Freiburg i. Br., 1896).

70. On Lamprecht see L. Schorn-Schütte, *Karl Lamprecht: Kulturgeschichtsschreibung zwischen Wissenschaft und Politik* (Göttingen, 1984); R. Chickering, *Karl Lamprecht: A German Academic Life (1856–1915)* (Atlantic Highlands, NJ, 1993); L. Raphael, 'Historikerkontroversen im Spannungsfeld zwischen Berufshabitus, Fächerkonkurrenz und sozialen Deutungsmustern. Lamprecht-Steit und französischer Methodenstreit der Jahrhundertwende in vergleichender Perspektive', in *Historische Zeitschrift* 252(1990), pp. 325–63.

71. W. Brönner, 'Zur Theorie der kollektiv-psychischen Erscheinungen', in *Zeitschrift für Philosophie und philosophische Kritik* 141(1911), pp. 1–40 at p. 13.

72. See R.M. Farr, *The Roots of Modern Social Psychology, 1872–1954* (Oxford, 1992); C.F. Graumann, *The Individualisation of the Social and the De-Socialisation of the Individual: Floyd H. Allport's Contribution to Social Psychology* (Heidelberg, 1984); F.H. Allport, *Social Psychology* (Boston, 1924).

73. W. Wundt, 'Über Ausfrageexperimente und über die Methoden der Psychologie des Denkens', in *Psychologische Studien* 3(1907), pp. 301–60.

74. S. Lukes, *Emile Durkheim, his Life and Work: A Historical and Critical Study*, second edition (London, 1992), pp. 86–98.

75. Th. Ribot, *La psychologie allemande contemporaine (Ecole expérimentale)* (Paris, 1879), pp. 215–97.

76. E. Durkheim, 'La science positive de la morale en Allemagne', in *Revue philosophique de la France et de l'étranger* 12(1887), pp. 33–58, 113–42, 275–84, at p. 37: 'Il est faux de dire qu'un tout soit égal à la somme de ses parties.' The second part of this essay was completely devoted to Wundt's *Ethics*.

77. Ibid., pp. 113, 116, 118–19.

78. Ibid., pp. 138.

79. Lukes, *Emile Durkheim*, p. 92. See S. Deploige, *Le conflit de la morale et de la sociologie* (Paris, 1912).

80. W. Lepenies, *Die drei Kulturen: Soziologie zwischen Literatur und Wissenschaft* (Frankfurt am Main, 2002), p. 50.

81. E. Durkheim, *De la division du travail social* [1893], seventh edition (Paris, 1960), pp. 213, 215; E. Durkheim, *The Elementary Forms of Religious Life* [1912], trans. C. Cosman (Oxford and New York, 2008), p. 128; R.A. Jones, 'The Positive Science of Ethics in France: German Influences on *De la division du travail social*', in *Sociological Forum* 9(1994), pp. 37–55.

82. E. Durkheim, 'Review of Wundt, *Elemente der Völkerpsychologie*', in *L'année sociologique* 12(1913), pp. 50–61.

83. Ibid., p. 51.

84. Ibid., pp. 60–61.

85. M. Mauss, 'L'art et le mythe d'après M. Wundt', in *Revue philosophique de la France et de l'étranger* 66(1908), pp. 48–78, translated as 'Art and Myth according to Wilhelm Wundt', in *Saints, Heroes, Myths, and Rites: Classical Durkheimian Studies of Religion and Society*, ed. and trans. A. Riley, S. Daynes and C. Isnart (Boulder, CO, and London, 2009), pp. 17–38.

86. Ibid., pp. 18, 21–22.

87. Lukes, *Emile Durkheim*, pp. 86–98; Lepenies, *Die drei Kulturen*, p. 82; E. Apfelbaum, 'Origines de la psychologie sociale en France: développements souterraines et discipline méconnue', in *Revue Française de Sociologie* 22(1981), pp. 397–407.

88. Weber's critique of Wundt's folk psychology is hidden within his extended review of Knies's 'System der Volkswirtschaft', one of the first of his famous methodological and epistemological essays. See M. Weber, 'Roscher und Knies und die logischen Probleme der Nationalökonomie', in M. Weber, *Gesammelte Aufsätze zur Wissenschaftslehre*, seventh edition (Tübingen, 1988), pp. 1–145, on Wundt pp. 49–63.

89. Ibid., p. 61. On Weber's critique of Wundt's psychology see W. Hennis, *Max Webers Wissenschaft vom Menschen: Neue Studien zur Biographie des Werks* (Tübingen, 1996), pp. 32–33, 37; on the context of Weber's *Seufzeraufsatz* see J. Radkau, *Max Weber: Die Leidenschaft des Denkens* (Munich and Vienna), 2005, pp. 399–407.

90. H. Lehmann, *Max Webers 'Protestantische Ethik': Beiträge aus der Sicht eines Historikers* (Göttingen, 1996); Radkau, *Max Weber*, pp. 316–50.

91. W. Sombart, *Die Juden und das Wirtschaftsleben* (Leipzig, 1911), pp. 296, 302.

92. F. Hertz, *Moderne Rassentheorien: Kritische Essays* (Vienna, 1904); J. Finot, *Le préjugé des races* (Paris, 1905).

93. Sombart, *Die Juden*, pp. 296–97; see F. Lenger, *Werner Sombart, 1863–1941: Eine Biographie* (Munich, 1994), pp. 197–201.

94. S. Freud, 'Totem und Tabu [1913]', in S. Freud, *Fragen der Gesellschaft. Ursprünge der Religion* (Studienausgabe, vol. 9) (Frankfurt am Main, 1997), pp. 287–444, at p. 291.

95. S.L. Gilman, *Freud, Race, and Gender* (New Haven, 1983). Gilman's characterization of Lazarus and Steinthal as 'Lamarckians', whose studies were 'highly medicalized', is misleading. See ibid., p. 27; D.J. Rosenberg, 'Patho-Teleology and the Spirit of War: The Psychoanalytic Inheritance of National Psychology',

in *Monatshefte* 100(2008), 213–25. For a contemporary and devastating critique of Freud's attempt to branch out into ethnology and anthropology see A.L. Kroeber, 'Totem and Taboo: An Ethnologic Psychoanalysis', in *American Anthropologist*, New Series, 22(1920), pp. 48–55.

96. Cf. M. Dierks, 'Thomas Mann und die "jüdische" Psychoanalyse. Über Freud, C.G. Jung, das "jüdische Unbewußte" und Manns Ambivalenz', in M. Dierks and R. Wimmer, eds, *Thomas Mann und das Judentum* (Frankfurt am Main, 2004), at p. 100.

97. S. Shamdasani, *Jung and the Making of Modern Psychology: The Dream of a Science* (Cambridge, 2003), pp. 278–82.

98. F.N. Hales, 'Review of Wundt, *Völkerpsychologie*, first vol.', in *Mind*, New Series 12(1903), pp. 239–45, at pp. 239–40.

99. W. Churchill, 'Review of Wundt, *Völkerpsychologie*, first and second volume: Die Sprache, third edition', in *Bulletin of the American Geographical Society* 47(1915), pp. 621–22; see also E.V. Arnold, 'Review of Wundt, *Völkerpsychologie*, vol. 1', in *The Classical Review* 15(1901), pp. 458–63; H.N. Gardiner, 'Review of Wundt, *Völkerpsychologie*, vol. 1', in *Philosophical Review* 11 (1902), pp. 497–514; H.N. Gardiner, 'Review of Wundt, *Völkerpsychologie*, vol. 2, first part, Myth and Religion, Leipzig, 1905', in *Philosophical Review* 16(2)(1907), pp. 200–4; H.N. Gardiner, 'Review of Wundt, *Völkerpsychologie*, vol. 2, third part, Leipzig 1909 and third volume, second edition, Leipzig 1908', in *Philosophical Review* 18(1909), pp. 543–48.

100. L. Bloomfield, 'Review of Wundt, *Elemente der Völkerpsychologie*', in *American Journal of Psychology* 24(1913), pp. 449–53.

101. R.R. Marett, 'Review of Wundt, *Elements of Folk Psychology*', in *Folklore* 27(1916), pp. 440–41.

102. T.S. Eliot, 'Review of Wundt, *Elements of Folk Psychology*', in *International Journal of Ethics* 27(1917), pp. 252–54.

103. G.H. Mead, 'A Translation of Wundt's "Folk Psychology"', in *American Journal of Theology* 23(1919), pp. 533–36. See Kroeber, 'The Possibility of a Social Psychology'.

104. H.K. Haeberlin, 'The Theoretical Foundations of Wundt's Folk Psychology', in *Psychological Review* 23(1916), pp. 279–302, reprinted in Rieber, ed., *Wilhelm Wundt and the Making of a Scientific Psychology*, pp. 229–49, here at pp. 235–36.

105. L.M. Easton, *Der rote Graf: Harry Graf Kessler und seine Zeit* (Stuttgart, 2005), pp. 56–59.

106. H. Graf Kessler, *Notizen über Mexiko* (Berlin, 1898); H. Graf Kessler, 'Nationalität', in *Die Zukunft* (April 1906); see Easton, *Der rote Graf*, p. 58.

107. S. Gordon, 'Reise westwärts, Blick ostwärts: Leipzig als Drehpunkt im Leben Martin Bubers', in S. Wendehorst, ed., *Bausteine einer jüdischen Geschichte der Universität Leipzig* (Leipzig, 2006), pp. 131–52, at pp. 146–47; M.S. Friedman, *Martin Buber's Life and Work* (Detroit, MI, 1988), pp. 23–24.

108. See the marketing text for the series in W. Sombart, *Das Proletariat. Bilder und Studien* (Frankfurt am Main, 1906); a best-seller of this collection was G. Simmel's *Die Religion* (Frankfurt am Main, 1906, third edition, 1922); Willy

Hellpach contributed a volume on *Die geistigen Epidemien* (Frankfurt am Main, 1906).

109. B. Beßlich, *Wege in den 'Kulturkrieg': Zivilisationskritik in Deutschland, 1890–1914* (Darmstadt, 2000); K. Flasch, *Die geistige Mobilmachung: Die deutschen Intellektuellen und der Erste Weltkrieg* (Berlin, 2000); H. Lübbe, *Politische Philosophie in Deutschland: Studien zu ihrer Geschichte* (Munich, 1974).

110. P. Hoeres, *Krieg der Philosophen: Die deutsche und die britische Philosophie im Ersten Weltkrieg* (Paderborn, 2004), pp. 276–81.

111. B. vom Brocke, '"Wissenschaft und Militarismus": Der Aufruf der 93 "An die Kulturwelt" und der Zusammenbruch der internationalen Gelehrtenrepublik im Ersten Weltkrieg', in W.M. Calder III, H. Flashaar and T. Lindken, eds, *Wilamowitz nach 50 Jahren* (Darmstadt, 1985), pp. 649–719; J. Ungern-Sternberg von Pürkel and W. von Ungern-Sternberg, *Der Aufruf 'An die Kulturwelt!' Das Manifest der 93 und die Anfänge der Kriegspropaganda im Ersten Weltkrieg* (Stuttgart, 1996).

112. Hoeres, *Krieg der Philosophen*.

113. W. Sombart, *Händler und Helden: Patriotische Besinnungen* (Munich, 1915); M. Scheler, *Der Genius des Krieges und der deutsche Krieg* (Leipzig, 1915); H. Oncken, *Unsere Abrechnung mit England* (Berlin, 1914).

114. W. Breitenbach, *England als Völkervernichter* (Bielefeld, 1917); E. Demolder, *Albions Todeskampf* (Munich, 1915); S. Gopcevic, *Aus dem Lande der unbegrenzten Heuchelei: Englische Zustände* (Berlin, 1915); E. Graf zu Reventlow, *England, der Feind* (Stuttgart, 1914).

115. W. Wundt, *Die Nationen und ihre Philosophie. Ein Kapitel zum Krieg*, [1915] (Leipzig, 1941).

116. Wundt, *Elemente der Völkerpsychologie*.

117. Wundt, *Die Nationen und ihre Philosophie*, p. 3.

118. Ibid., pp. 54–57.

119. Ibid., p. 124; this was a reference to the cultural critic Max Nordau, *Die conventionellen Lügen der Kulturmenschheit*, second edition (Leipzig, 1884).

120. See R. Bendix, *In Search of Authenticity: The Formation of Folklore Studies* (Madison, WI, 1997).

121. Wundt, *Die Nationen und ihre Philosophie*, pp. 124–25.

122. Ibid., pp. 126–27.

123. Th. Mann, *Betrachtungen eines Unpolitischen* (Berlin, 1918).

124. On the distinction between Kultur and Zivilisation in Germany see J. Fisch, 'Zivilisation, Kultur', in O. Brunner, W. Conze and R. Koselleck, eds, *Geschichtliche Grundbegriffe*, vol. 7 (Stuttgart, 1992), pp. 679–774.

125. See for instance J. Schreyer, *Die Judas-Briten: Ein zeitgemäßes Allerlei* (Kiel, 1917).

126. R. Thurnwald, 'Grundprobleme der vergleichenden Völkerpsychologie', in *Zeitschrift für die gesamte Staatswissenschaft* 87(1929), pp. 240–69. See R. Thurnwald, 'Geistesverfassung der Naturvölker', in K.T. Preuss, ed., *Lehrbuch der Völkerkunde* (Stuttgart, 1937), pp. 45–56, at p. 46; R. Thurnwald, 'Probleme der Völkerpsychologie und Soziologie', in *Zeitschrift für Völkerpsychologie und Soziologie* 1(1925), pp. 1–20; R. Thurnwald, 'Zum gegenwärtigen Stande der

Völkerpsychologie', in *Kölner Vierteljahreshefte für Soziologie* 3(1923–24), pp. 32–43. Thurnwald was also a co-editor of the *Archiv für Bevölkerungswissenschaft und Rassenhygiene*, the pre-eminent German journal for eugenics, founded by Alfred Ploetz. A representative of functionalist anthropology in Germany, he was well respected in the U.S.A. and the United Kingdom. His studies were regularly published in English, he was an Honorary Fellow of the Royal Anthropological Institute of Great Britain and Ireland, and spent the years from 1931 to 1933 as visiting professor at Yale and Harvard.

127. F. Krueger, *Über Entwicklungspsychologie, ihre sachliche und geschichtliche Notwendigkeit* (Leipzig, 1915); W. Wundt, 'Völkerpsychologie und Entwicklungspsychologie', in *Psychologische Studien* 10(1916), pp. 189–238; see A. Meischner-Metge, '"Völkerpsychologie" oder allgemeine "Entwicklungspsychologie"? Zur Wundt-Krueger-Deklarationsdiskussion', in Jüttemann, ed., *Wilhelm Wundts anderes Erbe: Ein Mißverständnis löst sich auf* (Göttingen, 2006), pp. 81–87.

128. F. Krueger, 'Wilhelm Wundt als deutscher Denker', in A. Hoffmann, ed., *Wilhelm Wundt: Eine Würdigung* (Erfurt, 1922), pp. 1–44 , at pp. 1–5.

129. Krueger, 'Wilhelm Wundt', p. 7, see ibid., pp. 14–16.

130. See M. Wundt, *Deutsche Weltanschauung: Grundzüge völkischen Denkens* (Munich, 1926); M. Wundt, *Was heißt völkisch?* (Langensalza, 1924); see C. Tilitzki, *Die deutsche Universitätsphilosophie in der Weimarer Republik und im Dritten Reich*, 2 vols (Berlin, 2002), vol. 1, pp. 123–25.

131. H. Volkelt, 'Die Völkerpsychologie in Wundts Entwicklungsgang', in *Wilhelm Wundt: Eine Würdigung*, pp. 74–105, at pp. 74–75.

132. Ibid., p. 76.

133. Ibid., p. 99.

134. Ibid., p. 104.

135. W. Moog, *Die deutsche Philosophie des 20. Jahrhunderts in ihren Hauptproblemen und Grundrichtungen* (Stuttgart, 1922), pp. 118, 120–21.

136. Ibid., p. 130.

137. See R. Müller-Freienfels, *Psychologie des deutschen Menschen und seiner Kultur: Ein volkscharakterologischer Versuch* (Munich, 1922).

138. E. Hurwicz, *Die Seelen der Völker: Ihre Eigenarten und Bedeutung im Völkerleben* (Gotha, 1920); E. Oberhummer, *Völkerpsychologie und Völkerkunde: Vortrag* (Vienna, 1923).

139. The monograph by H.-J. Lutzhöft, *Der Nordische Gedanke in Deutschland, 1920–1940* (Stuttgart, 1971), which focuses on Günther, is largely apologetic. See C.M. Hutton, *Race and the Third Reich: Linguistics, Racial Anthropology and Genetics in the Dialectic of the Volk* (Cambridge, 2005), pp. 35–63. On Clauss see P. Weingart, *Doppel-Leben. Ludwig Ferdinand Clauss: Zwischen Rassenforschung und Widerstand* (Frankfurt am Main, 1995); F. Wiedemann, 'Der doppelte Orient. Zur völkischen Orientromantik des Ludwig Ferdinand Clauß', in *Zeitschrift für Religions- und Geistesgeschichte* 61(2009), pp. 1–24.

140. H.F.K. Günther, *Rassenkunde des deutschen Volkes* [1922], seventeenth edition (Munich, 1933); L.F. Clauss, *Rasse und Seele. Eine Einführung in den Sinn der leiblichen Gestalt*, third edition (Munich, 1933).

141. Günther, *Rassenkunde des deutschen Volkes*, p. 197.

142. Examples of this attitude can be found in F. Keiter, *Rassenpsychologie: Einführung in eine werdende Wissenschaft* (Leipzig, 1941), p. 14; W.E. Mühlmann, *Rassen- und Völkerkunde:Lebensprobleme der Rassen, Gesellschaften und Völker* (Braunschweig, 1936); B. Petermann, *Das Problem der Rassenseele: Vorlesungen zur Grundlegung einer allgemeinen Rassenpsychologie* (Leipzig, 1935); E. Ortner, *Biologische Typen des Menschen und ihr Verhalten zu Rasse und Wert. Zugleich ein Beitrag zur Clauss'schen Rassenpsychologie* (Leipzig, 1937); K. Rau, *Untersuchungen zur Rassenpsychologie nach typologischer Methode* (Leipzig, 1936); O. Rutz, *Grundlagen einer psychologischen Rassenkunde* (Tübingen, 1934).

143. M.H. Boehm, *Das eigenständige Volk. Volkstheoretische Grundlagen der Ethnopolitik und Geisteswissenschaften* (Göttingen, 1932), pp. 265–310.

144. Ibid., p. 267–68.

145. Ibid., p. 283–84.

146. Ibid., p. 295.

147. Th. Waitz, *Anthropologie der Naturvölker*, 7 vols (Leipzig, 1859–71).

148. Eckardt, ed., *Völkerpsychologie;* Schneider, *Wilhelm Wundts Völkerpsychologie.*

149. F.K. Ringer, *The Decline of the German Mandarins: The German Academic Community, 1890–1933* (Cambridge, MA, 1969); K. Krause, *Alma Mater Lipsiensis: Geschichte der Universität Leipzig von 1409 bis zur Gegenwart* (Leipzig, 2003).

150. S. Hall, *The Founders of Psychology* (New York, 1912), p. 312. In 1909 Sigmund Freud accepted Hall's invitation after Wundt's rejection and used the occasion to advertise psychoanalysis in the U.S. with his *Five Lectures on Psychoanalysis.*

151. Danziger, *Constructing the Subject*, p. 34.

CHAPTER 3

Willy Hellpach and the Resurrection of Folk Psychology

In 1938 Willy Hellpach published a book entitled *Einführung in die Völkerpsychologie*. It was the first book-length study on folk psychology since Wilhelm Wundt's death and the first attempt to provide a concise introduction to the field suitable for university teaching.[1] This study turned Hellpach into the major representative of a discipline that did not really exist. Lacking an energetic and dedicated proponent, the field had not flourished after Wundt's death in 1920, despite the increased interest in 'differential' folk psychology during and after the First World War. By the 1930s Hellpach seemed an unlikely candidate to assume this role, despite his later efforts to present himself as a life-long adherent and champion of folk psychology. A founding member of the liberal Deutsche Demokratische Partei (German Democratic Party, DDP) in late 1918, he was best known for his political career: from 1922 to 1925 he was Minister for Education in the state of Baden, and in 1925 the candidate for the DDP in the first round of the elections for the Reich presidency. From 1928 to 1930 Hellpach, also a prolific political journalist and commentator on social affairs, was a member of the Reichstag for the DDP.[2]

By training, Hellpach was a psychologist and physician, and had been familiar with the idea and concept of folk psychology since his student years. In the 1890s he had enrolled at the University of Leipzig and studied with Wilhelm Wundt, who supervised his Ph.D. in experimental psychology. In 1913, as adjunct professor at the Technical College in Karlsruhe, Hellpach lectured on folk psychology, and in the 1920s and 1930s he continued to teach on the subject at the University of Heidelberg. Since the 1890s Hellpach had published countless books and articles, both in popular and academic form, on a wide range of topics, from environmental and climatic psychology to neurology, psychopathology, the psychology of work and psychotechnology. Still, none of the many studies on psychology and psychiatry he published before 1934 had made a contribution to *Völkerpsychologie*. Even in an early book on the 'neighbouring fields of psychiatry', Hellpach mentioned folk psychology only in passing. In that book he was quite dismissive of Wundt's approach to folk psychology and criticized his focus on language, myth and customs as too narrow. Instead, he preferred sociology as the discipline best suited to deal with the problem of 'elementary social-psychological events' (*sozialpsychische Elementarvorgänge*), a notion that was anathema to Wundt. Hellpach clearly favoured Karl Lamprecht's cultural history over Wundt's folk psychology, and while his book on the *Grenzwissenschaften der Psychologie* was dedicated to his teacher Wundt, he did not follow his path. At this stage he presented social psychology, not folk psychology as the future discipline that would study the historical-psychological development of mankind.[3]

It was only after the establishment of the Nazi regime that Hellpach made folk psychology the focus of his academic work and started working on the *Einführung* in a systematic way. This change of perspective was largely a result of his personal circumstances: as a former liberal politician and representative of the Weimar 'system', Hellpach was forced to abstain from any political work after 1933, and was not allowed to publish any political journalism, which had been his main occupation between 1926 and 1933. Despite these restrictions, however, he was allowed to keep his professorship at the University of Heidelberg, and to avoid conflict with the new regime, he reoriented his research towards folk psychology. The focus on *Völkerpsychologie*, then, was part of his personal strategy to adapt to the conditions of the Third Reich, and as such a clever choice. The topic fitted in neatly with Nazi-endorsed studies into the German *Volk*, *Volkstum* and *Volksgeschichte*, which were thriving on account of their – real or perceived – compatibility with the völkisch ideology of the Nazis.[4] Folk psychology thus provided Hellpach with an opportunity to reconcile himself with the Third Reich and to avoid denunciation and censorship. As long as he abstained from journalism and political statements in public, and concentrated on his academic work, Hellpach remained free in his choice of topics. He thus became increasingly well integrated into the German academic community, and the university provided him with the niche to survive the Third Reich unharmed.

While Hellpach convinced himself that he had kept his intellectual independence, even under the repressive conditions of the Nazi dictatorship, his folk psychology made clear concessions to Nazi ideology. Hellpach's version of folk psychology thus provides a telling case study of the behaviour of the majority of German academics (and intellectuals), who neither openly supported nor opposed the Third Reich. Moreover, it demonstrates the ease with which national-liberal intellectuals could adapt to the Nazi regime, on account of a substantial overlap between national-liberal and national-socialist ideas. While there were clear differences between Hellpach's academic and political views and Nazi ideology, in particular regarding anti-Semitism and political violence, there were also striking similarities. In particular, Hellpach agreed with one of the basic principles of the National Socialist German Workers' Party, namely that the workers had to be won for the national cause. With Friedrich Naumann (1860–1919), the left-liberal founder of the National-Sozialer Verein, Hellpach agreed strongly that the integration of the working class into the 'national community' was the most important social and political task of modern society.[5] But so did the National Socialists, despite the obvious difference in militancy and radicalism between them and the respectable middle classes. Hellpach's political *Weltanschauung*, then, differed not so much in substance, but in form and degree from the radical nationalism of the Nazis. In this respect, Hellpach's attitude was symptomatic of many disillusioned middle-class Germans in the Weimar Republic who sympathized with the NSDAP, or could at least understand their demands, but rejected the militant practice of the movement, in particular of the SA. Importantly, Hellpach was not an anti-Semite, and in the 1920s he had openly and at length criticized the popular theories of race as represented by Hans F.K. Günther and Ludwig Ferdinand Clauss. He did not deny, however, the importance of 'racial' or 'biological' factors in the make-up of a nation, or folk, and hence the need for the scientific study of race. For Hellpach, it proved dangerously easy to make his ideas about the folk, nation and race compatible with Nazi ideology. Slight, but decisive changes in focus and stress sufficed to achieve this task.[6]

Between Psychology and Politics

Hellpach came from a humble, petty-bourgeois family. Born in 1877 in the town of Oels in Silesia, he was raised by his mother after the early death of his father, who had been a middle-rank civil servant. Despite the difficult economic situation of his family, Hellpach took full advantage of the opportunities that opened up in higher education to talented and ambitious students during the German *Kaiserreich*. He became the first member of his family to attend a Gymnasium; he graduated with the *Abitur*, the entrance exam for the study at university, and went on to read medicine and psychology at Greifswald, Leipzig and Heidelberg between 1895 and 1903. At the University of Leipzig Hellpach became one of the many students who were attracted by Wundt's psychological laboratory. Under his supervision Hellpach was awarded a Ph.D. in psychology with a study on the perception of colours.[7] To conclude his medical studies Hellpach moved on to the University of Heidelberg, where he specialized in neurology. He was recommended by Wundt to Emil Kraepelin (1856–1926), one of Wundt's former students who had become one of the leading German neurologists; otherwise, Hellpach was not particularly close to Wundt.[8] Hellpach's hopes of becoming a salaried research assistant of Kraepelin in Heidelberg were disappointed, however. Undeterred, he spent a year as an intern at Kraepelin's hospital in Heidelberg and then moved on to Berlin to study with Hermann Oppenheim (1858–1919), another world-famous neurologist at the time. In 1903 Hellpach finished his prolonged course of study, when he passed his final exams in medicine at the University of Heidelberg. His second doctoral dissertation, this time in medicine, was dedicated to a then fashionable topic: 'Analytical Enquiries into the Psychology of Hysteria'.[9] The following year Hellpach published a 500-page book on the same topic, which demonstrated his talent for summarizing and popularizing scientific topics.[10] As early as 1902 Hellpach had published a short monograph on *Nervousness and Culture* which analysed 'neurasthenia' as a typical disease of modern civilization.[11] For Martin Buber's popular collection, *Die Gesellschaft*, Hellpach was invited to produce a volume on a related topic, entitled *Mental Epidemics* in 1906.[12] Despite – or because of – his remarkable publication record, however, Hellpach faced difficulties in finding the academic job he was hoping for, and in 1904, after getting married to his long-time fiancée, he decided to move to Karlsruhe, the capital of Baden, and to open a neurological practice.

By this time Hellpach had already established himself as a journalist and popular scientist with a distinguished record. As a student, he had supported himself as a freelance journalist and had published numerous essays using the pseudonym 'Ernst Gystrow' on social-political and popular-scientific topics – for some of the most respected journals in the German-speaking lands, such as *Die Grenzboten*, the Viennese *Zeit*, the *Gesellschaft*, Maximilian Harden's *Zukunft*, and the *Morgen*.[13] These early publications showed Hellpach as a talented science journalist. He made good use of his double qualification in medicine and philosophy, and excelled in explaining scientific topics to a general audience. Furthermore, Hellpach became a regular contributor to the *Sozialistische Monatshefte*, the journal of the revisionist wing of the German Social Democrats. During his time in Berlin Hellpach mingled with the group of intellectuals that had gathered around the editor of the journal, Joseph Bloch (1871–1936), and attended their regular meetings in the coffee houses of the German capital.[14] Led by Eduard Bernstein (1850–1932), the revisionists had criticized central parts of the official party programme of the SPD. The increasing prosperity of the German Empire called for a retraction from the Marxist strategy for realizing socialism, the revisionists argued. Instead of expecting a revolutionary 'big bang' that would necessarily lead to the demise and dissolution of the capitalist system and bring about socialism, Bernstein favoured and campaigned for a reformist strategy that would slowly transform the existing socio-economic order. Socialism was to be built from within capitalism, by means of co-operatives, the nationalization of industries and the further democratization of society.[15] Hellpach identified with the aims of the revisionists but never joined the SPD; indeed, he was extremely critical of the 'orthodox' leadership of the party under August Bebel (1840–1913) and its theoretical head Karl Kautsky (1854–1938): 'Socialism became a firm part of myself while my aversion against Social Democracy grew.'[16] One of his earliest contributions to the *Sozialistische Monatshefte* was a scathing review of the writings of Franz Mehring (1846–1919), who next to Kautsky had become one of the main interpreters of social-democratic Marxism and thus one of Hellpach's favourite enemies.[17]

In contrast to the 'orthodoxy' of the party, then, Hellpach followed his own definition of socialism that differed markedly from the Marxist position of the leadership of the SPD. With hindsight, he characterized his political stance before the First World War as a form of 'socialism of reason' (*Vernunftsozialismus*). He was convinced that the 'social question' was the most pressing national problem and that the future of Germany depended on a solution to this, but rejected any form of revolutionary socialism and ideas of class struggle. He sympathized with Friedrich Naumann's attempts to integrate the workers into the national community and thus solve the social question, and was deeply disappointed when the National-Sozialer Verein was dissolved after a crushing defeat at the national elections in 1903.[18] Reflecting his petty-bourgeois background, Hellpach's concern for the 'social question' had not been formed by personal experiences or by his reading of socialist theorists, but by the social realism he found in the novels of popular authors such as Gerhard Hauptmann (1862–1946), Henrik Ibsen (1828–1906) and Emile Zola (1840–1902).[19] Reflecting ideas of the circle around Joseph Bloch and the *Sozialistische Monatshefte*, Hellpach also called for a reconciliation of Nietzschean and socialist ideas as a solution to the 'social question'.[20] According to his memoirs, the defeat of the revisionist group within the SPD at the party conference in 1903 – which coincided with the demise of Naumann's National-Sozialer Verein – disillusioned Hellpach profoundly and had a major impact on his later career. After this event he severed his contact with the revisionist intellectuals in Berlin, stopped his collaboration with the *Sozialistische Monatshefte*, and abstained from political journalism until the First World War. Hellpach still published in non-academic journals, such as *Der Morgen*, but restricted his contributions to non-political topics. From 1907 he edited the *Ärtzliche Mitteilungen*, the journal of the Leipziger Verband, the German association of medical doctors later known as Hartmannbund after its founder, the physician Hermann Hartmann (1863–

1923). Hellpach depended on the regular income from this job to subsidize his fledgling career as a self-employed neurologist.[21]

Besides his day jobs as neurologist and journalist, Hellpach still tried to pursue an academic career. After moving to Karlsruhe, in 1903, he had started preparing a *Habilitation* at the Technical College, and after initial problems – for a lack of expertise at Karlsruhe, Hellpach's study on *General Ideas on the Methodology of Psychopathology*[22] had to be examined at the University of Heidelberg, where the matter was further delayed until Max Weber urged Wilhelm Windelband to support Hellpach – Hellpach became *Privatdozent* in psychology at Karlsruhe.[23] In 1911, after five years of teaching, he was awarded the prestigious title of adjunct professor. According to the requirements of the 'plumber's academy', as Hellpach sardonically referred to the Technical College in Karlsruhe, he mainly lectured on economic psychology and the psychology of work. With a characteristic lack of modesty, he later claimed to have introduced these fields single-handedly to higher education in Germany.[24]

Already in 1902 Hellpach had lifted his cover and revealed himself as the author 'Ernst Gystrow', when he published his first academic monograph. This was a decision he soon came to regret. His journalistic work, and in particular his affiliation with the *Sozialistische Monatshefte*, were met with deep suspicion by the academic establishment in Germany and jeopardized any realistic prospect of furthering his academic career.[25] A likely reason for Hellpach's abstention from political journalism after 1903 was his realization that an association with any form of socialism considerably diminished the chances of being appointed to a professorship. Decades later Hellpach still complained bitterly about the difficulties he encountered in starting an academic career, which, he claimed, were also due to the prejudices of the university establishment towards teachers at technical colleges, who were treated as 'second-class citizens'. Hellpach's many talents and his multiple occupations as neurologist, journalist, lobbyist and part-time lecturer seemed to have become an obstacle to his academic reputation, and he was accused of being a 'newspaper scribbler and a *Vielschreiber*'.[26]

With the beginning of the First World War, Hellpach was immediately called to duty and served as a military doctor for the German army for the length of the conflict. He spent the first months of the war behind the front line in the town of Lens in northern France, and then returned to Germany in 1915, when he was ordered to do service in military hospitals first in Staufen im Breisgau and later in Heidelberg. In this position he survived the hostilities unharmed. The war also renewed Hellpach's interest in politics, after his self-imposed abstention of ten years. During the war Hellpach contributed to the debates about Germany's future political outlook, notably in essays about the 'Bohemian Question' and on 'Conservative Thoughts'. With hindsight, he declared these articles the 'pillars' of his political thinking.[27] Shortly after the beginning of the war, he reported, the 'vision of a conservative democracy' as a solution to the crisis of the political system appeared to him for the first time. He would go on to advertise this concept as the 'royal road' to solve Germany's political difficulties, both before and after the Second World War. Hellpach's political writings during the First World War can be described as genuinely 'pan-German': he thought of himself as one of the very few Germans who 'really understood Austrian matters' because of his German-Bohemian family relations. In his youth he had regularly visited relatives who lived on the other side of the *Riesengebirge* in the Habsburg Empire, and his wife came from a German-Bohemian family from Prague. Through his in-laws, some of whom worked in the civil service of the Habsburg Empire, Hellpach claimed to have gained insight into 'the real weaknesses, but also the real value' of the Austrian mind which was regularly ignored in Prussian-dominated Germany.[28]

Hellpach's renewed concern with political problems during the First World War also spurred his interest in the study of national characters. The misjudgements of the German leadership during the war convinced him of the urgent need to study national characters as a means of political education. While stationed in Heidelberg, in 1916, Hellpach had attended a public lecture by the historian Hermann Oncken (1869–1945), and reacted with outrage to the praise Oncken found for the Reich chancellor Theobald von Bethmann-Hollweg (1856–1921). To Hellpach's mind, Oncken's speech had shown a naivety in foreign affairs that was characteristic of the German political elite and had proved fatal during the war. The 'extraordinary lack of psychological judgement of foreign nations and leaders, their moods and views' of Germany's political leadership had demonstrated the 'urgent need for educational improvement in this respect'. The idea to write contemporary folk psychology or *lebendige Völkerseelenkunde*, Hellpach claimed in his memoirs, was first conceived during the First World War and the political revelations he had experienced.[29]

Despite his renewed interest in politics during the First World War, Hellpach was still trying to become full professor at a German university. Several attempts during the war to install him as chair of psychology failed, however. Felix Krueger, since 1915 Wundt's successor on the renowned chair of psychology at the University of Leipzig, supported Hellpach's ambitions and suggested him as his successor at the University of Halle, but to no avail. Another attempt at the Technical College in Dresden failed, too.[30] After the end of the First World War, however, when Hellpach returned to Karlsruhe, he was soon able to concentrate fully on his academic work. Shortly after the war, and despite his rather idiosyncratic understanding of liberalism, Hellpach joined the left-liberal DDP, one of the founding parties of the Weimar

Republic, which had one of its strongholds in the state of Baden. Due to his good relations with the Ministry of Culture in Baden, his adjunct position at the Technical College in Karlsruhe was upgraded to a full professorship, enabling him to give up his position as editor of the *Ärtzliche Mitteilungen*. Hellpach became director of a new Institute of Social Psychology at the Technical College in Karlsruhe, where he concentrated on business psychology and the psychology of work, the focus of 'applied' psychology in the 1920s. In this new position he conducted empirical studies on the psychological effects of rationalized industrial work, and promoted 'group manufacturing' as an alternative to Taylorism, thus contributing to the quickly growing body of literature on industrial rationalization in the early Weimar Republic.[31]

At the time when he had finally reached his goal and had become a full-time professor, Hellpach's political career began to take shape. He was elected councillor of the city of Karlsruhe in 1920, and, allegedly to his own surprise, was offered the Ministry for Education and Culture in 1922 in the state of Baden, which was then governed by a Weimar coalition between the SPD, the DDP and the Catholic Centre Party. Hellpach duly accepted the offer, and during his time in office concentrated on educational and school reform, introduced the 'dual system' of apprenticeships and state schooling and thus developed another new field of expertise.[32] In 1924/5, in accordance with the constitutional arrangements of the state of Baden, he acted as president of state and became a member of the Reichsrat, the representation of the German states at federal level. After the surprising death of Reich president Friedrich Ebert (1871–1925) in 1925 – as state president of Baden, Hellpach gave a speech at the funeral in Ebert's hometown of Heidelberg – he agreed to his nomination as the candidate for the DDP in the upcoming elections. Even though he had no real chance of being elected, the electoral campaign made Hellpach known to a wider public and provided the talented speaker with a national platform. In the second round of the elections, the tactics and manoeuvring of the 'Weimar' parties failed when the surprise candidate of the right-wing parties, the war-hero general Paul von Hindenburg (1847–1934), beat the candidate of the democratic parties, Wilhelm Marx (1863–1946) of the Centre party, by a small margin. At the end of the same year Hellpach lost his position as Minister in Baden, not least because he had upset many of his party colleagues with his unorthodox views and overpowering personality. Since Hellpach had not kept open his professorship at Karlsruhe, in order to avoid a conflict of interest while Minister of Education, he could not return to his post, but he was entitled to a handsome pension as professor emeritus which made him financially independent. To compensate for the loss of his professorship, the University of Heidelberg agreed to appoint Hellpach to the rank of honorary chair in psychology (*ordentlicher Honorarprofessor*) after initial plans to make him full professor at the University of Heidelberg had met the resistance of the faculty of philosophy. When the attempt to install Hellpach to the chair of education at the University of Frankfurt in succession of Julius Ziehen (1864–1925) failed, he finally moved to Heidelberg and started teaching at the prestigious university in the autumn of 1926.[33]

With hindsight, Hellpach described the period between the end of his political career in Baden and the beginning of the Third Reich as the most comfortable and carefree time of his life. During the short period of prosperity of the Weimar Republic, between the Ruhr crisis and the Great Depression, Hellpach was in high demand as a public speaker, in Germany and abroad. His lectures and speeches were typical contributions of an 'elder statesman': he preferred to comment on current affairs and mostly avoided strictly academic topics. In addition, he became a regular contributor to the most respected German-language newspapers such as the *Vossische Zeitung*, the *Frankfurter Zeitung*, the *Neue Zürcher Zeitung* and the *Neue Freie Presse* in Vienna, which published Hellpach's comments on political developments. Before the Nazi regime Hellpach was thus more a public intellectual than an academic. His professorship at the University of Heidelberg was little more than a titular post that provided him with prestige and cultural capital, and he spent more time on his political writings than on research.[34]

His best-known book of the 1920s, entitled *Political Prognosis for Germany*, collected his political and journalistic works and provided a concise summary of his political views. It opened with a detailed critique of the popular race theories propagated by Hans F.K. Günther and Ludwig Ferdinand Clauss, and *völkisch* ideology in general. In order to reject the pseudo-scientific ideology of the Nordic Movement, Hellpach employed well-established arguments of traditional *Völkerpsychologie*. While he was not opposed to employing the category of 'race' in academic research, he dismissed the reductionism of Günther's theories and his *völkisch* followers. Instead, Hellpach stated that the German nation did not constitute a race.[35] Those who mixed up the present-day Germans with the allegedly blond and blue-eyed Germanic 'tribes' of ancient times acted against the national interest because they excluded millions of Germans who did not belong to this Nordic race from the German nation. History showed that nationhood (*Volkstum*) and race were never identical, and that the German lands had been at a crossroads of racial mixing for centuries, if not millennia. Therefore, the German nation was by definition a 'mixed race', in this respect not unlike the English 'race'. In the first place, Hellpach argued, it was language that constituted a nation: The term 'Germanic' originated, after all, in linguistics, and the mother tongue mattered much more to the character of a nation than blood and race. Indirectly, however, Hellpach showed that he agreed with the basic assumptions of 'race psychologists', namely that races were related to specific character traits. But to Hellpach, the mixture of races found in the German nation did not pose a political problem, as *völkisch* ideologues argued, but was an asset of the nation, since it assured a multitude of talents within the 'folk'. Hellpach did not forget to refer to Franz Boas, who had argued that even the physiognomy of a nation changed much more quickly than physical anthropologists assumed, as the study of American immigrants showed. The real enigma of the German *Volkstum* – that 'wonderful word' introduced by Friedrich Ludwig Jahn (1778–1852) – was not race, but the different 'tribes' (*Stämme*), Hellpach argued with reference to his own research.[36]

By the late 1920s Hellpach's political views were idiosyncratic to the degree that he did not fit into any of the established parties and began to feel politically homeless. In this respect he represented the crisis and the decline of political liberalism in Germany which accelerated after the onset of the economic crisis in 1929. Hellpach subscribed to a mixture of national and liberal ideas while paying attention to the 'social question'. With conservatives and liberals of all colours he shared a strong appreciation of the nation as an end to itself that was beyond criticism. Similarly, history and tradition represented independent values to Hellpach that needed no further justification. Generally speaking, he supported a democratic system of government, but, in line with a strong current of public opinion in Germany in the 1920s, he became increasingly critical of the parliamentarian system of the Weimar Republic. Instead of the anonymous and bureaucratic processes of a parliamentarian democracy, he favoured the direct interaction between the people and a strong political leadership. At the heart of his critique of the political system of the Weimar Republic lay his distrust of the powerful party 'machines', which he blamed for the 'depersonalization' of the political process. As with much of Hellpach's thinking, these views were hardly original, but reflected a widespread attitude that was not limited to radical enemies of Weimar democracy. Considering that Hellpach counted among the leading politicians of the DDP in the Weimar Republic, his idea of liberalism was odd, but similarly reflected a wider trend. He did not embrace or feel passionately about traditional liberal ideas and values such as a free market system, civil rights, or representative democracy. Instead, he explained his attachment to the liberal DDP as a purely personal decision that was more related to his instincts than to rational reasoning. During his military service, and again as a young academic, Hellpach explained, he had run into difficulties with his superiors and found it hard to follow orders. The problems he had encountered with authorities, Hellpach claimed, reflected his strong sense of individual freedom and independence, and were proof of his liberal instincts.[37]

Even though in the mid 1920s Hellpach might have been considered a 'republican of reason' who generally supported the Weimar Republic, by the late 1920s he had turned into a vociferous critic of the political system of the new German state.[38] His sharp and direct attacks on the workings of parliamentary democracy resembled those of open enemies of the Weimar Republic who wanted to get rid of a system that seemed alien to them and had allegedly been imposed on Germany by the Western Allies. In contrast to 'conservative revolutionaries' or even the *völkische* right, however, Hellpach did not oppose 'Western' democracy as such, but strongly detested the workings of the parliamentarian system that was introduced in the Weimar Republic. He admired the British system as superior because it produced stable majorities and governments and regularly produced a strong executive. As a remedy for the notorious instability of the Weimar Republic, Hellpach proposed reforms to the political system that would have further strengthened the executive – both the government and the president – at the expense of the power of parliament. In addition, he suggested the widening of the already considerable plebiscitary elements of the constitution in order to connect the *Volk* more to the political decision-making process. In contrast to more extreme right-wing opponents of the Weimar Republic, however, Hellpach insisted on reforming the democratic system and never envisioned a return to the semi-authoritarian system of the *Kaiserreich* or the introduction of an authoritarian dictatorship. The main target of Hellpach's scorn – and he was not alone with this view – were professional politicians who lived not only 'for politics' but also 'from politics'. To restrict the influence of the new political class – and thus to limit the influence of political parties and interest groups – he favoured a parliament that represented the 'estates' (*Stände*) and thus mirrored the social make-up of the German people more accurately. This suggestion was reminiscent of the ideas of the Austrian Catholic social philosopher Othmar Spann (1878–1950), the main supporter of a *Ständestaat* in the inter-war period, who became an inspiration for the Austro-fascist state after 1934, but was attenuated by Hellpach's general support for democracy.[39]

Despite his criticism of the parliamentarian system of the Weimar Republic, the ever-ambitious Hellpach made a surprise return to the political stage in 1928 when the DDP offered him the candidacy for a safe seat in the Reichstag, which he duly accepted. His short stint as a member of the Reichstag only re-enforced Hellpach's disdain for the professionalized and bureaucratic proceedings of the German parliament. He even detested the parliament's building, and saw the poor quality of the food served in the restaurant of the Reichstag as symptomatic of the institution. According to Hellpach, the 'philistinism of parliamentarianism' (*Verphilisterung des Parlamentarismus*) was mirrored in the 'worn-out jackets and the grumpy, sweating faces' of the waiters who served him mediocre lunches in the canteen of the parliament. The conduct of plenary sessions seemed undignified to Hellpach, because 'objective discussions and serious debates' were impossible. The public debates only served to cover up the horse-trading that went on behind closed doors in the committee rooms. Instead of an open and honest exchange of political views, parliament was dominated by the 'bartering behind the scenes' for which Hellpach held professional lobbyists responsible – a surprising view given his former employment by the main interest group of German medical doctors.[40] As a consequence, Hellpach resigned with aplomb from his seat in 1930, deeply frustrated by his experience as a parliamentarian, and left the quickly dissolving DDP. After his highly publicized retirement from active politics, Hellpach's criticism of the parliamentarian system grew even stronger.[41]

Similar to many of his contemporaries, and blinded by the double crisis of the political and economic system of the Weimar Republic after 1930, Hellpach underestimated the threat posed by the National Socialists. The 'Hitler party' appeared to him first of all as a generational phenomenon. The Nazis represented the young generation in Germany, with their activists between thirty to forty-five years old. Characteristic of youth was the search for the 'unconditional' (*das Unbedingte*), which explained the activism and the urgency of the national revolutionary movement. The main difference between the Nazis and other parties lay in their style of politics, Hellpach concluded, not in the substance of their demands or their main aims.[42] The Nazis and their followers might exaggerate their political demands in a typically youthful fashion, Hellpach opined, but they did raise serious and legitimate concerns about the political and economic crisis in Germany. For the same reason, Hellpach did not expect the Nazis to enjoy sustained success, but predicted their rapid decline, similar to that of the anti-Semitic parties of the 1880s and 1890s which had disappeared quickly after initial electoral successes.[43] To Hellpach, the NSDAP was merely a radical party of protest that would not have any long-term impact. Hence he did not take the Nazis' ideology seriously and thought it unnecessary to read Hitler's autobiography-cum-manifesto *Mein Kampf* – to which he referred as an 'opera score' – or to follow the National Socialist press.[44] In contrast to National Socialism, Hellpach regarded Italian fascism with more sympathy. In 1932 he had the opportunity to observe the Italian system and its representatives at first hand when he attended the second Volta conference in Rome on the future of Europe, a show-case for the Italian dictatorship to which Benito Mussolini (1883–1945) had invited him personally.[45] In Hellpach's judgement, the Italian fascists fared much better than the Nazis, since fascism was not based on a particular ideology or political philosophy but was merely a form of 'authoritarian pragmatism'. Compared to Hitler, Mussolini's obsession with power was limited, as evidenced by the fact that he had kept the monarchy intact and had found an arrangement with the Catholic Church. Towards the arts, culture and science Mussolini had shown an 'attitude of respect', in complete contrast to

Hitler and the National Socialists, who cultivated their proletarian, anti-bourgeois image and poked fun at intellectuals, artists and academics.[46]

After the hand-over of power to the Nazis, in 1933, Hellpach immediately ran into difficulties with the new government, not primarily because of his much publicized political opinions, but because of the offices he had held during the Weimar Republic as a member of the DDP. Despite his criticism of Weimar parliamentarianism that resembled the right-wing enemies of the state – in his autobiography Hellpach reported that the only speech he gave in parliament earned him applause from the National Socialists, to his own surprise and embarrassment[47] – the Nazis identified Hellpach as a former representative of the Weimar Republic and penalized him for this exposed position. On the basis of paragraph 12 of the 'Law for the Reinstitution of the Professional Civil Service' ('Reichsgesetz zur Wiederherstellung des Berufsbeamtentums'), introduced in April 1933, the pension he drew as professor emeritus at the Technical College of Karlsruhe was cut from 720 to 390 Reichsmark.[48] Hellpach took this decision as a political, disciplinary measure and considered himself a victim of the new regime. However, he did receive support from Paul Schmitthenner (1884–1963), an open supporter of the Nazis, who had been appointed as professor of military history at the University of Heidelberg in May 1933. Schmitthenner intervened on Hellpach's behalf at the Ministry of Education in Baden, and the Faculty of Philosophy at the University of Heidelberg was also supportive and extended his teaching assignment to 'social and folk psychology', which increased his annual honorarium from 1,920 to 2,400 Reichsmark, thus compensating him partly for his loss of earnings. Hellpach's financial position was further worsened since he had to give up his lucrative work as a freelance journalist during the Third Reich. For Hellpach, who had enjoyed a considerable income as a respected university professor, journalist and public speaker, the take-over of power by the Nazis brought about a serious deterioration of his standard of living and public status.[49]

Apart from the economic hardship he had to endure and the fact that two of his political books – *The Essence of the German School* and *Political Prognosis for Germany* – were subsequently banned by the Nazis, Hellpach did not suffer from further repression during the Third Reich. He was allowed to continue teaching, and after a brief period of disorientation and adaption, when the Hellpachs had to move to a smaller flat, and he described his mental state as confused and depressed, he refocused his energies on academic work. During the 1930s and 1940s Hellpach published several academic monographs, numerous articles and reviews in journals, and was, on his own account, free in the choice of his research topics. He became increasingly well integrated into the academic community, attended national and international conferences, and lectured at the University of Heidelberg without any interference from state officials or party authorities. Quite to the contrary, Hellpach's research interests proved to be perfectly compatible with the expectations of the Nazi regime.

From Physiognomy to *Völkerpsychologie*

In between his many other obligations, Hellpach occasionally found time to conduct research in the 1920s. A continuing project of his had been a study of the 'physiognomy of the German tribes' (*Physiognomik der deutschen Stämme*) to which he had referred in his *Political Prognosis for Germany*. While serving as a military doctor for the German army, during the First World War, Hellpach had gleaned 'characteriological data' of the 'diverse German tribes' from the patients in his care. He continued with this practice after the war, when he was researching the psychological effects of 'group production' and rationalization at the Technical College of Karlsruhe and used regular fieldtrips to factories and workshops to collect data for his studies on German physiognomies.[50] This 'counting at the street corners', as Hellpach referred to his rather unsystematic gathering of physiognomic-ethnographic information, formed the basis of a paper he presented to the Academy of Sciences at Heidelberg in 1921. In it, he compared the 'Franconian face' to the 'Swabian face' and argued that the physiognomies of German 'tribes' were characterized by different facial structures: 'In Germany (i.e., all the German-speaking lands) the diversity of faces seems extraordinary. Especially in the area from the centre of Germany to the foot of the Alps this diversity is so great that, on superficial inspection, it defies any rules or patterns. Patient, systematic and intensive observations, however, reveal the existence of well established physiognomic types.'[51] To explain these different types, Hellpach argued, physical-anthropological theories, 'morpho-chemical' explanations and environmental theories were all insufficient.[52] In contrast to the skull-measuring phrenologists who dominated physical anthropology in Germany, Hellpach was convinced of the plasticity of human physiognomy, thus following the German-American anthropologist Franz Boas and his teacher Wilhelm Wundt.[53] The obvious differences in the physiognomy of the German 'tribes' were due to 'social-psychological' factors, Hellpach maintained. The 'essential transformation of a Franconian face into a Swabian one' that he claimed to have observed was due to the influence of the social environment, 'through the influence of one's peers; it is a social-psychophysical process'.[54] The two forces that formed a face were 'temperament' and 'local dialect': 'The fact remains that temperaments differ a lot regionally, and "regions" of the same temperament are not constituted by similarities in climate or landscape, but through the unity of a tribe inhabiting the region; this unity in turn is characterized by a single criterion, dialect'.[55] Typical regional ways of speaking had 'physiognomo-plastic' effects; they 'formed' the faces predominant in a particular region. Conventions of gestures were in turn a consequence of temperament. Temperament and dialect, Hellpach explained, were cultural conventions and therefore products of the 'environment' that formed the physical appearance of man.[56]

In a second report on the progress of his research to the Academy in Heidelberg, Hellpach presented short characterizations of the Saxon, the 'Falic', and the Bavarian face.[57] The third instalment of his studies covered the Rhenish, the Falic and the 'Eastern' (*ostisch*) face.[58] The latter category he adopted from the popular race theorist Hans F.K. Günther, whose theories Hellpach generally rejected, in accordance with the majority of the academic community in Germany.[59] Despite his criticism of Günther, however, Hellpach's physiognomic studies provided no alternative to 'race psychology', but were based on a similar typology of the German 'tribes'. Hellpach was convinced that essential differences (*wesensmäßige Unterschiede*) between nations and between 'tribes' of the same nation existed. These could be established, he believed, by analysing the typical facial expressions and characteristics of these 'tribes'.[60] Despite subsequent attempts to present his studies of the German tribes as the 'empirical part' of his folk psychology,[61] they had more in common with Günther's and Clauss's racial studies, since Hellpach did not study the mind or spirit of the German 'tribes', but took them for granted and assumed that they 'moulded' the different 'facial expressions' prevalent in the regions of Germany. Nor was Hellpach's methodology, which he explained further in his third report to the Academy of Sciences in Heidelberg, any more sophisticated or systematic than Günther's. To the members of the Academy, he presented his random observations of people 'in the streets and at markets, on trains and in pubs, public meetings and at social events' cautiously as a necessary starting point and study aid. As his main method of collecting data he referred to 'systematic studies in schools', a by-product of his time as Minister of Education in Baden when Hellpach had used visits to schools to act as a 'participating observer' and classified the 'mimic expressions' of school children.[62] Despite thus building up a 'physiognomic collection', Hellpach did not gather data in a systematic and controlled way and ignored the standards of the fledgling social sciences of the 1920s and 1930s. In this, he continued the practice of his teachers, Wundt and Lamprecht, who had not shied away from bold speculations on a meagre empirical basis.[63] Despite the methodological weakness of Hellpach's 'physiognomy' and its questionable empirical basis, it was acknowledged as 'normal science' by the academic community. Hellpach was awarded the substantial sum of 5,000 Reichsmark to fund his research by the Notgemeinschaft der deutschen Wissenschaft (later to become the Deutsche Forschungsgemeinschaft), a vital resource for Hellpach who, as adjunct professor, did not have a research budget of his own.[64]

In 1934 Hellpach had overcome a period of disorientation and aimlessness following the Nazi take-over of power, and began to re-establish himself as an academic. The vehicle for this next step in his career was *Völkerpsychologie*. His role as the main representative of this field in Germany took shape when he was invited as a member of the official German delegation to the International Congress for Philosophy, in Prague, in 1934.[65] The simple fact that Hellpach, the former democratic minister, state president of Baden and candidate for the Reich presidency, officially represented National Socialist Germany at this event, caused a scandal. Hellpach was invited to share a podium at the conference with the American philosopher Thomas Vernor Smith (1890–1964); both speakers were asked to address 'the descriptive and the normative point of view in the social sciences'. The topic Hellpach had chosen for his lecture at the conference looked like a kowtow to the new German government: he spoke on 'The Folk as Natural Fact, Mental Form and Creation of the Will' ('Das Volk als Naturtatsache, geistige Gestalt und Willensschöpfung') and thus for the first time presented the three-fold definition of the concept *Volk* which would structure his book on folk psychology.[66] In order to defend this choice of topic, Hellpach insisted that he did not mean to flatter the National Socialists. It simply summarized his approach to folk psychology that he had already developed before the First World War. This explanation, however, did not convince his critics. To make matters worse, Hellpach ignored the sensitivities of the émigré community in Prague when he stated that every 'genuine culture was intolerant and totalitarian' (*intolerant und totalitär*), which suggested that he agreed with the violent persecution of the Nazis' opponents. In particular, his use of the term *totalitär* led to a heated debate at the conference. German academics and intellectuals who had fled from the Nazis were infuriated by Hellpach, who looked like a turncoat who had made his peace with the dictatorial regime in Germany. After his performance at the Prague congress, Hellpach's reputation amongst the German émigré community was irredeemably destroyed. He was considered nothing but a spineless opportunist who had accommodated himself with the Third Reich. Nobel Prize laureate Thomas Mann (1875–1955), for instance, on hearing the news about Hellpach's performance at the Prague conference in his Swiss exile, was outraged by the behaviour of the former Liberal Democrat.[67]

Hellpach, however, never prone to self-criticism, saw himself as the victor of the 'battle of speeches at Prague'. He insisted that his presentation had made no concessions to Nazi ideology since he had defined the *Volk* not from a purely biological point of view, as the racial ideology of the Nazis would have demanded, but had put equal emphasis on the 'mental form' of the folk. During the debate at the Prague conference, he had invoked the example of the legendary Czechoslovak president Tomáš G. Masaryk (1850–1937) to show that the Volk was the 'fundamental form of human communities': during the First World War, Hellpach explained, Masaryk had abandoned 'his family, his friends, his professorship and his students' in order to create a state 'for his *Volk*'.[68] Reichs-German members in the audience agreed that Hellpach had defended his ground well and saw his presentation as a success.[69] International observers, however, did not share this view of the proceedings in Prague. To the Czech philosopher Jan Blahoslav Kozák (1888–1974), reporting on the conference in the *Slavonic and East European Review*, Hellpach had provided a 'definition of sociology' that was 'entirely nationalistic and partial'. Kozák did not fail to mention that Hellpach had once been a democratic minister in Baden, but had now turned into a 'National Socialist'.[70] To an American observer Hellpach left the impression of providing 'a philosophical defence of the present government in Germany'.[71] Both sides of the debate in Prague had a point: Hellpach's argument that the study of the *Volk* had to be the starting point of any *social* science repeated the mantra of the *Völkerpsychologie* of Lazarus, Steinthal and Wundt, but could easily be adapted to the *völkisch* ideology of the Nazis. In contrast to earlier versions of folk psychology, Hellpach presented a formula for 'differential' folk psychology: he abandoned the universal perspective that had characterized Wundt's approach and stressed the uniqueness of each individual *Volk*. He also put more emphasis on the ethnic foundations of the folk and provided an essentialist definition of its nature. His version of folk psychology was thus fully compatible with the *völkisch* ideology of the Nazi government, despite Hellpach's insistence on his intellectual independence.

Hellpach's *Einführung in die Völkerpsychologie*, published in 1938, was based on the same three-fold definition of the Volk he had presented at the Prague conference in 1934. Designed as a textbook for teaching at universities, it provided yet another manifesto for a discipline-to-be and was built on a wide range of secondary literature, but contained no original research.[72] Similar to Lazarus, Steinthal and Wundt, Hellpach adamantly stressed the strictly academic character of his approach and distanced himself from travel writers and popular scientists who speculated about national characters. His folk psychology would not superficially sketch 'national characteristics', but provide a foundation on which any future research into the mind of the folk had to be built. Hellpach presented his book as part of a recent trend that studied the *Volk* from different angles: he mentioned Adolf Bach's *Deutsche Volkskunde*, Wilhelm Emil Mühlmann's *Rassen- und Volkskunde*, and Max Hildebert Boehm's *Volkskunde* as examples. Folk psychology, Hellpach explained, was part of this broader interest in German academia that put the study of the *Volk* at its centre. He was not interested in a scholastic debate about the legitimacy or even primacy of any of these approaches: 'I am not afraid to admit that I do not care at all whether folk psychology is called a "discipline" or a "branch" of psychology, sociology, or folklore (*Volkskunde*), or if it is referred to as an "approach" or a "point of view".'[73] This notion referred to critical remarks made by Max Hildebert Boehm in a private letter to Hellpach. Boehm had complimented Hellpach on his study of *Völkerpsychologie*, but expressed his concern that he had resurrected the 'fundamentally flawed term *Völkerpsychologie*'. Boehm reminded Hellpach that folk psychology had been invented by the Jewish scholars Lazarus and Steinthal, and that the term should, therefore, be avoided. Wundt had discredited the concept further, Boehm maintained, because he had written a social psychology and neglected the *Volk* in his studies. Using the term 'folk psychology' once again was even more regrettable since Hellpach had written a *Volkslehre*, not a study of folk psychology, Boehm argued. Hellpach replied that the concept of folk psychology had been 'in the air' in the mid nineteenth century; it was only coincidence that it was Lazarus and Steinthal who had introduced it to scholarly debates. It was now impossible to eradicate every term or every discovery made by Jews in the past century. Furthermore, Hellpach insisted that 'folk psychology' was the proper label for his study, while *Volkslehre* was both a larger concept – it studied more than just the 'basic psychological processes of *Volksleben*' – and more limited, since *Völkerpsychologie* dealt with all peoples, not just one. In this respect folk psychology was a branch of ethnology (*Völkerkunde*), not of folklore (*Volkskunde*).[74]

Still, Hellpach insisted that folk psychology was clearly distinguished from anthropology and ethnology, the disciplines in which the term *Völkerpsychologie* had been kept alive after Wundt's death in the 1920s and 1930s.[75] Repeating one of Wundt's arguments, Hellpach claimed that *Völkerkunde* was mainly concerned with studying the material culture of primitive, pre-literate civilizations and therefore a much more limited approach than folk psychology. The 'fantastic collections of tools and utensils' that were accumulated in museums of natural history were surely important sources for social anthropologists, but of very limited use for the study of the mental characteristics of nations – Hellpach ignored Lazarus's concept of *Verdichtung*, which aimed at including the study of material culture into folk psychology. Much more important and useful to Hellpach were the traditional 'documents' of *Völkerpsychologie*, which informed scholars about the mind of nations: languages, myths, religious beliefs, but also social rules and legal systems.[76]

Boehm had made a valid point when he characterized Hellpach's folk psychology as a *Volkslehre*: it was almost exclusively devoted to the definition of the concept *Volk*. Repeating the main argument of his speech at the Prague conference in 1934, Hellpach defined the *Volk* in three ways: it simultaneously constituted a 'natural fact' (*Naturtatsache*), a 'mental form' (*geistige Gestalt*) and a 'creation of the will' (*Willensschöpfung*). As a natural fact,

Hellpach understood the folk as a permanent and universal form of social organization that could be found throughout history. *Völker* were the 'really existing form of permanent communities in which the human race (*das Menschengeschlecht*) lives'. The folk constituted 'the natural and adequate community of fate for the hominid species' (*naturgegebene und geistgemäße Schicksalsgemeinschaft hominider Art*).[77] While the '*völkisch* form of life' was a basic phenomenon of human life, individual *Völker* were characterized by constant change. Hellpach thus repeated an idea of Lazarus and Steinthal's folk psychology: nations or *Völker* were created constantly, but they could also decline and 'disappear'. But regardless of the exact character and development of a folk, man had always organized his communal life in the form of *Völker*.[78]

Despite the axiomatic notion that the folk – the fact that people live together and organize themselves as a 'folk' – constituted a 'basic fact of human history', Hellpach struggled with providing a clear definition of the very term *Volk*. He rejected Heinrich von Treitschke's characterization of the 'folk' as 'multiple families living together permanently' for being too general and too formal; it lacked a 'psychological' element.[79] Generally, and despite its overall importance in the history of mankind, a 'folk' was such a complicated matter that it defied a short and simple definition. Like Lazarus, Steinthal and Wundt before him, Hellpach easily dismissed the argument that human beings belonged not only to a folk, but to a variety of communities that equally formed their mind. Families, 'tribes' and clans were essentially different forms of community. More importantly, they only existed within and as part of a *Volk*. The degree of direct relationships (*blutsverwandschaftliche Zusammenhänge*) within a folk, i.e., race and ethnicity, was a matter of great importance for folk psychology, Hellpach argued. The more a folk had developed out of real family relations, the more similar its members were in terms of hereditary traits, physical appearance, talents, will and character. But racial homogeneity was not necessarily an advantage for a folk, Hellpach explained, since it resulted in a one-sidedness of its capabilities and outlook, whereas a more racially mixed, heterogeneous folk might be less uniform in its talents, but more versatile.[80]

Hellpach was sometimes referred to as a representative of 'environmentalism' on account of his study of the 'geopsychological effects', i.e., the effects of the weather, climate and landscape, on the mind.[81] Since environmentalism argued that man was primarily formed by nurture, not by nature, and thus opposed the core idea of scientific racism, it was anathema to National Socialist ideology. In order not to be mistaken as an environmentalist, Hellpach duly considered the importance of the environment for the development of the folk, but did so in a way that fitted in with Nazi ideas of *Volk* and race. To this end, he incorporated the Nazi slogan of 'blood and soil' (*Blut und Boden*), into his definition of the folk. The make-up of the folk depended on nature and nurture, Hellpach explained, and the slogan *Blut und Boden* was just a different way of putting this simple fact. He thus shrewdly employed terms that were axiomatic to Nazi ideology and race theories. Furthermore, and following Friedrich Ratzel, one of his teachers at the University of Leipzig, Hellpach argued that the folk required an adequate *Lebensraum*, or living space, to prosper and develop. He conceded that there was a grain of truth in environmentalist theories of the folk since an intricate relationship existed between any biological species and its environment. Hence, not every human race (*hominide Rasse*) was able to survive in any living space. The racial structure of peoples confined them to certain areas: this was the essentially scientific meaning of the slogan 'blood and soil'.[82] Next to the climate and the landscape, the soil was an essential factor in forming a folk. Even though the impact of the soil on man was little studied, Hellpach speculated that it had a major impact on the constitution of human beings, and could modify their 'racial substance'.[83] Hellpach introduced the concept of 'constitution', which he had adopted from the works of the physiologist Ernst Kretschmer (1888–1963), as the key to understanding 'the folk as a natural fact'. It allowed consideration of race, climate, soil and landscape and their interrelationship as constituent factors in the formation of the folk.[84] While Hellpach had earlier agreed with Franz Boas's critique of simplistic theories of race, he now made sure to distance himself from the German-American anthropologist: Boas's idea that races were mere products of their physical environment (*Standortvarietäten*) was obviously flawed. Racial factors by far outweighed environmental factors in shaping a folk, Hellpach argued in accordance with Nazi ideas. The 'ability to form a folk and to exist in a *völkisch* way' was the yardstick to measure the ability of a race to adapt to an environment.[85]

Hellpach's book included a critical discussion of popular race theories, in particular of Ludwig Ferdinand Clauss's race psychology, which he had targeted already in the 1920s. Subsequently, he would present this discussion as proof of his opposition to the 'official' race ideology of the Nazis. However, his views on Clauss were wholly acceptable during the Third Reich and were shared by academics who were supporting the Nazi regime much more openly than Hellpach did. In order to criticize simplistic ideas of race, Hellpach distinguished strictly between 'race' and 'folk': 'We know of no race which, as a whole, lives as a uniform folk community. In those areas which are mainly inhabited by one race, we find this racially homogenous population divided into peoples and tribes which often are each other's fiercest enemies. Many peoples, on the other hand, who have formed the firm and conscious community of fate, the "nation", especially the leading nations of the occident, are mixtures of different races.'[86] Race was an important factor in forming a folk, but not the only one. Furthermore, 'races' were not to be confused with 'species'.[87] Races were not characterized by specific character traits, but by hereditary factors which could develop in different ways, depending on environmental factors. In accordance with contemporary studies of genetics, Hellpach stressed the difference between phenotype and genotype,[88] but did not deny the possibility that certain physical traits signified specific mental capabilities or characteristics, as race psychologists such as Egon von Eickstedt (1892–1964) had argued. It was for instance possible, Hellpach claimed, that blue eyes correlated with certain mental traits. It was only the popular, speculative 'physiognomy' of self-taught race psychologists like Clauss and Günther that had brought this kind of reasoning into disrepute. Against these successful amateurs Hellpach defended the legitimacy of scientific racial anthropology.[89] To a large degree, such criticism was a smoke screen which was widely used by the academic anthropologists and psychologists to distance themselves from the successful amateurs Günther and Clauss. Even Günther, famous for popularizing the six different racial 'types' in Europe, never confused 'race' and 'folk', but stressed their difference.[90]

Similar to most theorists of race, Hellpach chose a middling position concerning the question of 'nature and nurture' when he stressed that race was a major factor in the formation of the folk, but not the only one. A brief look at the fundamental changes in outlook of historical nations over relatively short periods of time would demonstrate this point. Hellpach pointed to the 'surprising turnaround' of the German *Volk* in modern times: the Germans of the eighteenth century had shown no talent for politics or economics but excelled in philosophy, music and the arts. From about 1850 this state of mind had suddenly given way to a one-sided focus on science, technology and business, which had led to the astonishing growth of the German economy in the second half of the nineteenth century. Such a profound change of mind and focus of a whole nation could not have been caused by a change in its racial structure, Hellpach argued. Rather, one had to assume a 'strong diversity of talents within the German folk': the different hereditary elements of the 'national genius' reacted to and were activated by different cultural circumstances.[91]

While Hellpach renewed his critique of simplistic race theories, he agreed with notions that were integral to scientific racism in the inter-war period. In particular, he was convinced that the 'clash' of different races necessarily led to 'psychological tensions', both within individuals and within nations. Whereas nations that consisted of very different 'racial groups' experienced internal tensions, individuals of mixed race showed a mental instability that increased the larger the 'distance' between the races was. Racists all over the world had used this notion in their campaign against the mixing of races, immigration and 'miscenigation', and Hellpach presented it as a fact that folk psychology had to reckon with.[92] In his judgement on the importance of race, then, Hellpach differed from traditional folk psychology. While he criticized the strict determinism of popular race theorists, he acknowledged that race was a decisive factor in the shaping of a folk and had to be fully taken into account by folk psychologists. Furthermore, Hellpach managed to appropriate seemingly environmentalist arguments into his version of folk psychology when he argued that living space and soil were integral factors in the formation of the folk.[93]

The second part of Hellpach's definition of the folk concentrated on more traditional aspects of folk psychology. Defining the folk merely by material conditions such as race and space, or blood and soil, remained incomplete, he argued. In addition, it was necessary to analyse and understand the 'mental form' of a folk, which represented its individuality and distinguished it from other nations. The development of peoples was conditioned and restricted by natural forces, but could not completely or essentially be deducted from these. All *Völker*, Hellpach argued, were defined by and developed five 'basic mental traits' (*geistige Urgüter*), namely language, clothing, tools, laws and commandments, and an idea of the beyond (*Jenseits*). Following in the footsteps of earlier folk psychology, Hellpach presented these 'basic mental traits' as a kind of universal minimum of civilization.[94] As such, they resembled the Volksgeist of Lazarus and Steinthal and the *Volksseele* of Wundt, but also C.G. Jung's psychological 'archetypes' or Oswald Spengler's *Ursymbole*.[95] He agreed with earlier folk psychology that language and speech were basic characteristics of any folk, since language distinguished man from animals: 'Only man, but all men, speak, and only peoples, but all peoples have their own particular language.' The ability to speak was the precondition to create and develop 'basic mental traits'. Therefore, Hellpach explained, it was no surprise that folk psychology had concentrated on the study of language for generations.[96] Following Lazarus and Steinthal, but without mentioning them, Hellpach maintained that the characteristics of language reflected the dual character of any *Volk*. Language changed and evolved gradually over time, partly by accident, partly according to strict rules; it was both a part of nature and a creation of the mind (*Doppelwesen als Naturereignis und als Geisteserzeugnis*).[97] As the *Volk* was constituted by language, language itself was both a 'natural fact' and a 'mental form'. To illustrate this point further, Hellpach referred to his studies of the physiognomy of the German 'tribes' and the 'face-modelling' qualities of language. Within the limits of biological heredity, common, spoken language 'modelled' faces and created the characteristic features of 'regional types'. Hence the study of language as well as of gestures and body language allowed for deep insights into the 'mental structure of a specific folk or "tribe"'.[98] Moreover, language was the precondition to formulate and communicate any human 'form of order' and thus served as a primary source for the study of folk psychology.[99]

All peoples developed a form of religion and an idea of the beyond, Hellpach explained. The latter was based on the idea of the 'second existence' of man after his death and had produced the concept of the soul, which could be found in the most primitive as well as in the most complex forms of religion.[100] Equally, all peoples believed in specific myths and showed forms of 'magical thinking'. According to Hellpach, myths were 'stories of world domination' (*Weltherrschaftsgeschichten*), i.e., attempts to make sense of history by positioning one's nation at its centre. Repeating the point that had caused such controversy at the Prague congress in 1934, Hellpach argued that a 'genuine myth' demanded universal truth and claimed to be the only true story of the origin of the world. For this reason, 'every real culture' was 'intolerant'.[101] Hellpach distinguished between five different 'founding myths' which had led to five great living orders of humanity throughout history, namely totemism, theocracy, polity (*Politie*), enlightenment, and *Volkstum*. Despite his rejection of any form of the philosophy of history, Hellpach thus adopted and expanded Wundt's concept of historical stages in the development of mankind. In order to make this model compatible with the Third Reich, he introduced a decisive change: instead of 'humanity', as in Wundt's folk psychology, history culminated in 'nationhood' (*Volkstum*). Hellpach thus put this hardly translatable German term *Volkstum*, which had been introduced by Friedrich Ludwig Jahn (1778–1853) in the nineteenth century and then been appropriated by the *völkisch* right a century later, at the centre of his folk psychology and presented it as the highest form of historical development.[102] To Hellpach, *Volkstum*, and not culture or humanity, defined the 'ultimate essence, the concept of the inner existence of any folk', as well as the *völkisch* order of life that was built on this essence.[103] He suggested replacing the controversial term 'folk soul', central to Wundt's folk psychology, but highly controversial, with the concept *Volkstum* since it comprised everything that was essential about a folk. The concept represented the 'unalienable physical and mental unity of the reality of the folk'.[104]

Volkstum, Hellpach argued, was clearly distinct from the nation: nationalism was only a partial aspect of the *Volkstum*, restricted to the polity and the constitutional organization of a folk within a state. But nationalism easily led to aggressive imperialism and denied other peoples their own *Volkstum*, while genuine *Volkstum* was tolerant and respected the rights of others. Hellpach thus repeated the central motifs of German *Volksgeschichte* of the 1920s and 1930s, which had strictly separated the nation from the folk. In this definition the nation was presented as a superficial, Western idea which was dependent on the state, whereas the *Volk* was an organic and authentic entity. This thinking had its roots in the romanticism of the nineteenth century and could be traced back to Fichte, Herder and Humboldt. After the First World War and during the intellectual fight against the Treaty of Versailles, however, it had taken on a new political meaning. Conveniently, the distinction between nation and folk supported German revisionist claims; the German *Volk* included the German-speaking minorities outside the German nation state. Echoing this argument, Hellpach contrasted the nation and its exclusive focus on the abstract organization of the state with the organic and creative genius of *Volkstum*. *Volkstum* represented the highest form of communal life, and had only been fully realized in Nazi Germany, Hellpach argued. He thus made another major concession to Nazi ideology when he called National Socialism 'the most passionate and unconditional idea and reality of the *Volkstum*'.[105]

The final part of Hellpach's study, and also its shortest, was devoted to the third 'basic fact' of all 'ethnic communities' and dealt with the folk as a 'creation of the will'. This chapter continued the discreet Nazification of his folk psychology. The 'leadership of the individual', Hellpach claimed, was essential for the formation of the folk. Only a leader (*Leitmensch*) could perform the action (*Tat*) necessary to create a folk. The folk as a 'creation of the will' depended on 'leaders of human beings' (*Menschenführer*). These outstanding individuals were the carriers of the will of the people. Hellpach thus assigned 'agency' of the folk to chosen individuals, not to its general members. Essential aspects of *völkisch* communal life did not originate with the people, he argued, but were created by exceptional personalities. Hellpach thus introduced a voluntaristic element into his definition of the folk, like Lazarus and in his wake Renan had done earlier. But instead of the 'daily plebiscite' of the members of the folk, who permanently recreated the nation, Hellpach introduced the 'leadership principle'. The folk was not the result of the shared will of its constituent members, he argued, but a 'creation of the will' of the leader.[106] The folk was shaped and formed by the actions of statesmen, generals, lawmakers, reformers or revolutionaries. These 'men of action' (*Tatmenschen*) were the true leaders of their folk because they were able to realize and implement their visions and ideas. The yardstick to measure the greatness of a leader was success: 'The creative man of action changes the world of his folk conclusively. He makes history for his folk, he never remains a mere episode.'[107] The leader did not even have to be representative of the characteristics of his folk. Quite in contrast, there was often an open tension between him and the majority of the people.[108] According to Hellpach, 'great individuals' could be found in all nations. They were characterized either by a commanding will or a by a creative, inventive mind; in special cases they showed a combination of both.[109] This was a clear reference to the German Führer, who presented himself as both the intellectual and political leader of the German people. At the same time the introduction of the *Führerprinzip* into folk psychology allowed Hellpach to provide a simple answer to one of the crucial problems of folk psychology, namely the relationship between the individual and the community. In contrast to Lazarus, Steinthal and Wundt, Hellpach argued that the individual – but only the exceptional leader, the 'man of action' – was the decisive force, not the community. To Hellpach, then, the interaction between individual and community was not complicated and complex, but simple, one-dimensional and hierarchical. He thus introduced notions of mass psychology into his folk psychology, with their air of elitism and cultural pessimism that looked at the 'masses' and the 'crowd' with suspicion and disdain. The character of the folk, Hellpach declared, was ultimately determined by the personality of its leader. The people themselves appeared as a passive, non-descript mass that depended on the action of an individual genius to turn them into a true *Volkstum*.

After 1945 Hellpach maintained that his studies on folk psychology and on the 'German physiognomy' had made no concessions to Nazi race theories, and some of his interpreters have believed his version. His publications and speeches during the Third Reich, however, did not constitute a subtle criticism of Nazism, as Horst Gundlach has argued, but rather a subtle, sometimes open adaptation to Nazi theory.[110] A thorough reading of Hellpach's *Einführung in die Völkerpsychologie* reveals it as a conscious attempt to make folk psychology compatible with Nazi ideology. In contrast to Lazarus, Steinthal and Wundt, Hellpach stressed the dependence of the *Volk* on racial and biological factors. While he clearly distinguished between race and folk, he attributed decisive importance to racial factors in the shaping of the folk. Hellpach then managed to marry environmental arguments, normally anathema to Nazi theorists, with racialist ideas when he argued that soil and living space were preconditions for the formation of the folk. Finally, he turned Lazarus's subjective and voluntaristic definition of the nation on its head and introduced the *Führerprinzip* into the definition of the *Volk*.

Not surprisingly, then, Hellpach's *Völkerpsychologie* received very positive reviews upon its publication. It did not 'cause a stir', as Gundlach has claimed, on account of its allegedly clever, but disguised criticism of Nazi race theories.[111] The reviewer of the *Anthropologischer Anzeiger* praised the way Hellpach had connected folk and race psychology, and commended his discussion of the relationship between race and *Volk*. The book included 'solid building material for the foundations of folk psychology as an exact discipline, which is without doubt a necessity'.[112] Hellpach's friend Karl Haushofer (1869–1946), the inventor of geopolitics, student of Friedrich Ratzel and erstwhile teacher of Rudolf Heß (1894–1987), was equally full of praise for Hellpach's *Völkerpsychologie*. It would be a useful aid for the study of geopolitics and, as a concise study, compared favourably with Wilhelm Wundt's overly lengthy contributions.[113] The statistician Friedrich Zahn (1869–1946) equally commended the brevity of Hellpach's *Völkerpsychologie*, compared to Wundt's ten volumes on the same topic, and was full of praise for his 'brilliant and stimulating remarks'.[114] The reviewer of the *Geographische Zeitschrift* praised Hellpach's 'brilliant and original presentation', but criticized his references to Franz Boas, who had become the arch-enemy of the Nazis because of his continued and dedicated fight against 'scientific racism'.[115] The *Zeitschrift für Ethnologie* stressed Hellpach's unique position in between the humanities and the sciences, which had enabled him to master the very complex subject matter of folk psychology. The book represented a major improvement over Wundt's work and constituted 'a masterpiece'.[116] Bruno Petermann (1898–1941), the author of a study on race psychology, wrote equally enthusiastically about Hellpach's 'highly recommendable' textbook: 'The result is a comprehensive psychological study of the being of the folk (*volkhaften Daseins*).'[117] The social anthropologist Richard Thurnwald (1869–1954) penned a positive review of Hellpach's *Völkerpsychologie* for the *Historische Zeitschrift*. While he found some errors in Hellpach's comments on ethnological knowledge, he praised his comprehensive treatment of the field. Readers would find a plethora of ideas that could be explored further.[118] Even though none of Hellpach's many publications were translated into English, some of them received attention in Britain and the U.S.A. and were reviewed in academic journals before the Second World War. In Britain, the reviewer for the journal of the International African Institute, who published his text in German, commended Hellpach's book.[119] Similarly, Charles Diserens, a psychologist at the University of Cincinnati who reviewed the book for the *American Journal of Psychology*, saw clear progress compared to Wundt's folk psychology, and agreed with Hellpach's treatment of the question of race in folk psychology.[120]

Hellpach acted inconspicuously during the Third Reich and avoided any conflict with the Nazi regime; his behaviour shows no signs of 'inner emigration' or secret opposition.[121] He regularly participated in international academic conferences – increasingly instrumentalized by the Nazis to disseminate propaganda to international audiences – at a time when only trusted academics were allowed to do so. For instance, in addition to the annual meetings of the German Association of Psychology, he participated in the congress of the International Union for the Scientific Investigation of Population Problems (IUSSIP), which was held in Berlin in 1935.[122] The anthropologist Eugen Fischer (1874–1967), director of the Kaiser Wilhelm Institute of Anthropology, Human Heredity and Eugenics, in Berlin, served as chairman of the congress, and used it as a forum to praise Adolf Hitler in front of the 500 international participants. The Führer, Fischer claimed, had 'clearly understood the deep and important meaning of population policies'.[123] In his everyday life Hellpach behaved inconspicuously, too. While he never joined the NSADP – indeed, it seems likely that he would not have been accepted by the party even if he had applied for membership, because of his past political activity – he had sworn the oath to the Führer that was required of civil servants, including university teachers, and signed his private letters with *Heil Hitler*.[124] In 1939, like the majority of Germans, Hellpach was delighted with the foreign policy successes of the Third Reich. In a letter to Karl Haushofer he showed himself pleased by the German occupation of the Czech lands, since now 'the old, honourable name "Bohemia" will be revered again in its German meaning'.[125] During the war Hellpach profited from the 'professionalization' of psychology in Germany. With the introduction of a new uniform degree structure for psychologists in 1942, Hellpach, then the only professor of psychology at the University of Heidelberg, became director of the newly established Psychological Institute. While plans to promote Hellpach to a full professorship were turned down, he thus still managed to improve his status and standing at the University.[126] The new degree programme (*Diplomprüfungsordnung*) responded to the demand for psychologists by the *Wehrmacht* during the war, and established psychology as an independent discipline at German universities, concluding its emancipation from departments of philosophy.[127]

In 1943 Hellpach came into direct contact with the race experts of the SS when he was invited to cooperate with the Reinhard Heydrich Foundation in Prague. This foundation, directed by the historian Hans-Joachim Beyer (1908–71) and the psychologist Rudolf Hippius (1906–45), was an independent research institute that functioned as a think tank of the SS, and was involved in plans to 'Germanize' the protectorate of Bohemia and Moravia after the war. Beyer, who had met Hellpach at a conference of the Deutsches Auslands-Institut in Stuttgart in 1938, had become interested in Hellpach's studies in the physiognomy of the German 'tribes', which had finally been published in 1942.[128] Beyer invited Hellpach to conduct similar studies in the 'Protectorate', funded by the Heydrich Foundation. Hippius, a former student of Felix Krueger, represented a form of *Völkerpsychologie* that included racial-psychological studies that he had conducted at the Reich University of Posen before moving on to Prague. It is unlikely that Hellpach did not realize the political function of this research institute, as he later claimed in his memoirs.[129]

Hellpach's behaviour and attitude both during and after the Third Reich show him as an intellectual fellow traveller of the regime. He acted in an opportunistic way, and successfully adapted to the new circumstances. In contrast to other intellectuals and academics, who, at least in the first years of the Third Reich, enthusiastically embraced the new regime and had high hopes for the promised 'national revolution', Hellpach was less exposed. He never tried to 'lead the leader' and influence politics directly with his advice and research – his history as a well-known democratic politician in the Weimar Republic prevented this option. But, quite in contrast to his later attempts to present himself as a victim of the regime, he did not oppose or resist the Nazis. After an initial period of depression and confusion, which was mainly caused by his loss of status, he prospered in the niche of the university and as a member of the academic community. Folk psychology became

Hellpach's vehicle for adaptation to the Third Reich. During the war he became increasingly well established within the well-funded academic apparatus of Nazi Germany, and had active contacts, even to the radical intellectuals of the SS, precisely when they were organizing the ethnic cleansing of large swathes of Central and Eastern Europe.

Hellpach after the Downfall

The end of the Second World War marked a clear break for Hellpach. The collapse of the Third Reich allowed him to make an astonishing come-back as a public intellectual, because of his former political career as a member of the DDP, which had made his position during the Third Reich more awkward than that of more apolitical academic colleagues. His democratic pedigree now provided Hellpach with massive social capital, restored his public image and elevated him to a position of moral authority in the early Federal Republic. In contrast to other members of his generation, most notably Konrad Adenauer (1876–1967) and Theodor Heuss (1884–1963), Hellpach did not return to active politics. Freed from the restrictions of the Nazi regime, however, he took up his political writing again and contributed to the soul-searching debates about Germany's future in the immediate post-war period. He also returned to religious topics – as he had done in the 1920s, but now answering increased popular demand – and resurrected his old idea of a 'conservative democracy' as the solution to the post-war crisis, which he promoted in a book entitled *Pax Futura*.[130]

In his memoirs Hellpach argued that the Nazis had not been interested in academic debates and remained ignorant towards the intricacies and subtleties of scholarly writing. As long as he stayed away from political journalism, he claimed, he was free to work on the academic topics of his own choice and did not experience any censorship.[131] This argument, however, was part of the *Entlastungstrategie* of German academics after the war, and belonged to the apologetic story that claimed that universities had provided a 'safe haven' during the Third Reich untouched by the regime, and hence did not need to be reformed or 'de-Nazified' in their organization and structure. In his *Völkerpsychologie* Hellpach had been very careful to present an interpretation that conformed to the stipulations of the Nazi regime. After the war, like many of his colleagues, he denounced Nazism as barbaric and primitive, while he presented German academia as part of a tradition of the 'good' Germany that had remained unaffected by the policies of the Third Reich. The involvement of German academics in the planning and implementation of Nazi policies, now closely researched and documented, has revealed this argument as a self-interested myth. It was little more than a reflex, and a largely apologetic position that bears little resemblance to the realities of the Third Reich.[132]

Even though immediately after the war he was briefly suspected of having been a collaborator with the Nazi regime, Hellpach was able to convince the authorities of his innocence. He was swiftly de-Nazified and allowed to continue teaching at the University of Heidelberg. His chair at the Technical College at Karlsruhe was restored, which allowed him to draw his full pension again. Throughout the post-war period Hellpach presented himself, with a good conscience, as a victim of the Nazi regime who had suffered from restrictions under the regime and lived in fear of further persecution. As proof of his suffering during the Third Reich, he repeatedly referred to the pay cut that had been imposed on him in 1933, and stressed that two of his books had been banned by the Nazis in 1936. He claimed that he was forced to give up his political journalism in 1933, and that he had never joined the NSDAP. He also defended his decision not to emigrate during the Nazi period, with arguments that had quickly become familiar in post-war Germany and were frequently used to justify the position of the majority of Germans: 'Only those who stayed are able to tell how the events that happened at the time were mirrored in living human beings, and how impressions, comments, attitudes fluctuated.'[133] Hellpach rarely commented on the Holocaust, and on the few occasions that he did, he used a maudlin tone that implied a comparison between the victims of the Nazi genocide and ordinary Germans, which reflected the general mood in post-war Germany: 'We now know every detail of what happened in the concentration camps, in the gas chambers, in the basements of the Security Service, in the "People's" court rooms, but we know damnably little about how those people fared who lived their simple middle-class lives and almost exclusively had to deal with the lowest strata of the dictatorship in their everyday lives.'[134]

Hellpach's newly acquired political-moral authority in post-war Germany led to a number of requests from former colleagues who had exposed themselves much more openly than he had done, and required *Persilscheine*, i.e., positive character references that attested their clean past during the proceedings of de-Nazification. One of the first academics to contact Hellpach was the former director of the Reinhard Heydrich Foundation in Prague, 'Himmler's professor' Hans-Joachim Beyer, who was evidently equipped with the right instinct regarding who could help his career after the collapse of the Third Reich. After his timely escape from Prague in 1945 Beyer, then staying at Innsbruck in the Tyrol, sent a detailed curriculum vitae to Hellpach, and asked for help and advice in his attempt to re-establish his career in West Germany.[135] The following year Hellpach received requests from Wilhelm Stählin (1883–1975), bishop of the Lutheran church in Oldenburg, and from the Lutheran church in Schleswig-Holstein, for a reference for Beyer. In his replies Hellpach stressed that he had met Beyer only on three or four occasions during the Third Reich. He considered him one of the most talented experts on questions of *Volkstum* and population policies, who had, even during the Third Reich, maintained the highest academic standards. In contrast to other academics, Hellpach explained, Beyer had abstained from making concessions to the 'official race ideology and phraseology'. Hellpach claimed that he had no knowledge of the political function of the Reinhard Heydrich Foundation. Still, he seemed to be aware of the political role Beyer had played when he recommended that he should stay in the background for a while and not expose himself too much and too early after the war. After a period of two to three years his expert knowledge on the ethnic make-up of central and Eastern Europe would be in demand again, in consideration of the open question of Germany's eastern borders: '"Silence! Don't make any noise!" is the best, and best intended, advice one can give him in the meantime'. In conclusion, Hellpach recommended giving Beyer a second chance, but to do so with caution.[136] This statement is remarkable, since Hellpach did not write positive references for anyone. For instance, he refused to provide references for the psychologist Gerhard Pfahler (1897–1976), who had openly supported the Third Reich and had become a genuine Nazi scientist, and for Friedrich Keiter (1906–67), who had exposed himself with studies on 'race psychology'.

After the Second World War Hellpach was quick to distance himself publicly from race ideology as propagated by the Nazis.[137] To achieve this aim he chose a strategy that many implicated professors followed: once again, the former stars of racial studies during the Third Reich, Hans F.K. Günther and Ludwig Ferdinand Clauss – irrespective of the fact that they did not represent the 'official' ideology of the regime – were singled out and denounced as pseudo-scientists who had perverted the standards of academic research. Since Günther and Clauss had always been outsiders to the academic establishment, their exclusion from the academic community came at little cost for the established professors. Hellpach chimed in with this widely held attitude. Importantly, he argued that the fact the Nazis had abused race theories for their own political purposes did not de-legitimate the study of race as such. Quite in contrast, and in line with his folk psychology, Hellpach maintained that race was a major factor in the make-up of the folk and had to be studied accordingly: 'The fact of race is and always will be a factor of immense importance for historical life, for the genesis and changes of culture, for the rise and fall of peoples and empires.'[138]

In the case of Clauss, Hellpach was officially asked to assess his career in 1952 by the West German Ministry of the Interior. Clauss had been appointed to a lectureship at the University of Berlin in 1936, but had been expelled from the Nazi party in 1943, after a denunciation by his former wife. Since the 1920s Clauss had employed Margarete Landé as a research assistant, who, according to the Nuremberg Laws, was considered a 'full Jew'. After his exclusion from the party Clauss had hidden Landé in his estate outside Berlin and thus protected her from arrest by the Gestapo and saved her life. After the war Clauss applied to the West German state for compensation since, he argued, he had lost his lectureship in 1943 and had been denied a chair in psychology because his theories had opposed Nazism. In order to receive compensation from the West German state, he had to prove that he had been disadvantaged by the Nazi regime. In 1952 Hellpach was asked to write a concluding reference (*Obergutachten*) in the complicated case. He denied Clauss's claims that his 'heterodox treatment of the phenomenon of race' had prevented him from being appointed to a chair in psychology during the Third Reich. Even then, Hellpach continued, no uniform or official approach to racial studies had prevailed. There was no evidence that Clauss's career had suffered because of his adverse views on the 'race question' during the Third Reich. In addition, Hellpach judged that Clauss was not appointable to a chair in psychology because he stubbornly focused on his idiosyncratic version of race psychology and ignored all other forms and methods of psychological research. Hellpach acknowledged Clauss's moral behaviour, however, as evidenced by the fact that he had taken a substantial personal risk when he saved M. Landé from the Gestapo, and suggested a compromise to settle the case. He recommended establishing a full-time lectureship for Clauss, which would allow him to continue his research and provide him with a regular income to support his family. In contrast to Hans F.K. Günther, who received a full pension as a former full professor, Clauss did not receive any payments from the German state. Hence Hellpach's solution would have acknowledged Clauss's moral behaviour, and compensated him adequately for his losses.[139]

After the establishing of the Federal Republic of Germany, in 1949, Hellpach received the highest awards, both for his academic work and for his role as a public intellectual: in 1952 he was the first recipient of the Wundt-Medaille from the German Association of Psychology, awarded for his life-time contributions to the study of psychology. In the same year he received the Großes Bundesverdienstkreuz of the young Federal Republic in recognition of his public engagement. As an academic, Hellpach remained active throughout the rest of his life. He served as a member of the editorial board of the *Zeitschrift für philosophische Forschung*, published from 1946, and continued publishing academic texts as well as books aimed at a wider audience.[140]

Ironically, in order to present himself as untainted by Nazism, Hellpach stressed the continuity of his studies in folk psychology. *Völkerpsychologie*, he claimed, had nothing to do with Nazi ideology; in fact, it had been the very opposite of the kind of race psychology that the Rassenpolitisches Amt of the NSDAP under Alfred Rosenberg had propagated. His focus on folk psychology, Hellpach now claimed, had been a long-standing interest of his, dating back to his time as a student of Wundt at the University of Leipzig and his lecture courses on the subject at the Technical College in Karlsruhe before the First World War. During the Third Reich, Hellpach explained, he had only continued and concluded his previous research, including the studies on the physiognomy of the German 'tribes'. As late as 1944 Hellpach had established a series of books *Schriftenreihe zur Völkerpsychologie*, which he continued after the war, even though, due to the economic and political circumstances, the series did not flourish and was dropped in 1947.[141] His monograph on *German Physiognomy* was republished in 1949 without major changes to the text. The second edition of the *Einführung in die Völkerpsychologie*, published as late as 1944, was accepted by the American authorities in occupied Germany as suitable for university teaching. Hellpach proudly reported this decision as further proof that his publications during the Third Reich had not been contaminated by Nazi ideology.[142] He was convinced that none of his academic or political views needed revision in the light of the collapse of National Socialism. Rather, his experiences re-enforced his belief in the 'basic facts' of folk psychology. In a paragraph on the SPD in his memoirs he argued that it was a 'natural' and 'primary phenomenon' of human life that man forms peoples and differentiates the meaning and forms of life according to *völkisch* principles. All people used language, but different peoples spoke different languages; different nations were characterized by different styles of buildings, different clothes, different customs and habits, also different levels of technology. These differences needed to be seen as a positive fact; without them, the world would be a boring and monotonous place.[143]

In 1954 the third edition of Hellpach's *Einführung in die Völkerpsychologie* was published, accompanied by a book on 'German character'.[144] Hellpach, as we have seen, seamlessly continued to promote and represent the approach in the Federal Republic, not least for personal reasons. In addition, the regulations for a degree in psychology (*Diplomprüfungsordnung*), introduced under the auspices of the National Socialists in 1942, were kept in place well into the 1960s, and since they included *Völkerpsychologie* as an elective subject that all students of psychology could be examined in, there was continued demand for Hellpach's *Einführung* as the only available textbook. The study on the 'German character' was designed to introduce the main tenets of his folk psychology to a non-specialist, general audience, with Hellpach assuming the role of the academic expert explaining the complicated subject matter of his discipline in simple terms to laymen. In this book Hellpach combined reflections on German peculiarities and the *Volkscharakter* of the Germans with comments on Germany's future outlook. In fact, the book was largely a collection of reflections, anecdotes and reminiscences typical of an aging scholar. Instead of showing how to analyse the German mind, Hellpach listed character traits of the Germans and their various 'tribes', very much in the fashion of 'national character studies' that his folk psychology was meant to supersede. Hellpach expanded on the mutability of a nation's character and used the same line of argument as in his *Einführung* : Between 1750 and 1830, he argued, the German character had been *schöngeistig*, dominated by the arts, philosophy and music. From 1830 to 1880 the Germans suddenly became *nutzgeistig*, absorbed by the economy, industry and technology. Between 1880 and 1945 the Germans had become *machtgeistig*, and were obsessed with power, the military, conquest and war. These quick changes over a relatively short period of time, Hellpach repeated, demonstrated the limited use of racial theories for analysing national characters.[145] In addition, Hellpach stressed that a nation's character was never uniform and coherent, but full of contradictions – a notion that should have raised doubts about the very idea of a national character. As he did in his autobiography, Hellpach dwelled on the failure to reconcile nationalism and socialism in a peaceful way, which he presented as the major problem of recent German history. The year 1903, when revisionism was voted down by the SPD and Friedrich Naumann's National-Social Association was dissolved, seemed to Hellpach as the fateful year in German history when a constructive and peaceful reconciliation of the two major forces of the nineteenth century was missed.[146] Hellpach had little to say about the personality of Hitler: in a chapter entitled 'Adolf Hitler: Ein Holzschnitt' he described the former Führer as a person full of contradictions, whose attraction to the masses remained a mystery even ten years after his downfall.[147] The study closed with another 'prognosis' on the future of Germany – Hellpach conceded that his predictions from the 1920s had been flawed. To the study of folk psychology, the book did not contribute. Hellpach showed little interest in analysing a nation in all its complexity, but testified to his elitist and individualist views when he polemicized against the 'crowd' in the tradition of mass psychology.

Some reviewers agreed with Hellpach's characterization of the German mind. Hans von Krannhals, in a double review of Hellpach's *Der deutsche Charakter* and the third edition of his *Völkerpsychologie*, praised the 'crystal-clear definitions' of difficult concepts such as Volk and race. Also, Hellpach's books included an 'objective and clarifying' interpretation of National Socialism, while the chapter on Adolf Hitler was a 'psychological-political essay' of outstanding quality.[148] Others were more sceptical of the aging scholar's studies and saw him as belonging to an older generation who could not contribute anymore to the study of present-day society. His views on German history were based on 'simplistic judgements' and outdated concepts such as the notion of society as a 'social organism'.[149] It was left to the French historian Henri Brunschwig (1904–89) to point out that Hellpach's folk psychology had rephrased the *quintessence* of Nazi ideology in his treatment of race, and express his surprise that the study could have been reprinted in largely unchanged form ten years after the collapse of the Third Reich.[150]

Notes

1. W. Hellpach, *Einführung in die Völkerpsychologie* (Stuttgart, 1938).
2. On Hellpach's political career see C.-A. Kaune, *Willy Hellpach (1877–1955). Biographie eines liberalen Politikers der Weimarer Republik* (Frankfurt am Main, 2005).
3. W. Hellpach, *Die Grenzwissenschaften der Psychologie: die biologischen und soziologischen Grundlagen der Seelenforschung, vornehmlich für die Vertreter der Geisteswissenschaften und Pädagogik* (Leipzig, 1902), pp. 470–79. Hellpach followed this principle until the hand-over of power to the Nazis in 1933; immediately beforehand he indeed published a textbook on social, not on folk, psychology, which was reprinted twice after the Second World War; see W. Hellpach, *Elementares Lehrbuch der Sozialpsychologie* (Berlin, 1933), second edition (Stuttgart, 1946), third edition (Stuttgart, 1951).
4. See T. Hauschild, ed., *Lebenslust und Fremdenfurcht: Ethnologie im Dritten Reich* (Frankfurt am Main, 1995); W. Oberkrome, *Volksgeschichte: Methodische Innovation und völkische Ideologisierung in der deutschen Geschichtswissenschaft, 1918–1945* (Göttingen, 1993); P. Schöttler, ed., *Geschichtsschreibung als Legitimationswissenschaft 1918–1945* (Frankfurt am Main, 1997); F.R. Hausmann, ed., *Die Rolle der Geisteswissenschaften im Dritten Reich* (Munich, 2002); C. Klingemann, *Soziologie im Dritten Reich* (Baden-Baden, 1996).
5. R. vom Bruch, ed., *Friedrich Naumann in seiner Zeit* (Berlin and New York, 2000). A similar case is the historian Friedrich Meinecke, see his *Die deutsche Katastrophe: Erinnerungen und Betrachtungen* (Wiesbaden, 1946).
6. See Hellpach's autobiography *Wirken in Wirren. Lebenserinnerungen. Eine Rechenschaft über Wert und Glück, Schuld und Sturz meiner Generation*, 2 vols (Hamburg, 1948). The third volume of this autobiography was only published posthumously in 1987; see C. Führ and H. G. Zier, eds, *Hellpach-Memoiren 1925–1945* (Cologne and Vienna, 1987). A full-scale academic biography of Hellpach is not available. See Kaune, *Willy Hellpach*; K.A. Lankenau, 'Willy Hellpach: Ein Leben zwischen Wissenschaft und Politik', in *Zeitschrift für die Geschichte des Oberrheins* 134(1986), pp. 359–75; W. Stallmeister and H.E. Lück, eds, *Willy Hellpach. Beiträge zu Werk und Biographie* (Frankfurt am Main, 1991).
7. W. Hellpach, *Die Farbenwahrnehmung im indirecten Sehen* (Leipzig, 1900).
8. W. Stallmeister and H.E. Lück, 'Die Völkerpsychologie im Werk von Willy Hellpach', in Jüttemann, ed., *Wundts anderes Erbe*, p. 123. See H. Steinberg, ed., *Wilhelm Wundt – Emil Kraepelin, Briefwechsel, 1880–1920: Zeugnis einer jahrzehntelangen Freundschaft* (Bern and Göttingen, 2002).
9. W. Hellpach, 'Analytische Untersuchungen zur Psychologie der Hysterie', Ph.D. dissertation (Heidelberg, 1903).

10. W. Hellpach, *Grundlinien einer Psychologie der Hysterie* (Leipzig, 1904).
11. W. Hellpach, *Nervosität und Kultur* (Berlin, 1902); see J. Radkau, *Das Zeitalter der Nervosität: Deutschland zwischen Bismarck und Hitler* (Darmstadt, 1998), pp. 14–15.
12. W. Hellpach, *Die geistigen Epidemien* (Frankfurt am Main, 1906).
13. Hellpach's bibliography lists 1,070 publications between 1895 and 1955. See Stallmeister and Lück, eds, *Willy Hellpach: Beiträge zu Werk und Biographie*, pp. 150–223.
14. Hellpach, *Wirken in Wirren*, vol. 1, pp. 370–82.
15. See F.L. Carsten, *Eduard Bernstein, 1850–1932: Eine politische Biographie* (Munich, 1993); P. Gay, *The Dilemma of Democratic Socialism: Eduard Bernstein's Challenge to Marx* (New York and London, 1962); I. Gilcher-Holtey, *Das Mandat des Intellektuellen: Karl Kautsky und die Sozialdemokratie* (Berlin, 1986); C.E. Schorske, *German Social Democracy 1905–1917: The Development of the Great Schism* (Cambridge, MA, 1955).
16. Hellpach, *Wirken in Wirren*, vol. 1, pp. 246–47.
17. E. Gystrow [i.e. ,W. Hellpach], 'Herr Mehring als Antiquarius: ein offener Brief', in *Sozialistische Monatshefte* 3 (1899), pp. 583–87.
18. Vom Bruch, ed. *Friedrich Naumann*.
19. Hellpach, *Wirken in Wirren*, vol. 1, p. 250.
20. E. Gystrow, 'Etwas über Nietzsche und uns Sozialisten', in *Sozialistische Monatshefte* 4(1900), pp. 630–40; see S.E. Aschheim, 'Nietzschean Socialism – Left and Right', in *Journal of Contemporary History* 23(1988), pp. 147–68, at pp. 153–54.
21. Hellpach, *Wirken in Wirren*, vol. 1, pp. 435–43; see H. Herold-Schmidt, 'Ärztliche Interessenvertretung im Kaiserreich, 1871–1914', in R. Jütte, ed., *Geschichte der deutschen Ärzteschaft* (Cologne, 1997), pp. 43–96.
22. W. Hellpach, *Grundgedanken zur Wissenschaftslehre der Psychopathologie* (Leipzig, 1906).
23. Hellpach had met Weber after moving to Karlsruhe. He had submitted an article to Weber and Sombart's journal *Archiv für Sozialwissenschaft und Sozialpolitik*, and started an exchange of letters with the eminent scholar. Because of his own illness, Weber was interested in Hellpach's expertise as a neurologist. Even though Weber helped Hellpach to get his *Habilitation* accepted, the latter's judgement of the German founding father of sociology was harsh. In contrast to admirers such as Karl Jaspers and Theodor Heuß, Hellpach accused Weber of not having reached a 'truly creative level' ('nicht bis zum wirklich Schöpferischen vorgedrungen') and not having finished any of his major works. Hellpach was particularly dismissive of Weber's methodological works, which were very critical of both Wundt and Lamprecht. Hellpach, *Wirken in Wirren*, vol. 1, p. 495.
24. Ibid., p. 486: 'Ich darf ohne Selbstüberhebung sagen, daß ich dieses Fach in den deutschen Hochschulunterricht eingeführt habe.'
25. Ibid., p. 441.
26. Hellpach, *Wirken in Wirren*, vol. 2, p. 83.

27. Ibid., p. 38; W. Hellpach, 'Böhmische Frage', in *Neue Preußische Kreuzzeitung*, 1 March 1917; W. Hellpach, 'Konservative Gedanken', in *Das neue Deutschland* 5(1917), pp. 458–64.
28. Hellpach, *Wirken in Wirren*, vol. 2, p. 18, see W. Hellpach, 'Deutschlands Österreichisches Gesicht', in *Akademische Rundschau* 3(1915), pp. 272–83.
29. Hellpach, *Wirken in Wirren*, vol. 2, pp. 56–57.
30. Ibid., pp. 77–78.
31. R. Lang and W. Hellpach, *Gruppenfabrikation* (Berlin, 1922). See R. Brady, *The Rationalization Movement in German Industry* (New York, 1933); E. Klautke, *Unbegrenzte Möglichkeiten: 'Amerikanisierung' in Deutschland und Frankreich, 1900–1933* (Stuttgart, 2003), pp. 183–91.
32. Hellpach, *Wirken in Wirren*, vol. 2, pp. 202–3; W. Hellpach, *Die Wesensgestalt der deutschen Schule* (Leipzig, 1925); see Lankenau, 'Willy Hellpach'.
33. Führ and Zier, eds, *Hellpach-Memoiren*, pp. 31–34.
34. See Hellpach's account in ibid., pp. 243–44.
35. W. Hellpach, *Politische Prognose für Deutschland* (Frankfurt, 1928), p. 9: 'Die Deutschen sind kein Rassevolk.'
36. Ibid., pp. 9–13, 16–17, 37–39. See F. Boas, 'Changes in the Bodily Form of Descendants of Immigrants', in *American Anthropologist*, New Series, 14(1912), pp. 530–62; W. Hellpach, *Das fränkische Gesicht: Untersuchungen zur Physiognomik der deutsche Volksstämme. 1. Folge* (Sitzungsberichte der Heidelberger Akademie der Wissenschaften) (Heidelberg, 1921).
37. Hellpach, *Wirken in Wirren*, vol. 2, pp. 43–48.
38. A. zu Dohna and W. Hellpach, *Die Krisis des deutschen Parlamentarismus: Vorträge auf der Tagung deutscher Hochschullehrer zu Weimar 1927* (Karlsruhe, 1927).
39. Hellpach, *Wirken in Wirren*, vol. 2, p. 11.
40. Führ and Zier, eds, *Hellpach-Memoiren*, pp. 64, 66, 69.
41. Ibid., p. 125.
42. W. Hellpach, 'Generationen', in *Vossische Zeitung*, 16 April 1933, pp. 1–2. See M. Wildt, *Generation des Unbedingten: Das Führungskorps des Reichssicherheitshauptamtes* (Hamburg, 2002).
43. R.S. Levy, *The Downfall of the Anti-Semitic Political Parties in Imperial Germany* (New Haven and London, 1975).
44. Führ and Zier, eds, *Hellpach-Memoiren*, p. 133.
45. Ibid., pp. 254–56; the conference is briefly discussed in J. Elvert, *Mitteleuropa! Deutsche Pläne zur europäischen Neuordnung, 1918–1945* (Stuttgart, 1999), pp. 201–3.
46. Führ and Zier, eds, *Hellpach-Memoiren*, p. 170.
47. Ibid., pp. 74–75; see Hellpach's Reichstag speech on education policy in *Stenographische Berichte über die Verhandlungen des Deutschen Reichstags, 4. Wahlperiode 1928*, vol. 425 (Berlin, 1928), pp. 2, 241–49.
48. See the text of the law in I. von Münch, ed., *Gesetze des NS-Staats: Dokumente eines Unrechtssystems*, third edition (Paderborn, 1994), pp. 26–28.
49. See the correspondence in Generallandesarchiv Karlsruhe, Bestand N Hellpach, No. 6; Führ and Zier, eds, *Hellpach-Memoiren*, pp. 275–77; H. Gundlach,

'Willy Hellpach; Attributionen', in C.F. Graumann, ed., *Psychologie im Dritten Reich* (Berlin, 1986) pp. 170–73.

50. Hellpach, *Wirken in Wirren*, vol. 2, pp. 116–18.

51. Hellpach, *Das fränkische Gesicht*, p. 3: 'In Deutschand (worunter das gesamte geschlossen deutsche Sprachgebiet begriffen ist) erscheint die Mannigfaltigkeit der Gesichter außerordentlich. Zumal im mitteldeutschen Gebiet bis in die Alpenvorlande hinauf wird sie so bunt, daß sie für den oberflächlichen Eindruck jeder Regel spottet. Dennoch gibt eine ausdauernde, planmäßige und eindringliche Beobachtung auch hier wohlausgeprägte physiognomische Typen.'

52. Ibid., pp. 9–10.

53. Ibid., pp. 5–6. See Boas, 'Changes in the Bodily Form of Descendants of Immigrants'.

54. Hellpach, *Das fränkische Gesicht*, pp. 10–11.

55. Ibid., pp. 11–12: 'Es bleibt der Tatbestand, daß die Temperamentsart regional sehr verschieden ist, und die "Regionen" gleichen Temperaments werden nicht bezeichnet durch klimatische oder landschaftliche Gleichförmigkeit, sondern durch die Stammeseinheit der die Region erfüllenden Bevölkerung, diese Stammeseinheit selber aber wird durch ein einziges Kriterium, die Mundart, charakterisiert.'

56. Ibid., p. 18.

57. W. Hellpach, *Zweite Mitteilung zur Physiognomik der deutschen Stämme* (Sitzungsberichte der Heidelberger Akademie der Wissenschaften) (Berlin and Leipzig, 1925). Hellpach now used Ernst Kretschmer's concept of the human 'constitution' to criticize physical anthropology, and quoted Franz Boas's studies, to which he owed a lot. See also Hellpach, *Die geopsychischen Erscheinungen: Wetter, Klima und Landschaft in ihrem Einfluß auf das Seelenleben*, third edition (Leipzig, 1923), p. 344.

58. W. Hellpach, *Dritte Mitteilung zur Statik und Dynamik der deutschen Stammesphysiognomien*, (Sitzungsberichte der Heidelberger Akademie der Wissenschaften, mathematisch-naturwissenschaftliche Klasse) (Berlin and Leipzig, 1931).

59. E. Klautke, 'German Race Psychology and its Implementations in Central Europe: Egon von Eickstedt and Rudolf Hippius', in M. Turda and Paul Weindling, eds, *'Blood and Homeland': Eugenics and Racial Nationalism in Central and Southeast Europe, 1900–1940* (Budapest, 2007), pp. 23–40, at pp. 24–25.

60. For example Hellpach, *Einführung in die Völkerpsychologie*, p. 45: 'Der Unterschied ist gekennzeichnet durch ein psychologisches Vorwiegen der Verstandes- und Willensseite bei den Nordteilen und der Phantasie- und Gemütsseite bei den Südteilen der Völker.'

61. Hellpach, *Wirken in Wirren*, vol. 2, pp. 56–57. In his inaugural lecture at the University of Heidelberg, in 1926, Hellpach presented his studies on the physiognomy of the German 'tribes' as the 'central theme' of his future research under the title 'Appearance and Creation of the Volkstum'. See Führ and Zier, eds, *Hellpach-Memoiren*, p. 248.

62. Hellpach, *Dritte Mitteilung*, pp. 4–5.

63. W. Hellpach, *Deutsche Physiognomik: Grundlegung zu einer Naturgeschichte der Nationalgesichter* (Berlin, 1942), p. iii.

64. Führ and Zier, eds, *Hellpach-Memoiren*, pp. 244–46. The anthropologist Eugen Fischer had provided Hellpach with the decisive, positive reference, after Rudolf Martin, a physical anthropologist at the University of Munich, had rejected Hellpach's initial application because of misgivings regarding the suggested research methods. On Fischer see N.C. Loesch, *Rasse als Konstrukt: Leben und Werk Eugen Fischers* (Frankfurt am Main, 1997).

65. W. Stallmeister, 'Willy Hellpachs Auftritt beim Internationalen Kongreß für Philosophie in Prag 1934', in Stallmeister and Lück, eds, *Willy Hellpach. Beiträge zu Werk und Biographie*, pp. 46–58; Klingemann, *Soziologie im Dritten Reich*, pp. 236–39. Cf. H. Gundlach, 'Willy Hellpachs Sozial- und Völkerpsychologie unter dem Aspekt der Auseinandersetzung mit der Rassenideologie', in C. Klingemann, ed., *Rassenmythos und Sozialwissenschaften in Deutschland: Ein verdrängtes Kapitel sozialwissenschaftlicher Wirkungsgeschichte* (Opladen, 1987), pp. 242–76, at pp. 256–63. Hellpach's use of the term *Eugenik* instead of *Rassenhygiene* at a conference in 1934 hardly marks him as 'an opponent of national socialism', contrary to Gundlach's claims, p. 254.

66. Hellpach's lecture was published as W. Hellpach, 'Volk als Naturtatsache, geistige Gestalt und Willensschöpfung', in *Volksspiegel* 1(1934), pp. 209–17; a shortened version appeared under the same title in *Forschungen und Fortschritte* 10(1934), pp. 389–90.

67. T. Mann, *Tagebücher 1933–1934*, ed. P. de Mendelssohn (Frankfurt am Main, 1977), pp. 32, 526.

68. Führ and Zier, eds, *Hellpach-Memoiren*, pp. 278–82.

69. H. Hartmann, *Begegnung mit Europäern: Gespräche mit Gestaltern unserer Zeit* (Thun, 1954), p. 119: 'Schon die Tatsache der einhelligen Begeisterung über diesen Vortrag zeigt, daß es bei einigem Mut auch für deutsche Forscher möglich war, weiter ihrer Linie treu zu bleiben.' See H. Driesch, *Lebenserinnerungen: Aufzeichnungen eines Forschers und Denkers in entscheidender Zeit* (Munich and Basel 1951), p. 274.

70. J.B. Kozák, 'The Prague Congress of Philosophy', in *Slavonic and East European Review* 13(1935), pp. 330–36, at p. 333. See L.J. Walker, 'The International Congress on Philosophy held at Prague, September 2–7, 1934', in *Philosophy* 10(1935), pp. 3–14.

71. C. Krusé, 'The Eighth International Congress of Philosophy', in Philosophical Review 44(1935), pp. 46–56, at p. 49. Similarly, see E. Nagel, 'The Eighth International Congress of Philosophy', in *Journal of Philosophy* 31(1934), pp. 589–601, at p. 593.

72. Hellpach, *Einführung in die Völkerpsychologie*, p. iv.

73. Ibid., p. v; see A. Bach, *Deutsche Volkskunde: Ihre Wege, Ergebnisse und Aufgaben* (Leipzig, 1937); W.E. Mühlmann, *Rassen- und Völkerkunde: Lebensprobleme der Rassen, Gesellschaften und Völker* (Braunschweig, 1936); M.H. Böhm, *Volkskunde* (Berlin, 1937). See W. Hellpach, 'Volkswissenschaften, Völkerwissenschaften, Bevölkerungswissenschaft und die gesamte Psychologie', in *Archiv für die gesamte Psychologie* 100(1938), pp. 554–89. In this review article Hellpach dis-

cussed the above-mentioned titles in detail and compared them to his own *Einführung in die Völkerpsychologie*.

74. Generallandesarchiv Karlsruhe, N Hellpach, No. 277 (allgemeine Korrespondenz), Professor Dr Max H. Boehm, Jena, to Hellpach, 19 November 1937; Hellpach to Boehm, 31 December 1937. Hellpach mentioned Boehm's private letter in his review article 'Volkswissenschaften, Völkerwissenschaften, Bevölkerungswissenschaft', p. 577.

75. Despite his critical attitude towards folk psychology, Richard Thurnwald established and edited the *Zeitschrift für Soziologie und Völkerpsychologie* from 1925 until 1931, when he changed its name to *Sociologus*.

76. Hellpach, *Einführung in die Völkerpsychologie*, pp. 67–68.

77. Ibid., p. 1.

78. Ibid.: 'Die Menschheit lebt in Völkern. Sie existiert praktisch nur als ein riesiges Nebeneinander, Miteinander, oft auch Gegeneinander von zahllosen Völkern.' See ibid. pp. 22–24.

79. Ibid., p. 2.

80. Ibid., p. 18.

81. See Hellpach, *Die geopsychischen Erscheinungen* (Leipzig, 1911). This study was Hellpach's longest-selling book; it remained in print until 1977 under the title *Geopsyche: Die Menschenseele unter dem Einfluß von Klima und Wetter, Boden und Landschaft*, eighth edition (Stuttgart, 1977). It was translated into French as *Géopsyché. L'âme humaine sous l'influence du temps, du climat, du sol et du paysage* (Paris,1943), as well as into Italian and Dutch.

82. Hellpach, *Einführung in die Völkerpsychologie*, pp. 42–43.

83. Ibid., p. 48.

84. Ibid., pp. 49–50: 'Auch die Völker, als die natürlichen Lebenseinheiten des Menschengeschlechts, würden, sobald sie wandern, umsiedeln, in großen Teilen kolonisieren, neue Heimaten sich schaffen, dafür eine mehr oder weniger eingreifende Umwandlung ihrer leiblichen und seelischen Konstitution hinnehmen müssen. … Die Rasse wird dadurch nicht verwandelt, so wenig wie das Familienerbgut oder -ungut. Die Neger sind auch (sofern sie sich nicht mit den Weißen oder Roten vermischten) in Amerika Neger geblieben. Aber der amerikanische Schwarze ist von anderer Konstitution als der afrikanische.'

85. Hellpach, *Einführung in die Völkerpsychologie*, p. 43: 'die Fähigkeit, Völker zu bilden und völkisch zu existieren, ist der Maßstab für die Standorteignung einer Rasse'.

86. Hellpach, *Einführung in die Völkerpsychologie*, p. 36: 'Wir kennen keine Rasse, die als Ganzes in einer geschlossenen Volksgemeinschaft lebte. Innerhalb der Räume, die von wesentlich einer Rasse bewohnt sind, ist diese rassisch homogene Bevölkerung in Völker, Völkerschaften, Völkerstämme aufgegliedert, die teilweise in grimmiger Feindseligkeit miteinander leben. Umgekehrt sind viele Völker, welche den sehr festen und bewußten Schicksalszusammenhang der "Nation" in sich ausgebildet haben, aus verschiedenen Rassen gemischt, wie wir es bei den führenden Nationen des Abendlandes feststellen können.'

87. Hellpach, *Einführung in die Völkerpsychologie*, p. 31.

88. Ibid., pp. 32–33.

89. Ibid., p. 34.
90. See H.F.K. Günther, *Rassenkunde des deutschen Volkes*, seventeenth edition (Munich, 1933) [1922].
91. Hellpach, *Einführung in die Völkerpsychologie*, p. 35.
92. Ibid., pp. 36–37.
93. Gundlach's attempt to present Hellpach's folk psychology as a subtle criticism of Nazi race ideologies, on account of his use of 'chiffres' and 'codes', is not convincing. See Gundlach, 'Willy Hellpach's Sozial- und Völkerpsychologie', pp. 264–70.
94. Hellpach, *Einführung in die Völkerpsychologie*, p. 52.
95. Ibid., p. 52. See C.G. Jung, 'Über die Archetypen des kollektiven Unbewußten [1934]' and 'Der Begriff des kollektiven Unbewußten', in C.G. Jung, *Archetypen* (Munich, 2001), pp. 7–43 and 44–56; O. Spengler, *Der Untergang des Abendlandes: Umriß einer Morphologie der Weltgeschichte* (Munich, 1995) [1918–1922], pp. 226–27. Spengler argued that each civilization developed a different *Ursymbol*.
96. Hellpach, *Einführung in die Völkerpsychologie*, p. 53.
97. Ibid., p. 58.
98. Ibid., p. 66.
99. Ibid., p. 85.
100. Ibid., p. 89.
101. Ibid., p. 93; see also pp. 146–47.
102. Ibid., pp. 98–99.
103. Ibid., p. 106: 'das letzthin Wesenhafte, gleichsam den innerlichen Existenzbegriff eines jeden Volkes – und die völkische Lebensordnung, die sich hierauf gründet'.
104. Hellpach, *Einführung in die Völkerpsychologie*, p. 106: 'die unauflösliche leib-seelische Einheit der Volkswirklichkeit'.
105. Hellpach, *Einführung in die Völkerpsychologie*, p. 108.
106. Ibid., pp. 5, 6.
107. Ibid., pp. 124–25.
108. Ibid., p. 133.
109. Ibid., p. 143.
110. Cf. Gundlach, 'Willy Hellpach – Attributionen'; Klingemann, *Soziologie im Dritten Reich*; and Kaune, *Willy Hellpach*, have followed Gundlach without testing his argument.
111. Cf. Gundlach, 'Willy Hellpach's Sozial- und Völkerpsychologie', p. 264.
112. A. Harasser, 'Review of Hellpach, *Völkerpsychologie*', in *Anthropologischer Anzeiger* 15(1938), p. 81.
113. K. Haushofer, 'Review of Hellpach, *Völkerpsychologie*', in *Zeitschrift für Geopolitik* 15(1938), p. 133.
114. F. Zahn, 'Review of Hellpach, *Völkerpsychologie*', in *Allgemeines Statistisches Archiv* 27(1938), p. 475.
115. G. Spannhaus, 'Review of Hellpach, *Völkerpsychologie*', in *Geographische Zeitschrift* 47(1941), p. 236.

116. J. Glück, 'Review of Hellpach, *Völkerpsychologie* and *Geopsyche*, fifth edition', in *Zeitschrift für Ethnologie* 73 (1941) [published 1944], pp. 122–23.

117. B. Petermann, 'Review of Hellpach, *Völkerpsychologie*', in *Zeitschrift für Rassenkunde* 7(1938), p. 308.

118. R. Thurnwald, 'Review of 'Hellpach, *Völkerpsychologie*', in *Historische Zeitschrift* 159(1939), pp. 103–5.

119. P.A.H. Werder, 'Review of Hellpach, *Einführung in die Völkerpsychologie*', in *Africa: Journal of the International African Institute* 11(1938), pp. 516–17.

120. C. Diserens, 'Review of Hellpach, *Einführung in die Völkerpsychologie*', in *The American Journal of Psychology* 51(1938), pp. 774–75. See, more critical, J.R. Kantor, 'Review of Hellpach, *Elementares Lehrbuch der Sozialpsychologie*', in *American Journal of Psychology* 46(1934), p. 534; G. Saenger, 'Review of Hellpach, *Schöpferische Unvernunft*', in *Journal of Philosophy* 35(1938), pp. 446–47.

121. Hellpach himself rejected the 'pompous' label 'inner emigration' for his behaviour during the Third Reich: see Führ and Zier, eds, *Hellpach-Memoiren*, p. 195.

122. See. W. Hellpach, 'Entstehung und Ausformung von Großstadtgauschlägen', in H. Harmsen and F. Lohse, eds, *Bevölkerungsfragen: Bericht des Internationalen Kongresses für Bevölkerungsfragen, Berlin 1935* (Munich, 1936), pp. 221–27; on the development of academic psychology in Germany during the Third Reich see M.G. Ash, 'Psychologie', in F.R. Hausmann, ed., *Die Rolle der Geisteswissenschaften im Dritten Reich, 1933–1945* (Munich, 2002), pp. 229–64; C.F. Graumann, ed., *Psychologie im Nationalsozialismus* (Berlin, 1985).

123. S. Kühl, *Die Internationale der Rassisten: Aufstieg und Niedergang der internationalen Bewegung für Eugenik und Rassenhygiene im 20. Jahrhundert* (Frankfurt am Main, 1997), pp. 131–37; H. Kaupen-Haas and C. Saller, eds, *Wissenschaftlicher Rassismus: Analysen einer Kontinuität in den Human- und Naturwissenschaften* (Frankfurt am Main, 1997).

124. Gundlach, 'Hellpach – Attributionen', pp. 178–79. See Generallandesarchiv Karlsruhe, N Hellpach, No. 279–96.

125. See Hellpach's letter to Karl Haushofer in H.A. Jacobsen, ed., *Karl Haushofer: Leben und Werk*, vol. 2: *Ausgewählter Schriftwechsel 1917–1946* (Boppard, 1979), pp. 371–73: 'daß der herrliche, altehrwürdige Name "Böhmen" in seiner deutschen Bedeutung wieder zu Ehren gekommen ist'.

126. Gundlach, 'Hellpach – Attributionen', p. 186.

127. U. Geuter, *Die Professionalisierung der deutschen Psychologie im Nationalsozialismus* (Frankfurt am Main, 1988), p. 359.

128. Hellpach, *Deutsche Physiognomik*; Gundlach, 'Hellpach – Attributionen', p. 187.

129. See A. Wiedemann, *Die Reinhard-Heydrich-Stiftung in Prag (1942–1945)* (Dresden, 2000); K.H. Roth, 'Heydrichs Professor. Historiographie des "Volkstums" und der Massenvernichtungen: Der Fall Hans-Joachim Beyer', in P. Schöttler, ed., *Geschichtsschreibung als Legitimationswissenschaft*, pp. 262–342; Klautke, 'German Race Psychology', pp. 29–36.

130. W. Hellpach, *Pax Futura: Die Erziehung des friedlichen Menschen durch eine konservative Demokratie* (Braunschweig, 1949); W. Hellpach, *Der deutsche*

Charakter (Bonn, 1954). See A. Rabinbach, *In the Shadow of Catastrophe: German Intellectuals, Apocalypse and Enlightenment* (Berkeley and London, 1997); J.W. Müller, *German Ideologies since 1945: Studies in the Thought and Political Culture of the Bonn Republic* (New York, 2003).

131. Führ and Zier, *Hellpach-Memoiren*, p. 296.

132. I. Haar and M. Fahlbusch, eds, *German Scholars and Ethnic Cleansing (1920–1945)* (New York and Oxford, 2004); Hausmann, ed. *Geisteswissenschaften*; S.P. Remy, *The Heidelberg Myth: The Nazification and Denazification of a German University* (Cambridge, 2002); P. Weingart, J. Kroll and K. Bayertz, *Rasse, Blut und Gene: Geschichte der Eugenik und Rassenhygiene in Deutschland* (Frankfurt am Main, 1988); Schöttler, ed., *Geschichtsschreibung*.

133. Führ and Zier, eds, *Hellpach-Memoiren*, p. 4: 'Nur wer dageblieben ist, vermag zu erzählen, wie sich im lebendigen Menschen die Ereignisse spiegelten, die sich damals zutrugen, und wie die Schwankungen der Eindrücke, der Stellungsnahmen, der Haltungen sich vollzogen.'

134. Ibid., p. 6: 'Wie es in den Konzentrationslagern, den Vergasungskammern, den Kellern des Sicherheitsdienstes, vor den Volksgerichtshöfen zuging, das wissen wir nun bis ins I-Tüpfelchen hinein, aber wir wissen verdammt wenig, wie es denen erging und wie ihnen zumute war, die ihr einfaches bürgerliches Dasein lebten und es fast nur mit der untersten Schicht der Diktatur im Alltag zu tun bekamen.'

135. Beyer to Hellpach, 19 June 1945, in Generallandesarchiv Karlsruhe, N Hellpach, No. 442.

136. See the copies of Hellpach's references in ibid., Nachlaß Hellpach, No. 442: '"Stille! Kein Geräusch gemacht!" ist der beste, der bestgemeinte Rat, den man ihm vorerst machen kann.'

137. W. Hellpach, 'Logos und Pragma', in W. Hellpach, *Universitas Litterarum* (Stuttgart, 1948), pp. 367–75, at p. 373–74. Similar in Führ and Zier, eds, *Hellpach-Memoiren*, p. 303.

138. Ibid., p. 301: 'Die Rassentatsache ist und bleibt ein außerordentlich bedeutungsvoller Faktor im geschichtlichen Geschehen, in aller Kulturwerdung und –wandlung, im Aufbau und Verfall der Völker und Reiche.' For the same reason, Hellpach saw no reason to avoid terms such as 'rassisch' and 'völkisch' in academic writing.

139. See Hellpach's memorandum in Generallandesarchiv Karlsruhe, N Hellpach, No. 438. Clauss's story has been retold, in a strange kind of non-fictional novel, by P. Weingart, *Doppel-Leben. Ludwig Ferdinand Clauss: Zwischen Rassenforschung und Widerstand* (Frankfurt am Main, 1995); on Hellpach's involvment see pp. 215–21. See C.M. Hutton, *Race and the Third Reich: Linguistics, Racial Anthropology and Genetics in the Dialectic of the Volk* (Cambridge, 2005), pp. 183–86.

140. See the brief curriculum vitae of Hellpach on the occasion of his seventieth birthday, which stressed his versatility and his striving for a synthesis of the sciences and the humanities: 'Willy Hellpach zum 70. Geburtstag', in *Zeitschrift für philosophische Forschung* 1(1946), pp. 404–7.

141. Only two pamphlets, both authored by Hellpach, were published in this 'series': W. Hellpach, *Völkerentwicklung und Völkergeschichte unterm Walten und Wirken von bindendem Gesetz und schöpferischer Freiheit im Völkerseelenleben* (Stuttgart, 1944) (*Schriftenreihe zur Völkerpsychologie*, vol. 1–2); W. Hellpach, *Das Magethos. Eine Untersuchung über Zauberdenken und Zauberdienst als Verknüpfung von jenseitigen Mächten mit diesseitigen Pflichten; für die Entstehung und Befestigung von Geltungen und Setzungen, Brauch und Recht, Gewissen und Gesittungen, Moralen und Religionen* (Stuttgart, 1947) (*Schriftenreihe zur Völkerpsychologie*, vol. 3–4). For a contemporary view see E. Maste, Review of 'Hellpach, *Völkerentwicklung*', in *Zeitschrift für philosophische Forschung* 1(1946), pp. 433–34.

142. Führ and Zier, eds, *Hellpach-Memoiren*, p. 197.

143. Hellpach, *Wirken in Wirren*, vol 1, p. 205: 'Aber es ist doch eben naturgegeben, ein Urphänomen des Menschengeschlechts, daß es in Völkern lebt und alle seine Lebensinhalte und Lebensformen danach "völkisch" differenziert.'

144. W. Hellpach, *Deutsche Physiognomik*; W. Hellpach, *Der Deutsche Charakter*.

145. Ibid., pp. 83–118.

146. Ibid., pp. 131.

147. Ibid., p. 139: 'Hitler ist nämlich ein sozialpsychologisches, noch richtiger gesagt, ein sozialcharakterologisches Phänomen seltsamster Prägung darin, daß er je nach der Umwelt, in der er sich befindet, einen ganz anderen Menschen zeigt.'

148. H. von Krannhals, 'Review of Hellpach, *Völkerpsychologie* and *Der deutsche Charakter*', in *Welt und Wort: Literarische Monatsschrift* 10(1954), pp. 376–77. See F. Würzbach, Review of Hellpach, *Kultur-Psychologie*', in Welt und Wort 9(1954), pp. 63–64.

149. R. Meister, 'Review of Hellpach, *Völkerpsychologie*, third edition', in *Wiener Zeitschrift für Philosophie, Psychologie, Pädagogik* 6(1956), pp. 144–45. See R. Heberle, 'Review of Hellpach, *Kultur-Psychologie*', in *American Journal of Sociology* 60(1954), pp. 194–95.

150. H. Brunschwig, 'Psychologie d'avant guerre', in *Annales: Histoire, Sociétés* 10(1955), pp. 455–56.

Völkerpsychologie after the Catastrophe

At first sight it seems that the efforts by Lazarus, Steinthal and Wundt to promote and establish *Völkerpsychologie* ended in complete failure. After the Second World War it was all too easy to dismiss folk psychology since it had not been established as a discipline at university level, but remained a mere 'approach'. So while in the 1950s and 1960s the social sciences finally became part of the university curriculum and expanded greatly during the course of the twentieth century, folk psychology was left out of this process. Instead, other disciplines became fully institutionalized, with their own university departments, dedicated chairs, degree programmes, academic journals and associations. Social psychology, sociology and political science as well as social and cultural anthropology succeeded in this way. The institutional failure of folk psychology, in contrast to competing social scientific disciplines, was not the result of its 'defeat' on the 'marketplace of ideas'. Sociologists, political scientists and social psychologists did not always have more convincing answers to the main problems raised by the social sciences, which they often shared with folk psychology; neither were they equipped with more adequate methods to study the 'mind of the nation'. Often, the champions of those social sciences that did succeed found themselves under more favourable circumstances and could better meet the expectations for a new academic discipline. Without an institutional base, the intrinsic weaknesses and outright flaws of folk psychology weighed even more and contributed to the repudiation of the whole approach. Still, for an historical understanding of the social sciences, an apparent academic and institutional 'failure' such as folk psychology will prove to be as useful as the histories of more successful disciplines.

After the collapse and destruction of the Third Reich the reputation of *Völkerpsychologie* declined further: academics and intellectuals increasingly viewed it as part of the legacy of the Third Reich, understood it as a form of national stereotyping, or even associated it with the racist ideology of the

Nazis, and deemed it not worthy of the status of an academic discipline. This judgement, as has been shown, was misguided, and did not reflect the intentions of its founders or the nature of their research: neither Lazarus and Steinthal's, nor Wundt's, folk psychology had been a forerunner of scientific racism. Quite to the contrary, *Völkerpsychologie* had provided authors who were opposed to racist theories of the nation with a welcome alternative. Even more so than Lazarus and Steinthal themselves, some of their followers, for instance Alfred Fouillée in France or W.I. Thomas in America, had referred to folk psychology in this way and employed it in their struggle against scientific racism.[1] Lazarus and Steinthal had dismissed not only biological-racial definitions of the nation, but any 'objective' definition of the folk as insufficient. Instead, they argued that the very existence of the 'folk' depended on the will of its members to form a community. They thus introduced a 'subjective', or 'voluntaristic', view of the nation which resembled – maybe even inspired – Ernest Renan's famous definition of the nation as a 'daily plebiscite'; as such, it resonates with modern theories of nationalism that stress the 'constructed' and 'imagined' character of national communities. A product of the Jewish background of Lazarus and Steinthal, their 'voluntaristic' definition of the nation thus assured an important, but hidden legacy of folk psychology.

Lazarus and Steinthal's dismissal of objective definitions of the nation, including biological or racist ones, however, did not prevent them from essentializing the 'folk' and its 'spirit'. Based on the notion of a harmonic plurality of nations, which they had inherited from Herder, Lazarus and Steinthal viewed the folk as an irreducible historical force which, monad-like, would explain the development of culture and civilization. Even though Lazarus and Steinthal prided themselves on their academic approach to the study of folk psychology and distanced themselves from political propagandists who employed the notion of a folk spirit to great effect, they were unable to escape the spectre of politics. They eventually abandoned their universalist outlook when they employed folk psychology for particularistic ends – even though they did so for an honourable cause, i.e., as a Jewish defence against anti-Semitism in the 1880s. The universalist claims of folk psychology had always presupposed the particularistic frame of the nation and had created an inner conflict that could never be resolved. Lazarus remained indifferent towards questions of academic objectivity that would vex future generations of social scientists, and ignored this conceptual problem of folk psychology. Unable to distinguish between political and academic concerns, he never doubted the moral value of the folk, or nation. Studying the folk spirit in a systematic and 'scientific' way, he was convinced, would improve the folk spirit and thus contribute to the common good. In the view of its founders, then, the repackaging of central ideas of folk psychology to counter anti-Semitism did not pose a problem, but demonstrated the usefulness and legitimacy of their approach. In this light, Willy Hellpach's adaptation of *Völkerpsychologie* to the needs and requirements of the Third Reich was not so much an aberration, but continued a possibility that had always been part of folk psychology.

Lazarus and Steinthal's aim was to create a comprehensive discipline based on the notion of man as a social being, which would summarize the results and insights of the humanities in a systematic and rigorous way. In the scientific age they were convinced it was imperative to study and understand the laws according to which the folk spirit developed: to them, the discovery of these laws constituted the scientific character of folk psychology and distinguished it from more established disciplines, which remained descriptive. Educated in the humanities, however, both scholars treated methodological questions only casually and superficially. Their understanding of *Wissenschaft* did not extend to the natural sciences and showed little grasp for the new empirical and experimental methods on which the natural sciences were building their success. Hence their methodology was the weakest part of *Völkerpsychologie*: it appeared outdated almost upon its publication and did not convince contemporary commentators. Similarly, the idea to create a super-discipline that would be based on the findings of established disciplines such as history, linguistics and philosophy proved to be overambitious and unrealistic, as many critics observed, and met with stern opposition. Lazarus and Steinthal remained indebted to the language of romantic philosophy, stuck to politically loaded concepts such as the *Volksgeist*, and struggled to distance folk psychology clearly from popular nationalism. Still, Lazarus and Steinthal's folk psychology was an integral part of the wide-spanning debates that inaugurated the social sciences in the nineteenth century and contributed to their eventual establishment, albeit in an indirect, mediated way. Not surprisingly, important and canonized scholars such as Georg Simmel, Emile Durkheim and Franz Boas, who adopted central aspects of folk psychology, avoided the peculiar language of *Völkerpsychologie*. Important legacies of folk psychology have thus remained hidden and disguised. It provided a link between the philosophy of Lazarus and Steinthal's teachers – above all Johann Herbart and Wilhelm von Humboldt – with the pioneers of the social sciences in the early twentieth century. While many of their peers agreed with Lazarus and Steinthal's focus on the community, few were convinced of the importance, or even the existence, of a folk spirit.

As a powerful professor at one of Imperial Germany's leading universities, Wilhelm Wundt was much better placed to establish *Völkerpsychologie* as an academic discipline than the Jewish scholars Lazarus and Steinthal, who always operated on the margins of the academic establishment. However, even though he was equally versed in the sciences and the humanities, and devoted decades of his academic life to writing a comprehensive multi-volume folk psychology, he had no intention of doing so.

Hence, for his role in the development of modern psychology, Wundt has been aptly described as the 'sorcerer's apprentice'.[2] By introducing experimental methods to the study of the human mind, he was instrumental in emancipating psychology as a discipline and moving it away from the humanities, closer to the sciences. While providing the paradigm to turn psychology into a science, however, Wundt remained opposed to the attempts of establishing it as an independent discipline solely based on experimental methods. Despite his scientific training, he remained critical of his many enthusiastic followers who wanted to cut the ties between psychology and philosophy. To him, psychology remained an integral part of philosophy, which he conceived in a broad way. The problems of Wundtian folk psychology and its reception can be located in this setting; Wundt appears as a reluctant modernizer who found himself caught between 'scientific' psychologists who championed the use of experimental methods as the only possible way to study the human mind, and philosophers who wanted psychology to remain a part of the humanities and employed hermeneutic methods. With his folk psychology Wundt remained loyal to the epistemological traditions of the nineteenth century and thus confused and disappointed the majority of his students, who in turn largely ignored the philosophical part of his *œuvre*. Many of his followers looked at *Völkerpsychologie* as an unwelcome return to the kind of metaphysical speculation they wanted to leave behind. Despite Wundt's standing and his reputation as the founder of scientific psychology, then, his folk psychology found only few genuine followers amongst psychologists. The majority of his own students, including the many Americans who would transplant the 'psychological laboratory' across the Atlantic, were only interested in experimental or physiological psychology and ignored folk psychology. Most of them came to Leipzig to learn experimental, physiological psychology and to work in his laboratory.[3] The forgetting and suppression of Wundt's *Völkerpsychologie* by psychologists starts with this uneven reception of his works. Even his most devoted American followers regularly played down the importance and significance of his 'ethnic anthropology'. Wundt's notion that 'comparative analysis' and observation in folk psychology were the equivalents of experimental methods in individual psychology did not convince those of his students who were fascinated by the idea of a truly scientific psychology, in Germany and abroad.[4]

The very term *Völkerpsychologie* quickly disappeared from academic discourse with the death of its last representative, Willy Hellpach, in 1955. His continued academic activity after 1945, when he was publicly held in high esteem and had a vested interest in stressing the continuities of his academic work, had kept folk psychology alive for a while. Indeed, he found one of his most enthusiastic followers in post-war France where Abel Miroglio

(1895–1978) founded a French journal dedicated to the study of 'psychologie des peuples' that continued the traditional French love affair with German folk psychology. The journal was published by Miroglio's Institut havrais de sociologie économique et psychologie de peuples from 1946 until 1970, when it was renamed and published under the more inconspicuous title *Ethnopsychologie* until 1982. Even though Miroglio operated on the margins of French academia, his research institute was acknowledged and sponsored by Centre National de la Recherche Scientifique (CNRS), the central funding body of scientific research in France, and he published a volume on folk psychology in the popular series of pocketbooks *Que sais-je?*, used by A-level and university students to prepare for their exams.[5]

Despite this acknowledgement of Hellpach's folk psychology, his essayistic approach quickly lost its appeal in post-war Germany. Few reviewers drew connections between the legacy of the Nazi period and Hellpach's works, but they increasingly saw his psychology as inadequate and outdated. No German scholar tried to develop the concept of folk psychology further, or reform and adapt it to the changed intellectual conditions of the increasingly stable Federal Republic. Instead, a new generation of academics began to understand the very term *Völkerpsychologie* as shorthand for reductionist and simplistic theories about national characters and associated it with Nazi ideology and racial theories. Folk psychology seemed to belong to a bygone era as part of an intellectual heritage that might not have been directly responsible for Nazism, but had been incapable of preventing it. A major concern of the new generation of academic psychologists in post-war Germany who set out to transform the discipline was the methodological naivety of folk psychology. In the 1950s and 1960s German psychology was finally, but slowly, turned into a social science based on quantitative, empirical methods. The traditional 'hermeneutic' approach of folk psychology, which used qualitative, interpretive methods prevalent in the humanities, did not fit into this reconceptualization of psychology.[6] The transformation of psychology into a modern, 'Americanized' discipline reflected the eagerness of younger German scholars to integrate their discipline into Western traditions; it also cut the ties with the traditional topics of folk psychology – language, myth, religion and customs – which were now delegated to disciplines other than psychology, insofar as they could not be conceptualized with quantitative, statistical methods.

Despite its apparent disappearance from academia in the 1950s and 1960s, however, folk psychology was not so much abandoned and forgotten, as transformed – sometimes beyond recognition. While the association of *Völkerpsychologie* with Nazi ideology made its continuation after the Second World War particularly awkward, scholars of the humanities and the social sciences remained interested in studying the 'mind of the nation'. In particular the German mind needed explanation, since, it was assumed, it had allowed the rise and the success of Nazism in Germany. This led to a paradoxical situation in which the language of traditional *Völkerpsychologie* became highly suspicious and was shunned by the majority of academics, while the themes, topics and questions of this 'failed' discipline remained highly relevant. Frederick Hertz (1878–1964), for instance, the British-Austrian doyen of the study of nationalism who had already written a systematic critique of race theories before the First World War, published another major study on *Nationality in History and Politics* in his English exile in 1944. In this work Hertz argued that the very term 'national character' should be replaced by a less ambiguous one. As a substitute, he suggested speaking of a 'national mentality', since this term would reflect national traditions, but also social structures and the influence of 'powerful individuals' on the mind of a nation – a definition that came close to Lazarus's 'folk spirit' and Hellpach's *Volkstum*, but avoided the biologism of the latter.[7]

Regardless of Hertz's criticism, the concept of a national character remained a central concern of scholars during the 1950s and 1960s. A number of historians – some of them emigrants, such as George Mosse (1918–99), Hans Kohn (1891–1971) and Fritz Stern (b. 1926), who had escaped Nazi Germany and established themselves at American universities – produced studies of the German mind that could easily have qualified as contributions to folk psychology.[8] In the tradition of the history of ideas, they wrote case studies of modern German history and ignored the theoretical and methodological problems of a theory of national characters, even though their approaches depended on the assumption of a more or less stable German mind. American social scientists were equally interested in developing a 'science of national character', as the psychologists Otto Klineberg (1899–1992) called it. During the war, studies in national character were in high demand by political and military authorities in the U.S.A. who asked for reliable information about foreign nations. Anthropologists of the 'culture and personality' school, such as Margaret Mead (1901–78), Gregory Bateson (1904–80) and Ruth Benedict (1887–1948) responded to these demands: having formed a Committee on National Morale in 1939 which aimed to study domestic American culture during the war, they provided the U.S. Navy's Office of War Information with interpretations of the German and Japanese characters based on their unique fusion of anthropological fieldwork and Freudian theories. Thus, cultural anthropology would demonstrate its practical usefulness.[9] While he treated these attempts with respect, the behaviourist psychologist Otto Klineberg remained sceptical about the cultural anthropologists' methodology of studying national characters. Following a critical-rationalist, empirical approach to social psychology that asked for hard evidence, figures and quantitative data, Klineberg was not impressed with most of the available literature on national character. Still, he insisted that such a science was necessary and possible. He thus repeated the attitude with which *Völkerpsychologie* had been promoted by its champions and criticized by its sympathetic readers. His article ended on a note that sounded very similar to the programmatic manifestos Lazarus and Steinthal had published almost one hundred years before: 'I am reasonably pessimistic about the present status of our "science", but I have considerable hope for its future. Difficult, yes; complicated, certainly; impossible, no. Given enough time, patience, and the collaboration of psychologists in other countries as well as of our fellow social scientists here, we *can* have a science of national character.'[10]

Some German scholars, not least because of the conflation of folk psychology with Nazism, had more scruples than their American colleagues. Left-wing and liberal authors in particular, who were desperate to avoid any association with intellectual traditions tainted by Nazi ideologies, frequently found themselves in an uncomfortable position when they were trying to study and understand the German mind. The journalist, sociologist and philosopher of history Siegfried Kracauer (1889–1966), who was forced to emigrate from Nazi Germany first to France, then to the U.S.A., struggled with this dilemma when he prepared the study on German cinema that was soon to become the classic *From Caligari to Hitler*. This book was based on reviews of German films he had written for newspapers in the 1920s and 1930s, and tried to explain the peculiarities of the German mind as reflected by national cinema. In this respect he followed a recipe of traditional folk psychology when he studied the *Volksgeist* of the Germans through the prism of its cultural 'emanations', in his case German films. Kracauer was well aware of the fact that his study was a piece of *Völkerpsychologie*, but felt uneasy about it: in a draft of his 'book on film', he stated that 'the films of a nation reflect the mentality of this nation in a more direct way than other artistic media' since they were the results of a collective effort, of 'team work'. Films, Kracauer continued, offered an 'incomparable means of access to the mentality they reflect' since they revealed 'those deep layers of collective mentality which more or less extend below the dimension of consciousness'. Still, he was adamant to distance himself from the idea of a fixed 'national character', which he associated with racialism. His interest lay 'exclusively in such collective dispositions or tendencies as prevail within a nation at a certain stage of its historic development':

> I am not stipulating a National Character. Against Anthropologists. They more or less eliminate History, and my modest task is simply to make visible the psychological factor instrumental in historic developments. I do not set apart German mentality as isolated entity. Certain German traits may appear everywhere (for instance Paralysis, double personality), and

we are all human beings. On the other hand, it cannot be denied that, owing to its history, its geographical situation, the German people – any people – develops certain predilections, habits, idiosyncrasies, connected with certain stages of its history.[11]

So while the reputation of *Völkerpsychologie* declined steadily in the 1950s and 1960s, the search for the German mind continued. Despite the disappearance of traditional folk psychology from academia in the post-war era, the central questions it had posed remained central to the humanities and the social sciences: what characterized a nation, what distinguished it from other nations, and how could it be studied? The peculiar language which had been introduced by the champions of *Völkerpsychologie* changed: concepts such as 'folk spirit' or 'national soul' were now avoided in academic discourse. But the desire to find an accurate and objective approach to characterize nations and explain their behaviour did not disappear. The sociologist Ralf Dahrendorf (1929–2009), a rising star of the emerging social sciences in West Germany in the 1950s and 1960s, represents this process. A member of the generation of '45ers' who set out to integrate the Federal Republic firmly into the Western alliance, he openly and at length criticized folk psychology in his influential study on 'Society and Democracy in Germany', one of the seminal German texts of the interpretation of German history as a *Sonderweg*. Dahrendorf's aim was to locate the reasons for the German 'divergence from the West' which, he was convinced, had made the rise of Nazism possible.[12] In order to expose the futility of studying national characters, he opened his study with a damning critique of Willy Hellpach's folk psychology. Dahrendorf chose Hellpach's weakest text, the popular study on the 'German character' from 1954, and used it to highlight the fundamental flaws of any *Völkerpsychologie*. Ignoring earlier versions of the approach, Dahrendorf erroneously maintained that folk psychology had always operated with the concept of an immutable 'national character', and was therefore 'tautological'. He had no difficulties ridiculing the shortcomings of Hellpach's study, but ignored the long and venerable tradition of folk psychology from Lazarus and Steinthal to Wundt. Dahrendorf also avoided a detailed critique of Hellpach's *Einführung in die Völkerpsychologie*, the more advanced and sophisticated text on the subject, and thus missed the chance to draw a direct line between folk psychology and Nazi ideology. He clearly felt uneasy about the whole idea of *Völkerpsychologie*, which seemed simplistic, outdated and dangerous, since it was based on speculations about character traits that could only be hypothesized, but not proven. To Dahrendorf, Hellpach belonged to a generation of scholars that had not kept abreast with developments in the West, and whose value-laden concepts needed to be replaced by truly modern approaches to the social sciences.[13]

The main questions that Hellpach and any folk psychology before him had posed, however, were of central interest to Dahrendorf's own research. After all, his aim was to analyse 'the peculiarities of German history', and these included, he was convinced, the mentality and political attitudes of the Germans.[14] In the course of his study, then, he was forced to re-introduce the very idea of a specific German character, which was necessary to identify and explain the mental deformations of the German nation that had allowed National Socialism to rise to power. The obvious solution to Dahrendorf was to take the American social sciences as the role model for the study of national characters: instead of speculations about the German 'spirit' and its essence, modern-day social scientists needed to employ empirical research methods, and base their judgements about German character traits on quantitative data. This step would allow him to drop the language of folk psychology with its romantic and idealist connotations, and at the same time to keep its conceptual frame in place.[15] It was only a half-hearted solution that did not solve the problem Dahrendorf had identified, since even studying the German mind through opinion polls and surveys, by the 1960s the generally accepted standard of the social sciences in the 'West', did not provide a safeguard against essentializing the German, or any other nation's, character.

Dahrendorf's position was typical for the general climate in which folk psychology was dropped, and the dilemma his generation of scholars was faced with: the very term 'folk psychology' reminded them of Nazi theories, and its main concepts stemmed from a bygone era that had been imbued with 'irrational', romantic traditions which were now identified as a central problem of German history, because they had prevented, it was assumed, Germany's development into a 'normal' Western nation. This view of German history, albeit highly critical of German traditions and character traits, rested as much on notions of a German character as those of the German nationalists it criticized. It offered no clear solution to the fundamental paradox posed by the notion of a German *Sonderweg* – to explain and at the same time overcome Germany's troubled national traditions. Dahrendorf's text, however, became a major point of reference for a generation of German historians and social scientists whose main aim was to end this 'special path' and integrate Germany firmly into Western traditions. Their view of German history, of German traditions and of the German mind included a form of inverted folk psychology: while highly critical of anything deemed typically German – from militarism to authoritarianism, from anti-Semitism to anti-Americanism – this world view still depended on the notion of a unique German character.

Studying a nation's mind by employing the quantitative methods of the social sciences was not the only substitute for folk psychology after 1945. An alternative option could be found in the 'history of mentalities' which developed in the inter-war period around Marc Bloch (1886–1944) and Lucien

Febvre's (1878–1956) journal *Annales*, the most advanced interdisciplinary approach to historical studies in the early twentieth century. Of particular importance to the approach of Bloch and Febvre was the Durkheim school of sociology; their colleagues at the University of Strasbourg, the sociologist Maurice Halbwachs (1877–1945) and the psychologist Charles Blondel (1876–1939) held similar interests in the study of the 'collective mind'. Via Durkheim, the 'history of mentalities' can be linked to Wundt's folk psychology. Febvre championed the study of the historical development of national mentalities and ascribed historical agency to the 'collective consciousness', a view he derived from Durkheim's theory of 'collective representations' – which, as we have seen, owed much to Wundt's concept of a *Volksseele*. Historians of the *Annales* school transformed this concept into a theory of 'mentalities', often conceptualized on a national basis, and thus provided a proxy for notions of a 'national spirit' or 'character'. Not surprisingly, as Volker Sellin has shown, the very concept of a national 'mentality' proved as elusive and difficult to define as the 'folk spirit' or a 'national soul'. While the champions of the history of mentalities agreed that a 'mentality' differed from 'ideas' and 'ideologies', there was little agreement about the precise meaning of the term, which could include emotions, attitudes, representations, perceptions, and any views held by historical actors. Hence, the language employed by historians of mentalities often only pretended to have overcome the predicament of essentializing the 'mind of the nation'.[16]

A similar, but even more successful term is the now ubiquitous 'national identity', which often replaced older concepts such 'folk spirit' or 'national character'. One of the most successful catchphrases of contemporary social sciences, it has been popularized, if not introduced, by the German-American psychoanalyst Erik H. Erikson (1902–94), most notably in his study on *Childhood and Society*, first published in 1950. Originally meant to describe stages in the normal development of a person from childhood to adulthood, it was employed by Erikson himself to describe whole societies and nations. A normal nation at ease with itself, it was thus implied, was a nation that had overcome or avoided a 'crisis of identity'. 'National identity' can easily be seen as the modern-day equivalent of Lazarus and Steinthal's *Volksgeist* and Wundt's *Volksseele*. Lacking a precise definition, it suggests accuracy and academic erudition, but only covers up the problems involved in defining and studying the 'mind of the nation'. Erikson had committed one of the simplest errors of any form of folk psychology: he had simply applied a term developed in individual psychology to the study of a group, thus treating the nation as an individual.[17]

The main questions of folk psychology, then – the development and formation of nations, the relationship between the individual and the community, and the questions of national differences and a national 'mind' – could not be as easily abandoned as the language of *Völkerpsychologie*. They continue to intrigue social scientists and make regular returns in academic discourse, albeit often disguised by fashionable jargon.[18] Hence, while folk psychology became a taboo in serious academic discourse and remains dubious to scholars who are adamant to break with any tradition related to National Socialism, the modes of thinking that had underpinned this approach have been kept alive until the present day. Therefore, the dismissive attitude of modern historians, literary critics and social scientists towards *Völkerpsychologie* appears presumptuous. While there is little reason to try to resurrect folk psychology in its original form, its history tells us as much about the origins of the social sciences as about the present-day study of the 'mind of the nation'.

Notes

1. Cf. M. Dierks, 'Thomas Mann und die "jüdische" Psychoanalyse. Über Freud, C.G. Jung, das "jüdische Unbewußte" und Manns Ambivalenz', in M. Dierks and R. Wimmer, eds, *Thomas Mann und das Judentum* (Frankfurt am Main, 2004), pp. 97–126, at p. 100; see A. Brock, 'Was Wundt a "Nazi"?', in *Theory and Psychology* 2(1992), pp. 205–23.

2. K. Danziger, *Constructing the Subject: Historical Origins of Psychological Research* (Cambridge, MA, 1990) p. 34.

3. For a list of Wundt's doctoral students and their dissertation topics, which included fourteen American scholars, see M.A. Tinkler, 'Wundt's Doctorate Students and their Theses, 1875–1920', in *American Journal of Psychology* 44(1932), pp. 630–37.

4. E.B. Titchener, 'Wilhelm Wundt', in *American Journal of Psychology* 32(1921), pp. 161–78, on *Völkerpsychologie* pp. 165–66. See S. Feldman, 'Wundt's Psychology', in *American Journal of Psychology* 44(1932), pp. 615–29; Anon., 'Death of Wundt', in *Mind*, New Series, 30(1921), pp. 123–24.

5. A. Miroglio, *La psychologie des peuples* (Paris, 1958). This study was reprinted three times, with the last edition published in 1971.

6. A. Métraux, 'Der Methodenstreit und die "Amerikanisierung" der Psychologie in der Bundesrepublik, 1950–1970', in M.G. Ash and U. Geuter, eds, *Geschichte der deutschen Psychologie im 20. Jahrhundert*, pp. 225–51.

7. F. Hertz, *Nationality in History and Politics: A Study of the Psychology of National Sentiment and Character* (London, 1944), p. 41.

8. L. Krieger, *The German Idea of Freedom* (Boston, 1957); H. Kohn, *The German Mind* (New York, 1960); G.L. Mosse, *The Crisis of German Ideology: Intellectual Origins of the Third Reich* [1964] (New York, 1981); F. Stern, *The Politics of Cultural Despair: A Study in the Rise of the Germanic Ideology* [1961] (Berkeley, Los Angeles and London, 1974).

9. F. Neiburg and M. Goldman, 'Anthropology and Politics in Studies of National Character', in *Cultural Anthropology* 13(1998), pp. 56–81; P. Gleason,

'Identifying Identity: A Semantic History', in *Journal of American History* 69(1983), pp. 910–31.

10. O. Klineberg, 'A Science of National Character', in *American Scientist* 32(1944), pp. 273–85, at p. 285.

11. Deutsches Literaturarchiv Marbach, Nachlaß Kracauer, 72.3572/1: 'Von Caligari bis Hitler, handschriftlicher Entwurf, abgeschlossen 7 April 1946'. See S. Kracauer, *From Caligari to Hitler: A Psychological History of the German Film* (Princeton, 1947).

12. A.D. Moses, *German Intellectuals and the Nazi Past* (New York and Cambridge, 2007).

13. See R. MacLeod, 'Review of Hellpach, *Grundriß der Religionspsychologie* and *Grundriß der Sozialpsychologie*', in *American Journal of Psychology* 66(1953), p. 168, who concluded that Hellpach's works showed 'little appreciation of recent developments in psychology'.

14. This is the title of the classic critique of the theory of a German Sonderweg, which introduced this very term in the first place: D. Blackbourn and G. Eley, *The Peculiarities of German History: Bourgeois Society and Politics in Nineteenth Century Germany* (Oxford, 1984). See E. Klautke, 'Auf den Spuren des Sonderwegs: Zur Westorientierung der deutschen Geschichtswissenschaft in der Bundesrepublik', in M. Berg and P. Gassert, eds, *Deutschland und die USA in der internationalen Geschichte des 20. Jahrhunderts* (Stuttgart, 2004), pp. 98–112.

15. R. Dahrendorf, *Gesellschaft und Demokratie in Deutschland* (Munich, 1965), pp. 36–37.

16. V. Sellin, 'Mentalität und Mentlitätsgeschichte', in *Historische Zeitschrift* 241(1985), pp. 555–98; see U. Raulff, ed., *Mentalitäten-Geschichte. Zur politischen Rekonstruktion geistiger Prozesse* (Berlin, 1987).

17. Niethammer has produced an exhaustive study of the murky pre-history of the concept of a 'collective' or 'national identity'. He has traced the 'secret origins' of these terms to the 1920s; the academic and public success of the catchphrase, however, started with Erikson's adoption of the term. See L. Niethammer, *Kollektive Identität: Heimliche Quellen einer unheimlichen Kultur* (Reinbek bei Hamburg, 2000).

18. There are numerous examples of studies that continue the tradition of folk psychology without acknowledging it: see for example R. Blomert, H. Kuzmics and A. Treibel, eds, *Transformationen des Wir-Gefühls: Studien zum nationalen Habitus* (Frankfurt am Main, 1993); W. Lepenies, *Kultur und Politik: Deutsche Geschichten* (Munich and Vienna, 2006); P. Watson, *The German Genius: Europe's Third Renaissance, the Second Scientific Revolution, and the Twentieth Century* (New York, 2010). A 'classic' of this kind is N. Elias, *Studien über die Deutschen: Machtkämpfe und Habitusentwicklung im 19. und 20. Jahrhundert* (Frankfurt am Main, 1989).

Bibliography

Unpublished Sources

Generallandesarchiv Karlsruhe, N Hellpach.

Literaturarchiv Marbach, Nachlaß Siegfried Kracauer.

Published Sources

Allgemeine Deutsche Biographie: Nachträge bis 1899, vol. 51 (Berlin, 1906), pp. 738–39.

Allport, F.H. *Social Psychology* (Boston, 1924).

Anon. 'Zur Völkerpsychologie und Sprachwissenschaft', in *Blätter für literarische Bildung* 1 (1861), p. 355.

_____. 'Review of Wundt, Vorlesungen über die Menschen- und Thieseele, II', in *Literarisches Centralblatt für Deutschland* 15(1864), pp. 964–66.

_____. 'Death of Wundt', in *Mind*, New Series, 30(1921), pp. 123–24.

Arnold, E.V. 'Review of Wundt, Völkerpsychologie, vol. 1', in *The Classical Review* 15 (1901), pp. 458–63.

Bach, A. *Deutsche Volkskunde: Ihre Wege, Ergebnisse und Aufgaben* (Leipzig, 1937).

Bachmann, A. 'Einiges über die bisherige Entwicklung der Völkerpsychologie und deren Verhältnis zur Geschichte', in F. Dworzak, *Erster Jahresbericht des Staats-Unterrealgymnasiums in Arnau* (Arnau, 1873).

Bakhtin, M.M. *Speech Genres and other late Essays*, eds C. Emerson and M. Holquist (Austin, TX, 1986).

Barth, P. *Die Philosophie der Geschichte als Sociologie. Erster Teil: Einleitung und kritische Übersicht* (Leipzig, 1897).

Bastian, A. 'Zur vergleichenden Psychologie', in *ZfVS* 5(1868), pp. 153–80.

_____. 'Der Baum in vergleichender Ethnologie', in *ZfVS* 5(1868), pp. 287–316.

Belke, I. ed., *Moritz Lazarus und Heymann Steinthal: Die Begründer der Völkerpsychologie in ihren Briefen*, 3 vols (Tübingen, 1971–86).

Below, G. von, 'Review of Deutsche Geschichte, von Karl Lamprecht', in *Historische Zeitschrift* 71(1893), pp. 465–98.

Beneke, F.E. *Lehrbuch der Psychologie als Naturwissenschaft* (Berlin, 1833).

Bernheim, E. *Lehrbuch der historischen Methode und Geschichtsphilosophie: Mit Nachweis der wichtigsten Quellen und Hilfsmittel zum Studium der Geschichte*, third and fourth edition (Leipzig, 1903).

Berr, H. *L'avenir de la philosophie. Esquisse d'une synthèse des connaissances fondée sur l'histoire* (Paris, 1899).

_____. *La synthèse en histoire. Essai critique et théorique* (Paris, 1911).

Bloomfield, L. 'Review of Wundt, *Elemente der Völkerpsychologie*', in *American Journal of Psychology* 24(1913), pp. 449–53.

Boas, F. 'The History of Anthropology', in *Science* 20(1904), pp. 513–24.

_____. 'Changes in the Bodily Form of Descendants of Immigrants', in *American Anthropologist*, New Series, 14(1912), pp. 530–62.

Boeckh, R. 'Die statistische Bedeutung der Volkssprache als Kennzeichen der Nationalität', in *ZfVS* 4(1866), pp. 259–402.

Boehlich, W. ed. *Der Berliner Antisemitismusstreit* (Frankfurt am Main, 1965).

Boehm, M.H. *Das eigenständige Volk: Volkstheoretische Grundlagen der Ethnopolitik und Geisteswissenschaften* (Göttingen, 1932).

_____. *Volkskunde* (Berlin, 1937).

Boring, E.G. *A History of Experimental Psychology* [1929], second edition (New York, 1950).

Bouglé, C. *Les sciences sociales en Allemagne: les méthodes actuelles* (Paris, 1896).

Breitenbach, W. *England als Völkervernichter* (Bielefeld, 1917).

Brönner, W. 'Zur Theorie der kollektiv-psychischen Erscheinungen', in *Zeitschrift für Philosophie und philosophische Kritik* 141(1911), pp. 1–40.

Brunschwig, H. 'Psychologie d'avant guerre', in *Annales: Histoire, Sociétés* 10(1955), pp. 455–56.

Churchill, W. 'Review of Wundt, *Völkerpsychologie*, first and second volume: Die Sprache, third edition', in *Bulletin of the American Geographical Society* 47(1915), pp. 621–22.

Clauss, L.F. *Rasse und Seele. Eine Einführung in den Sinn der leiblichen Gestalt*, third edition (Munich, 1933).

Cohen, H. 'Die platonische Ideenlehre psychologisch entwickelt', in *ZfVS* 4(1866), pp. 403–64.

_____. 'Die dichterische Phantasie und der Mechanismus des Bewußtseins', in *ZfVS* 6(1869), pp. 171–263.

_____. 'Mythologische Vorstellungen von Gott und Seele', in *ZfVS* 5(1868), pp. 396–434 and 6 (1869), pp. 113–31.

_____. 'Ein Bekenntnis in der Judenfrage [1880]', in W. Boehlich, ed., *Der Berliner Antisemitismusstreit*, pp. 124–49.

_____. 'Das Problem der jüdischen Sittenlehre: Eine Kritik von Lazarus' Ethik des Judentums [1899]', in H. Cohen, *Jüdische Schriften*, vol. 3 (Berlin, 1924), pp. 1–35.

Dahrendorf, R. *Gesellschaft und Demokratie in Deutschland* (Munich, 1965).

Delbrück, B. 'Die Entstehung des Mythos bei den indogermanischen Völkern', in *ZfVS* 3(1865), pp. 266–99.

_____. 'Über das Verhältnis zwischen Religion und Mythologie', in *ZfVS* 3(1865), pp. 487–97.

_____. *Grundfragen der Sprachforschung. Mit Rücksicht auf W. Wundts Sprachpsychologie erörtert* (Straßburg, 1901).

Demolder, E. *Albions Todeskampf* (Munich, 1915).

Deploige, S. *Le conflit de la morale et de la sociologie* (Paris, 1912).

Dilthey, W. 'Zur Kritik der Völkerpsychologie von Lazarus und Steinthal', in W. Dilthey, *Psychologie als Erfahrungswissenschaft, zweiter Teil: Manuskripte zur Genese der deskriptiven Psychologie*, eds G. van Kerckhoven and H.-U. Lessing (Gesammelte Schriften 22) (Göttingen, 2005), pp. 1–6.

Diserens, C. 'Review of Hellpach, *Einführung in die Völkerpsychologie*', in *American Journal of Psychology* 51(1938), pp. 774–75.

Dittrich, O. 'Review of Wundt, *Völkerpsychologie*, Band 1: Die Sprache, Leipzig 1900', in *Zeitschrift für Romanische Philologie* 27(1903), pp. 198–210.

Dohna A. zu and W. Hellpach, *Die Krisis des deutschen Parlamentarismus: Vorträge auf der Tagung deutscher Hochschullehrer zu Weimar 1927* (Karlsruhe, 1927).

Driesch, H. *Lebenserinnerungen: Aufzeichnungen eines Forschers und Denkers in entscheidender Zeit* (Munich and Basel, 1951).

Drobisch, M.W. 'Über den neuesten Versuch, die Psychologie naturwissenschaftlich zu begründen', in *Zeitschrift für exacte Philosophie* 4(1864), pp. 313–48.

Durkheim, E. 'La science positive de la morale en Allemagne', in *Revue philosophique de la France a de l'étranger* 12(1887), pp. 33–58, 113–42, 275–84.

_____. 'Review of Wundt, *Elemente der Völkerpsychologie*', in *L'année sociologique* 12(1913), pp. 50–61.

_____. *De la division du travail social* [1893], seventh edition (Paris, 1960).

_____. *The Elementary Forms of Religious Life* [1912], trans. C. Cosman (Oxford and New York, 2008).

Eliot, T.S. 'Review of Wundt, *Elements of Folk Psychology*', in *International Journal of Ethics* 27(1917), pp. 252–54.

Feldman, S. 'Wundt's Psychology', in *American Journal of Psychology* 44(1932), pp. 615–29.

Finot, J. *Le préjugé des races* (Paris, 1905).

Fontane, T. *Von Zwanzig bis Dreißig: Autobiographisches* [1898] (Munich, 1973).

Fouillée, A. *L'évolutionisme des idées-forces* (Paris, 1890).

_____. *La psychologie des idées-forces*, 2 vols (Paris, 1893).

_____. *Psychologie du peuple français* (Paris, 1898).

_____. *Esquisse psychologique des peuples européens* (Paris, 1903).

Frauenstädt, J. *Blicke in die intellectuelle, physische und moralische Welt nebst Beiträgen zur Lebensphilosophie* (Leipzig, 1869).

Freud, S. 'Totem und Tabu [1913]', in S. Freud, *Fragen der Gesellschaft. Ursprünge der Religion* (Studienausgabe, vol. 9) (Frankfurt am Main, 1997), pp. 287–444.

Führ, C. and H.G. Zier, eds, *Hellpach-Memoiren 1925–1945* (Cologne and Vienna, 1987).

Gabelentz, G. von der, 'Ideen zu einer vergleichenden Syntax', in *ZfVS* 6(1869), pp. 376–84.

Gardiner, H.N. 'Review of Wundt, *Völkerpsychologie*, vol. 1', in *Philosophical Review* 11(1902), pp. 497–514.

_____. 'Review of Wundt, *Völkerpsychologie*, vol. 2, first part, Myth and Religion, Leipzig, 1905', in *Philosophcal Review* 16(2) (1907), pp. 200–4.

_____. 'Review of Wundt, *Völkerpsychologie*, vol. 2, third part, Leipzig 1909 and third volume, second edition, Leipzig 1908', in *Philosophical Review* 18(1909), pp. 543–48.

Glück, J. 'Review of Hellpach, *Völkerpsychologie* and *Geopsyche*, fifth edition', in *Zeitschrift für Ethnologie* 73(1941) [published 1944], pp. 122–23.

Gopcevic, S. *Aus dem Lande der unbegrenzten Heuchelei: Englische Zustände* (Berlin, 1915).

Graf zu Reventlow, E. *England, der Feind* (Stuttgart, 1914).

Günther, H.F.K. *Rassenkunde des deutschen Volkes* [1922], seventeenth edition (Munich, 1933).

Gystrow E. [i.e., W. Hellpach] 'Herr Mehring als Antiquarius: ein offener Brief', in *Sozialistische Monatshefte* 3 (1899), pp. 583–87.

Gystrow, E. [i.e., W. Hellpach] 'Etwas über Nietzsche und uns Sozialisten', in *Sozialistische Monatshefte* 4(1900), pp. 630–40.

Haeberlin, H.K. 'The Theoretical Foundations of Wundt's Folk Psychology', in *Psychological Review* 23(1916), pp. 279–302, reprinted in Rieber, ed., *Wilhelm Wundt and the Making of a Scientific Psychology*, pp. 229–49.

Hales, F.N. 'Review of Wundt, *Völkerpsychologie*, vol. 1', in *Mind*, New Series 12(1903), pp. 239–45.

Hall, S. *The Founders of Psychology* (New York, 1912).

Harasser, A. 'Review of Hellpach, *Völkerpsychologie*', in *Anthropologischer Anzeiger* 15(1938), p. 81.

Hartmann, E. von, 'Das Wesen des Gesammtgeistes. (Eine kritische Betrachtung des Grundbegriffes der Völkerpsychologie) [1869]', in E. von Hartmann, *Gesammelte Studien und Aufsätze gemeinverständlichen Inhalts* (Berlin, 1876), pp. 504–19.

Hartmann, H. *Begegnung mit Europäern: Gespräche mit Gestaltern unserer Zeit* (Thun, 1954).

Haushofer, K. 'Review of Hellpach, *Völkerpsychologie*', in *Zeitschrift für Geopolitik* 15(1938), p. 133.

Heberle, R. 'Review of Hellpach, *Kultur-Psychologie*', in *American Journal of Sociology* 60(1954), pp. 194–95.

Heidegger, M. 'Probleme der Völkerpsychologie. Von Wilhelm Wundt [1915]', in M. Heidegger, *Gesamtausgabe, 1. Abteilung: Veröffentlichte Schriften 1910–1976*, vol. 36, (Frankfurt am Main, 2000), pp. 33–35.

Hellpach, W. *Die Farbenwahrnehmung im indirecten Sehen* (Leipzig, 1900).

_____. *Die Grenzwissenschaften der Psychologie: die biologischen und soziologischen Grundlagen der Seelenforschung, vornehmlich für die Vertreter der Geisteswissenschaften und Pädagogik* (Leipzig, 1902).

_____. *Nervosität und Kultur* (Berlin, 1902).

_____. 'Analytische Untersuchungen zur Psychologie der Hysterie', Ph.D. dissertation (Heidelberg, 1903).

_____. *Grundlinien einer Psychologie der Hysterie* (Leipzig, 1904).

_____. *Grundgedanken zur Wissenschaftslehre der Psychopathologie* (Leipzig, 1906).

_____. *Die geistigen Epidemien* (Frankfurt am Main, 1906).

_____. 'Deutschlands Österreichisches Gesicht', in *Akademische Rundschau* 3(1915), pp. 272–83.

_____. 'Böhmische Frage', in *Neue Preußische Kreuzzeitung*, 1 March 1917.

_____. 'Konservative Gedanken', in *Das neue Deutschland* 5(1917), pp. 458–64.

_____. *Das fränkische Gesicht: Untersuchungen zur Physiognomik der deutsche Volksstämme, 1. Folge* (Sitzungsberichte der Heidelberger Akademie der Wissenschaften) (Heidelberg, 1921).

_____. *Die geopsychischen Erscheinungen: Wetter, Klima und Landschaft in ihrem Einfluß auf das Seelenleben* (Leipzig, 1911), third edition (Leipzig, 1923).

_____. *Die Wesensgestalt der deutschen Schule* (Leipzig, 1925).

_____. *Zweite Mitteilung zur Physiognomik der deutschen Stämme* (Sitzungsberichte der Heidelberger Akademie der Wissenschaften) (Berlin and Leipzig, 1925).

_____. *Politische Prognose für Deutschland* (Frankfurt, 1928).

_____. *Dritte Mitteilung zur Statik und Dynamik der deutschen Stammesphysiognomien* (Sitzungsberichte der Heidelberger Akademie der Wissenschaften, mathematisch-naturwissenschaftliche Klasse) (Berlin and Leipzig, 1931).

_____. *Elementares Lehrbuch der Sozialpsychologie* (Berlin, 1933), second edition (Stuttgart, 1946), third edition (Stuttgart, 1951).

_____. 'Generationen', in *Vossische Zeitung*, 16 April 1933.

_____. 'Volk als Naturtatsache, geistige Gestalt und Willensschöpfung', in *Volksspiegel* 1(1934), pp. 209–17.

_____. 'Enstehung und Ausformung von Großstadtgauschlägen', in H. Harmsen and F. Lohse eds, *Bevölkerungsfragen: Bericht des Internationlen Komgresses für Bevölkerungsfragen, Berlin 1935* (Munich, 1936), pp. 221–27.

_____. 'Volkswissenschaften, Völkerwissenschaften, Bevölkerungswissenschaft und die gesamte Psychologie', in *Archiv für die gesamte Psychologie* 100(1938), pp. 554–89.

_____. *Einführung in die Völkerpsychologie* (Stuttgart, 1938), second edition (Stuttgart, 1944), third edition (Stuttgart, 1954).

_____. *Deutsche Physiognomik: Grundlegung zu einer Naturgeschichte der National-gesichter* (Berlin, 1942), second edition (Berlin, 1949).

_____. *Völkerentwicklung und Völkergeschichte unterm Walten und Wirken von binden-dem Gesetz und schöpferischer Freiheit im Völkerseelenleben* (Stuttgart, 1944).

_____. *Das Magethos: Eine Untersuchung über Zauberdenken und Zauberdienst als Verknüpfung von jenseitigen Mächten mit diesseitigen Pflichten; für die Entstehung und Befestigung von Geltungen und Setzungen, Brauch und Recht, Gewissen und Gesittungen, Moralen und Religionen* (Stuttgart, 1947).

_____. 'Logos und Pragma', in W. Hellpach, *Universitas Litterarum* (Stuttgart, 1948), pp. 367–75.

_____. *Wirken in Wirren: Lebenserinnerungen. Eine Rechenschaft über Wert und Glück, Schuld und Sturz meiner Generation*, 2 vols (Hamburg, 1948).

_____. *Pax Futura: Die Erziehung des friedlichen Menschen durch eine konservative Demokratie* (Braunschweig, 1949).

_____. *Der deutsche Charakter* (Bonn, 1954).

Herbart, J.F. *Psychologie als Wissenschaft, neu gegründet auf Erfahrung, Metaphysik und Mathematik*, 2 vols (Königsberg, 1824–25).

_____. *Lehrbuch zur Einleitung in die Philosophie*, third edition (Königsberg, 1834).

Hertz, F. *Moderne Rassentheorien: Kritische Essays* (Vienna, 1904).

_____. *Nationality in History and Politics: A Study of the Psychology of National Sentiment and Character* (London, 1944).

Heyse, C.W.L. *System der Sprachwissenschaft. Nach dessen Tod herausgegeben von H. Steinthal* (Berlin, 1856).

Hillebrand, K. *Zeiten, Völker und Menschen*, 6 vols (Berlin, 1873–86).

Hume, D. 'On National Characteristics [1777]', in D. Hume, *Essays: Moral, Political and Literary*, ed. E.F. Miller (Indianapolis, n. d.), pp. 197–215.

Hurwicz, E. *Die Seelen der Völker: Ihre Eigenarten und Bedeutung im Völkerleben* (Gotha, 1920).

Jacobsen, H.A. ed., *Karl Haushofer – Leben und Werk, vol. 2: Ausgewählter Schriftwechsel 1917–1946* (Boppard, 1979).

Jung, C.G. 'Über die Archetypen des kollektiven Unbewußten [1934]', and 'Der Begriff des kollektiven Unbewußten', in C.G. Jung, *Archetypen* (Munich, 2001), pp. 7–43, 44–56.

Kantor, J.R. 'Review of Hellpach, *Elementares Lehrbuch der Sozialpsychologie*', in *American Journal of Psychology* 46(1934), p. 534.

Kauffmann, F. 'Review of Wundt, *Völkerpsychologie*, Band 2: Mythus und Religion, 1. Teil, Leipzig 1905', in *Zeitschrift für deutsche Philologie* 38(1906), pp. 558–68.

_____. 'Review of Wundt, *Völkerpsychologie*, 2. Band: Mythus und Religion, 2. Auflage, Leipzig 1906-1909', in *Zeitschrift für deutsche Philologie* 41(1909), pp. 361–72.

Keiter, F. *Rassenpsychologie: Einführung in eine werdende Wissenschaft* (Leipzig, 1941).

Kessler, H. Graf, *Notizen über Mexiko* (Berlin, 1898)

_____. 'Nationalität', in *Die Zukunft* (April 1906).

Klemm, O. *G.B. Vico als Geschichtsphilosoph und Völkerpsycholog* (Leipzig, 1906).

_____. *A History of Psychology* (New York, 1914).

Klineberg, O. 'A Science of National Character', in *American Scientist* 32 (1944), pp. 273–85.

Kohn, H. *The German Mind* (New York, 1960).

Kozák, J.B. 'The Prague Congress of Philosophy', in *Slavonic and East European Review* 13(1935), pp. 330–36.

Kracauer, S. *From Caligari to Hitler: A Psychological History of the German Film* (Princeton, 1947).

Krannhals, H. von, 'Review of Hellpach, *Völkerpsychologie* and *Der deutsche Charakter*', in *Welt und Wort: Literarische Monatsschrift* 10(1954), pp. 376–77.

Krieger, L. *The German Idea of Freedom* (Boston, 1957).

Kroeber, A.L. 'The Possibility of a Social Psychology', in *American Journal of Sociology* 23(1918), pp. 633–50.

_____. 'Totem and Taboo: An Ethnologic Psychoanalysis', in *American Anthropologist*, New Series, 22(1920), pp. 48–55.

Krueger, F. *Über Entwicklungspsychologie, ihre sachliche und geschichtliche Notwendigkeit* (Leipzig, 1915).

_____. 'Wilhelm Wundt als deutscher Denker' in A. Hoffman, ed., *Wilhelm Wundt: Eine Würdigung* (Erfurt, 1922), pp. 1–44.

Krusé, C. 'The Eighth International Congress of Philosophy', in *Philosophical Review* 44(1935), p. 46.

Lamprecht, K. *Was ist Kulturgeschichte? Beitrag zu einer empirischen Historik* (Freiburg i. Br., 1896)

_____. *Die historische Methode des Herrn von Below: eine Kritik* (Berlin, 1899).

_____. *Die kulturhistorische Methode* (Berlin, 1900).

_____. *Americana* (Freiburg, 1906).

Lang R. and W. Hellpach, *Gruppenfabrikation* (Berlin, 1922).

Lasson, [A.] 'Review of *Zeitschrift für Völkerpsychologie und Sprachwissenschaft*', in *Archiv für das Studium der Neueren Sprachen und Literaturen* 27(1860), pp. 209–16.

Lazarus, M. 'De educatione aesthetica', Ph.D. dissertation (Halle, 1849).

_____. *Die sittliche Berechtigung Preußens in Deutschland* (Berlin, 1850).

_____. 'Über den Begriff und die Möglichkeit einer Völkerpsychologie', in *Deutsches Museum: Zeitschrift für Literatur, Kunst und öffentliches Leben* 1 (1851), pp. 112–26.

_____. 'Mathematische Psychologie', in *Cottas Morgenblatt für gebildete Leser*, 1855, pp. 481–86, 513–19.

_____. *Das Leben der Seele*, 2 vols (Berlin, 1856–57).

_____. 'Über das Verhältniß des Einzelnen zur Gesammtheit', in *ZfVS* 2(1862), pp. 393–453.

_____. 'Verdichtung des Denkens in der Geschichte. Ein Fragment', in *ZfVS* 2(1862), pp. 54–62.

_____. 'Einige synthetische Gedanken zur Völkerpsychologie', in *ZfVS* 3(1865), pp. 1–94.

_____. 'Was heißt national? [1880]', in M. Lazarus, *Treu und Frei*, pp. 53–113.

_____. 'Unser Standpunkt. Zwei Reden an seine Religionsgenossen am 1. und 16. Dezember 1880', in M. Lazarus, *Treu und Frei*, pp. 115–55.

_____. *Treu und Frei: Gesammelte Reden und Vorträge über Juden und Judenthum* (Leipzig, 1887).

_____. *Die Ethik des Judenthums*, vol. 1 (Frankfurt am Main, 1898).

_____. *Aus meiner Jugend*, ed. N. Lazarus (Frankfurt am Main, 1913).

_____. *Grundzüge der Völkerpsychologie und Kulturwissenschaft*, ed., C. Köhnke (Hamburg, 2003).

Lazarus, M. and H. Steinthal, 'Einleitende Gedanken über Völkerpsychologie, als Einladung zu einer Zeitschrift für Völkerpsychologie und Sprachwissenschaft', in *ZfVS* 1 (1860), pp. 1-73.

Lazarus, N. *Ein deutscher Professor in der Schweiz: Mit Briefen und Dokumenten im Nachlaß ihres Gatten* (Berlin, n.d.).

Lazarus, N. and A. Leicht, eds, *Moritz Lazarus' Lebenserinnerungen* (Berlin, 1906).

Leicht, A. *Lazarus, der Begründer der Völkerpsychologie* (Leipzig, 1904).

Lenz, M. 'Lamprechts Deutsche Geschichte, 5. Band', in *Historische Zeitschrift* 77(1896), pp. 385–447.

Lindner, G. *Das Problem des Glücks: Psychologische Untersuchungen über die menschliche Glückseligkeit* (Vienna, 1868).

_____. *Ideen zur Psychologie der Gesellschaft als Grundlage der Sozialwissenschaft* (Vienna, 1871).

MacLeod, R. 'Review of Hellpach, *Grundriß der Religionspsychologie* and *Grundriß der Sozialpsychologie*', in *American Journal of Psychology* 66(1953), p. 168.

Mann, Th. *Betrachtungen eines Unpolitischen* (Berlin, 1918).

_____. *Tagebücher 1933–1934*, ed. P. de Mendelssohn (Frankfurt am Main, 1977).

Marett, R.R. 'Review of Wundt, *Elements of Folk Psychology*', in *Folklore* 27(1916), pp. 440–41.

Maste, E. 'Review of Hellpach, *Völkerentwicklung*', in *Zeitschrift für philosophische Forschung* 1(1946), pp. 433–34.

Mauss, M. 'L'art et le mythe d'après M. Wundt', in *Revue philosophique de la France et de l'étranger* 66(1908), pp. 48–78; ['Art and Myth according to Wilhelm Wundt'], in *Saints, Heroes, Myths, and Rites: Classical Durkheimian Studies of Religion and Society* ed. and trans. A. Riley, S. Daynes and C. Isnart (Boulder, CO, and London, 2009), pp. 17–38.

Mead, G.H. 'A Translation of Wundt's "Folk Psychology"', in *American Journal of Theology* 23(1919), pp. 533–36.

Meinecke, F. *Die deutsche Katastrophe: Erinnerungen und Betrachtungen* (Wiesbaden, 1946).

Meister, R. 'Review of Hellpach, *Völkerpsychologie*, third edition' in *Wiener Zeitschrift für Philosophie, Psychologie, Pädagogik* 6 (1956), pp. 144-45.

Meumann, E. 'Review of W. Wundt, *Völkerpsychologie*, Band 3: Die Kunst, 2. Auflage, Leipzig 1908', in *Archiv für die gesamte Psychologie* 14(1909), pp. 46–48.

Mill, J.St. *A System of Logic. Ratiocinative and inductive* [1843], vol. 2, seventh edition (London, 1868).

Miroglio, A. *La psychologie des peuples* (Paris, 1958).

Misch, C. ed., *Der junge Dilthey. Ein Lebensbild in Briefen und Tagebüchern, 1852–1870* (Leipzig and Berlin, 1933).

Moog, W. *Die deutsche Philosophhie des 20. Jahrhunderts in ihren Hauptproblemen und Grundrichtungen* (Stuttgart, 1922).

Mosse, G.L. *The Crisis of German Ideology: Intellectual Origins of the Third Reich* [1964] (New York, 1981).

Mühlmann, W.E. *Rassen- und Völkerkunde: Lebensprobleme der Rassen, Gesellschaften und Völker* (Braunschweig, 1936).

Müller-Freienfels, R. *Psychologie des deutschen Menschen und seiner Kultur: Ein volkscharakterologischer Versuch* (Munich, 1922).

Münch, I. von, ed., *Gesetze des NS-Staats: Dokumente eines Unrechtssystems*, third edition (Paderborn, 1994).

Nagel, E. 'The Eighth International Congress of Philosophy', in *Journal of Philosophy* 31(1934), pp. 589–601.

Noack, L. 'Die Idee der Völkerpsychologie', in *Psyche: Zeitschrift für die Kenntnis des Seelen- und Geisteslebens* 2,1(1859), 161–65.

Nordau, M. *Die conventionellen Lügen der Kulturmenschheit*, second edition (Leipzig, 1884).

_____. *Der Sinn der Geschichte* (Berlin, 1909).

Oberhummer, E. *Völkerpsychologie und Völkerkunde: Vortrag* (Vienna, 1923).

Oncken, H. *Unsere Abrechnung mit England* (Berlin, 1914).

Ortner, E. *Biologische Typen des Menschen und ihr Verhalten zu Rasse und Wert: Zugleich ein Beitrag zur Clauss'schen Rassenpsychologie* (Leipzig, 1937).

Ostwald, W. *Der energetische Imperativ* (Leipzig, 1912).

_____. *Lebenslinien: Eine Selbstbiographie*, 3 vols (Berlin, 1926–27).

Paul, H. *Prinzipien der Sprachgeschichte*, fourth edition (Halle an der Saale, 1909).

_____. 'Über Völkerpsychologie: Rektoratsrede', in *Süddeutsche Monatshefte* 7(1910), pp. 363–73.

Petermann, B. *Das Problem der Rassenseele: Vorlesungen zur Grundlegung einer allgemeinen Rassenpsychologie* (Leipzig, 1935).

_____. 'Review of Hellpach, *Völkerpsychologie*', in *Zeitschrift für Rassenkunde* 7(1938), p. 308.

Rau, K. *Untersuchungen zur Rassenpsychologie nach typologischer Methode* (Leipzig, 1936).

Renan, E. *Nouvelles considérations sur le caractère général des peuples sémitiques, et en particulier leur tendance au monothéisme* (Paris, 1859).

_____. *Qu'est-ce qu'une nation? Conférence faite en Sorbonne, le 11 mars 1882* (Paris, 1882).

Ribot, Th. *L'hérédité, étude psychologique: sur ses phénomènes, ses lois, ses causes, ses conséquences* (Paris, 1873).

_____. *La psychologie allemande contemporaine (Ecole expérimentale)* (Paris, 1879).

_____. *Les maladies de la mémoire* (Paris, 1881).

_____. 'Philosophy in France', in *Mind* 2(1877), pp. 366–86.

Rutz, O. *Grundlagen einer psychologischen Rassenkunde* (Tübingen, 1934).

Saenger, G. 'Review of Hellpach, *Schöpferische Unvernunft*', in *Journal of Philosophy* 35(1938), 446–47.

Scheler, M. *Der Genius des Krieges und der deutsche Krieg* (Leipzig, 1915).

Schreyer, J. *Die Judas-Briten: Ein zeitgemäßes Allerlei* (Kiel, 1917).

Schweiger, L. *Philosophie der Geschichte, Völkerpsychologie und Soziologie in ihren gegenseitigen Wechselbeziehungen* (Bern, 1899).

Sganzini, C. *Die Fortschritte der Völkerpsychologie von Lazarus bis Wundt* (Bern, 1913).

Simmel, G. 'Psychologische und ethnologische Studien über Musik', in *ZfVS* 13(1882), pp. 261–305.

_____. 'Über sociale Differenzierung. Sociologische und psychologische Untersuchungen [1890]', in G. Simmel, *Aufsätze 1887 bis 1890. Über sociale Differenzierung. Die Probleme der Geschichtsphilosophie*, ed. H.-J. Dahme (Frankfurt am Main, 1989), pp. 109–295.

_____. Die Großstädte und das Geistesleben [1903]', in G. Simmel, *Aufsätze und Abhandlungen 1901–1908*, vol. 1, eds R. Kramme, A. Rammstedt and O. Rammstedt (Frankfurt am Main, 1995), pp. 116–31.

_____. *Die Religion* (Frankfurt am Main, 1906), third edition (Frankfurt am Main, 1922).

_____. 'Der Krieg und die geistigen Entscheidungen. Reden und Aufsätze [1917]', in G. Simmel, *Der Krieg und die geistigen Erscheinugen. Grundfragen der*

Soziologie. Vom Wesen des historischen Verstehen. Der Konflikt der modernen Kultur. Lebensanschauung, ed. G. Fitzi and O. Rammstedt (Frankfurt am Main, 1999), pp. 7–58.

Sombart, W. *Das Proletariat: Bilder und Studien* (Frankfurt am Main, 1906).

_____. *Die Juden und das Wirtschaftsleben* (Leipzig, 1911).

_____. *Händler und Helden: Patriotische Besinnungen* (Munich, 1915).

Spannhaus, G. 'Review of Hellpach, *Völkerpsychologie*', in *Geographische Zeitschrift* 47(1941), p. 236.

Spengler, O. *Der Untergang des Abendlandes: Umriß einer Morphologie der Weltgeschichte* [1918–1922] (Munich, 1995).

Stehlich, F. *Die Sprache in ihrer Beziehung zum Nationalcharakter* (Berlin, 1882).

Steinberg, H., ed., *Wilhelm Wundt – Emil Kraepelin, Briefwechsel, 1880–1920: Zeugnis einer jahrzehntelangen Freundschaft* (Bern and Göttingen, 2002).

Steinthal, H. *De pronomine relativo commentatio philosophico-philologica, cum excursu de nominativi particula* (Berlin, 1847).

_____. *Die Sprachwissenschaft Wilhelm von Humboldts und die Hegel'sche Philosophie* (Berlin, 1848).

_____. *Die Classification der Sprachen, dargestellt als die Entwickelung der Sprachidee* (Berlin, 1850).

_____. *Der Ursprung der Sprache, im Zusammenhange mit den letzten Fragen alles Wissens: Eine Darstellung der Ansicht Wilhelm von Humboldts, verglichen mit denen Herders und Hamanns* (Berlin, 1851).

_____. *Die Entwicklung der Schrift, nebst einem offenen Sendschreiben an Herrn Professor Pott* (Berlin 1852).

_____. *Die Wurzeln der verschiedenen chinesischen Dialekte* (Berlin, 1854).

_____. *Grammatik, Logik und Psychologie, ihre Prinzipien und ihr Verhältnis zu einander* (Berlin, 1855).

_____. 'Zur Charakteristik der semitischen Völker', in *ZfVS* 1(1860), pp. 328–45.

_____. *Geschichte der Sprachwissenschaft bei den Griechen und Römern mit besonderer Rücksicht auf die Logik*, 2 vols (Berlin, 1863).

_____. *Philologie, Geschichte und Psychologie in ihren gegenseitigen Beziehungen: Ein Vortrag gehalten in der Versammlung der Philologen zu Meissen 1863* (Berlin, 1864).

_____. *Die Mande-Neger-Sprachen: Psychologisch und phonetisch betrachtet* (Berlin, 1867).

_____. ed., *Die sprachphilosophischen Werke Wilhelm von Humboldts* (Berlin, 1884).

_____. 'Begriff der Völkerpsychologie', in *ZfVS* 17(1887), pp. 223–64.

_____. 'Judentum und Patriotismus [1892]', in H. Steinthal, *Über Juden und Judentum. Vorträge und Aufsätze*, ed. G. Karpels (Berlin, 1906), pp. 67–70.

_____. 'Herrn Prof. Dr. M. Lazarus zu seinem fünfundzwanzigjährigem Doktorjubiläum am 30. November 1874', in H. Steinthal, *Über Juden und Judentum. Vorträge und Aufsätze*, ed. G. Karpels (Berlin, 1906), pp. 238–42.

_____. *Über Juden und Judentum: Vorträge und Aufsätze*, ed. G. Karpeles (Berlin, 1906).

Stenographische Berichte über die Verhandlungen des Deutschen Reichstags, 4. Wahlperiode 1928, vol. 425 (Berlin, 1928).

Stern, F. *The Politics of Cultural Despair: A Study in the Rise of the Germanic Ideology* [1961] (Berkeley, Los Angeles and London, 1974).

Sütterlin, L. *Das Wesen der sprachlichen Gebilde: Kritische Bemerkungen zu Wilhelm Wundts Sprachpsychologie* (Heidelberg, 1902).

Thomas, W.I. 'The Province of Social Psychology', in *American Journal of Sociology* 10(1905), pp. 445–55.

Thomas, W.I. 'The Scope and Method of Folk-Psychology', in *American Journal of Sociology* 1(1896), pp. 434–45.

Thurnwald, R. 'Zum gegenwärtigen Stande der Völkerpsychologie', in *Kölner Vierteljahreshefte für Soziologie* 3(1923–24), pp. 32–43.

_____. 'Probleme der Völkerpsychologie und Soziologie', in *Zeitschrift für Völkerpsychologie und Soziologie* 1(1925), pp. 1–20.

_____. 'Grundprobleme der vergleichenden Völkerpsychologie', in *Zeitschrift für die gesamte Staatswissenschaft* 87(1929), pp. 240–69.

_____. 'Geistesverfassung der Naturvölker', in K.T. Preuss, ed., *Lehrbuch der Völkerkunde* (Stuttgart, 1937), pp. 45–56.

_____. 'Review of 'Hellpach, *Völkerpsychologie*', in *Historische Zeitschrift* 159(1939), pp. 103–5.

Titchener, E.B. 'Wilhelm Wundt', in *American Journal of Psychology* 32(1921), pp. 161–78.

Tobler, L. 'Zeitschrift for Völkerpsychologie und Sprachwissenschaft', in *Neue Jahrbücher für Philologie und Pädagogik* 83(1861), pp. 257–80.

_____. 'Ueber die dichterische Behandlung der Thiere', in *ZfVS* 2(1862), pp. 211–24.

_____. 'Uebergang zwischen Tempus und Modus', in *ZfVS* 2(1862), pp. 29–53.

_____. 'Das Wort in der Geschichte der Religion', in *ZfVS* 3(1865), pp. 257–66.

_____. 'Ueber das volkthümliche Epos der Franzosen', in *ZfVS* 4(1866), pp. 139–210.

_____. 'Ueber die psychologische Bedeutung der Wortzusammensetzung, mit Bezug auf nationale Charakteristik der Sprachen', in *ZfVS* 5(1868), pp. 205–31.

Trebitsch, R. 'Wilhelm Wundts "Elemente der Völkerpsychologie" und die moderne Ethnologie', in *Zeitschrift für angewandte Psychologie* 8(1914), pp. 275–309.

Treitschke, H. von, 'Noch einige Bemerkungen zur Judenfrage [1880]', in W. Boehlich, ed., *Der Berliner Antisemitismusstreit* (Frankfurt am Main, 1965), pp. 77–90.

_____, 'Unsere Aussichten [1879]', in W. Boehlich, ed., *Der Berliner Antisemitismusstreit* (Frankfurt am Main, 1965), pp. 5–12.

Vico, G. *Grundzüge einer neuen Wissenschaft über die gemeinschaftliche Natur der Völker*, trans. W.E. Weber (Leipzig, 1822).

Vierkandt, A. *Naturvölker und Kulturvölker: Ein Beitrag zur Sozialpsychologie* (Leipzig, 1896).

_____. 'Review of W. Wundt, *Elemente der Völkerpsychologie* and *Probleme der Völkerpsychologie*', in *Zeitschrift für Psychologie und Physiologie der Sinnesorgane*, 1. Abteilung 72(1915), pp. 428–29.

Volkelt, H. 'Die Völkerpsychologie in Wundts Entwicklungsgang', in A. Hoffmann, ed., *Wilhelm Wundt: Eine Würdigung* (Erfurt, 1922), pp. 74–105.

Waitz, Th. *Anthropologie der Naturvölker*, 7 vols (Leipzig, 1859–71).

Walker, L.J. 'The International Congress on Philosophy held at Prague, September 2–7, 1934', in *Philosophy* 10(1935), pp. 3–14.

Weber, M. 'Roscher und Knies und die logischen Probleme der Nationalökonomie', in M. Weber, *Gesammelte Aufsätze zur Wissenschaftslehre*, seventh edition (Tübingen, 1988), pp. 1–145.

_____. 'Wissenschaft als Beruf [1917]', in M. Weber, *Gesammelte Aufsätze zur Wissenschaftslehre*, seventh edition (Tübingen, 1988), pp. 582–613.

Werder, P.A.H. 'Review of Hellpach, *Einführung in die Völkerpsychologie*', in *Africa: Journal of the International African Institute* 11(1938), pp. 516–17.

'Willy Hellpach zum 70. Geburtstag', in *Zeitschrift für philosophische Forschung* 1(1946), pp. 404–7.

Windelband, W. 'Die Erkenntnislehre unter dem völkerpsychologischen Gesichtspunkte', in *ZfVS* 8(1875), pp. 166–78.

Wundt, M. *Was heißt völkisch?* (Langensalza, 1924).

Wundt, M. *Deutsche Weltanschauung: Grundzüge völkischen Denkens* (Munich, 1926).

Wundt, W. 'Untersuchungen über das Verhalten der Nerven in entzündeten und degenerirten Organen', Ph.D. dissertation (Heidelberg, 1856).

_____. *Die Lehre von der Muskelbewegung, nach eigenen Untersuchungen* (Braunschweig, 1858).

_____. 'Der Mund. Physiognomische Studie', in *Unterhaltungen am häuslichen Herd*, 1862, pp. 503–10.

_____. 'Die Geschwindigkeit des Gedankens', in *Die Gartenlaube*, 1862, pp. 263–65.

_____. 'Der Blick. Eine physiognomische Studie', in *Unterhaltungen am häuslichen Herd*, 1863, pp. 1028–33.

_____. *Vorlesungen über die Menschen- und Thierseele*, 2 vols (Leipzig, 1863).

_____. *Grundzüge der physiologischen Psychologie* (Leipzig, 1873).

_____. *Ethik: Eine Untersuchung der Tatsachen und Gesetze des sittlichen Lebens* (Stuttgart, 1886).

_____. 'Über das Verhältnis des Einzelnen zur Gemeinschaft', in *Deutsche Rundschau* 18(1891), pp. 190–206.

_____. *Vorlesungen über die Menschen- und Thierseele*, second edition (Hamburg and Leipzig, 1892).

_____. *Sprachgeschichte und Sprachpsychologie: Mit Rücksicht auf B. Delbrücks 'Grundfragen der Sprachforschung' erörtert* (Leipzig, 1901).

_____. *Logik: Eine Untersuchung der Prinzipien der Erkenntnis und der Methoden wissenschaftlicher Forschung*, third edition, 3 vols, (Stuttgart, 1906)

_____. 'Über Ausfrageexperimente und über die Methoden der Psychologie des Denkens', in *Psychologische Studien* 3(1907), pp. 301–60.

_____. 'Sprachwissenschaft und Völkerpsychologie', in *Indogermanische Forschungen. Zeitschrift für indogermanische Sprach- und Altertumskunde* 28(1911), pp. 205–19.

_____. 'Ziele und Wege der Völkerpsychologie [1886]', in W. Wundt, *Probleme der Völkerpsychologie* (Leipzig, 1911), pp. 1–35.

_____. *Elemente der Völkerpsychologie: Grundlinien einer psychologischen Entwicklungsgeschichte der Menschheit* (Leipzig, 1912).

_____. *Elements of Folk Psychology: Outlines of a Psychological History of the Development of Mankind* (London, 1916).

_____. 'Völkerpsychologie und Entwicklungspsychologie', in *Psychologische Studien* 10(1916), pp. 189–238.

_____. *Völkerpsychologie: Eine Untersuchung der Entwicklungsgesetze von Sprache, Mythus und Sitte*, 10 vols (Leipzig, 1900–1920).

_____. *Erlebtes und Erkanntes* (Stuttgart, 1920).

_____. *Die Nationen und ihre Philosophie: Ein Kapitel zum Krieg* [1915] (Leipzig, 1941).

Würzbach, F. 'Review of Hellpach, *Kultur-Psychologie*', in *Welt und Wort* 9 (1954), pp. 63–64.

Zahn, F. 'Review of Hellpach, *Völkerpsychologie*', in *Allgemeines Statistisches Archiv* 27(1938), p. 475.

Secondary Literature

Allesch, C.G. 'Johann Friedrich Herbart als Wegbereiter der Kulturpsychologie', in A. Hoeschen and L. Schneider, eds, *Herbarts Kultursystem: Perspektiven der Transdisziplinarität im 19. Jahrhundert* (Würzburg, 2001), pp. 51–67.

Alt, P.-A. *Franz Kafka: Der ewige Sohn* (Munich, 2005).

Anderson, B. *Imagined Communities: Reflections on the Origin and Spread of Nationalism*, revised edition (London, 1991).

Apfelbaum, E. 'Origines de la psychologie sociale en France: développements souterraines et discipline méconnue', in *Revue Française de Sociologie* 22(1981), pp. 397–407.

Aschheim, S.E. 'Nietzschean Socialism – Left and Right', in *Journal of Contemporary History* 23(1988), pp. 147–68.

Ash, M.G. 'Academic Politics in the History of Science: Experimental Psychology in Germany 1871–1941', in *Central European History* 13(1980), pp. 255–86.

_____. 'Psychologie', in F.R. Hausmann, ed., *Die Rolle der Geisteswissenschaften im Dritten Reich, 1933–1945* (Munich, 2002), pp. 229–64.

Baumgardt, D. 'The Ethics of Lazarus and Steinthal', in *Yearbook of the Leo Baeck Institute* 2(1957), pp. 205–17.

Becker, P. *Verderbnis und Entartung: Eine Geschichte der Kriminologie des 19. Jahrhunderts als Diskurs und Praxis* (Göttingen, 2002).

Bendix, R. *In Search of Authenticity: The Formation of Folklore Studies* (Madison WI, 1997).

Beßlich, B. *Wege in den 'Kulturkrieg': Zivilisationskritik in Deutschland, 1890–1914* (Darmstadt, 2000).

Beuchelt, E. *Ideengeschichte der Völkerpsychologie* (Meisenheim am Glan, 1974).

Biard, A. et al., eds, *Henri Berr et la culture du XXe siècle: histoire, science et philosophie* (Paris, 1994).

Blackbourn D., and G. Eley, *The Peculiarities of German History: Bourgeois Society and Politics in Nineteenth Century Germany* (Oxford, 1984).

Blomert, R., H. Kuzmics and A. Treibel, eds, *Transformationen des Wir-Gefühls: Studien zum nationalen Habitus* (Frankfurt am Main, 1993).

Blumenthal, A.L. 'A Reappraisal of Wilhelm Wundt', in *American Psychologist*, November 1975, pp. 1081–88.

Brady, R. *The Rationalization Movement in German Industry* (New York, 1933).

Brandist, C. 'The Rise of Soviet Sociolinguistics from the Ashes of Völkerpsychologie', in *Journal of the History of the Behavioral Sciences* 42(2006), pp. 261–77.

Bringmann, W.G., W.D.G. Balance and R.B. Evans, 'Wilhelm Wundt 1832–1920: A Brief Biographical Sketch', in *Journal of the History of the Behavioral Sciences* 11(1975), pp. 287–97.

Brock, A. 'Was Wundt a "Nazi"?', in *Theory and Psychology* 2(1992), pp. 205–23.

Brocke, B. vom, '"Wissenschaft und Militarismus". Der Aufruf der 93 "An die Kulturwelt" und der Zusammenbruch der internationalen Gelehrtenrepublik im Ersten Weltkrieg', in W.M. Calder III, H. Flashaar and T. Lindken, eds, *Wilamowitz nach 50 Jahren* (Darmstadt, 1985), pp. 649–719.

Bruch, R. vom, ed. *Friedrich Naumann in seiner Zeit* (Berlin and New York, 2000).

Bruch, R. vom, F.W. Graf and G. Hübinger, eds, *Kultur und Kulturwissenschaften um 1900: Krise der Moderne und Glaube an die Wissenschaft* (Stuttgart, 1989).

Bulmer, M. *The Chicago School of Sociology: Institutionalisation, Diversity, and the Rise of Sociological Research* (Chicago, 1984).

Bumann, W. *Die Sprachtheorie Heymann Steinthals: Dargestellt im Zusammenhang mit seiner Theorie der Geisteswissenschaft* (Meisenheim am Glan, 1966).

Bunzl, M. 'Franz Boas and the Humboldtian Tradition: From *Volksgeist* and *Nationalcharakter* to an Anthropological Concept of Culture', in G.W. Stocking Jr., ed., *Volksgeist as Method and Ethic: Essays on Boasian Ethnography and the German Anthropological Tradition* (Madison, WN, 1996), pp. 17–78.

_____. 'Völkerpsychologie and German-Jewish emancipation', in H.G. Penny and M. Bunzl, eds, *Worldly Provincialism: German Anthropology in the Age of Empire* (Ann Arbor, MI, 2003), pp. 47–85.

Buttmann, G. *Friedrich Ratzel: Leben und Werk eines deutschen Geographen* (Stuttgart, 1977).

Carsten, F.L. *Eduard Bernstein, 1850–1932: Eine politische Biographie* (Munich, 1993).

Chickering, R. *Karl Lamprecht: A German Academic Life (1856–1915)* (Atlantic Heights, NJ, 1993).

_____. 'Das Leipziger "Positivisten-Kränzchen" um die Jahrhundertwende', in G. Hübinger, R. vom Bruch and F.W. Graf, eds, *Kultur und Kulturwissenschaften um 1900, II: Idealismus und Positivismus* (Stuttgart, 1997), pp. 227–45.

Coen, D. *Vienna in the Age of Uncertainty: Science, Liberalism and Private Life* (Chicago and London, 2007).

Cole, M. *Cultural Psychology: A Once and Future Discipline* (Cambridge, Mass. and London, 1996).

Conry, Y. *L'introduction du darwinisme en France au XIXe siècle* (Paris, 1974).

Danziger, K. *Constructing the Subject: Historical Origins of Psychological Research* (Cambridge, MA, 1990).

Diamond, S. 'Wundt before Leipzig', in R.W. Rieber, ed., *Wilhelm Wundt and the Making of a Scientific Psychology* (New York and London, 1980), pp. 3–70.

Dierks, M. 'Thomas Mann und die "jüdische" Psychoanalyse. Über Freud, C.G. Jung, das "jüdische Unbewußte" und Manns Ambivalenz', in M. Dierks and R.

Wimmer, eds, *Thomas Mann und das Judentum* (Frankfurt am Main, 2004), pp. 97–126.

Digeon, C. *La crise allemande de la pensée française (1870–1914)* (Paris, 1959).

Easton, L.M. *Der rote Graf: Harry Graf Kessler und seine Zeit* (Stuttgart, 2005).

Echternkamp, J. *Der Aufstieg des deutschen Nationalismus, 1770–1840* (Frankfurt am Main, 1998).

Eckardt, G. ed., *Völkerpsychologie: Versuch einer Neuentdeckung* (Weinheim, 1997).

Elias, N. *Studien über die Deutschen: Machtkämpfe und Habitusentwicklung im 19. und 20. Jahrhundert* (Frankfurt am Main, 1989).

Elvert, J. *Mitteleuropa! Deutsche Pläne zur europäischen Neuordnung, 1918–1945* (Stuttgart, 1999).

Espagne, M. *Les transferts culturels franco-allemand* (Paris, 1999).

_____. *En-deça du Rhin: L'Allemagne des philosophes français au XIXe siècle* (Paris, 2004).

Espagne, M. and M. Werner, eds, *Transferts: les relations interculturelles dans l'espace franco-allemand* (Paris, 1988).

Eßbach W. 'Vernunft, Entwicklung, Leben: Schlüsselbegriffe der Moderne', in W. Eßbach, *Die Gesellschaft der Dinge, Menschen, Götter* (Wiesbaden, 2001), pp. 131–40.

Evans, R.J. *The Third Reich in Power, 1933–1939* (London, 2005).

Farr, R.M. *The Roots of Modern Social Psychology, 1872–1954* (Oxford, 1992).

Fisch, J. 'Zivilisation, Kultur', in O. Brunner, W. Conze and R. Koselleck, eds, *Geschichtliche Grundbegriffe*, vol. 7 (Stuttgart, 1992), pp. 679–774.

Fischer, H. *Völkerkunde im Nationalsozialismus: Aspekte einer Anpassung, Affinität und Behauptung einer wissenschaftlichen Disziplin* (Berlin and Hamburg, 1990).

Fischer, M., P. Bolz and S. Kamel, eds, *Adolf Bastian and his Universal Archive of Humanity: The Origins of German Anthropology* (Hildesheim and New York, 2007).

Flasch, K. *Die geistige Mobilmachung: Die deutschen Intellektuellen und der Erste Weltkrieg* (Berlin, 2000).

Friedman, M.S. *Martin Buber's Life and Work* (Detroit, MI, 1988).

Frisby, D. *Simmel and Since: Essays on Georg Simmel's Social Theory* (London and New York, 1992).

Gardt, A. *Geschichte der Sprachwissenschaft in Deutschland vom Mittelalter bis zum 20. Jahrhundert* (Berlin, 1999).

Gay, P. *The Dilemma of Democratic Socialism: Eduard Bernstein's Challenge to Marx* (New York and London, 1962).

_____. 'Begegnung mit der Moderne – Deutsche Juden in der deutschen Kultur', in W.E. Mosse and A. Paucker, eds, *Juden im Wilhelminischen Deutschland, 1890–1914*, second edition (Tübingen, 1998), pp. 241–311.

Gerhardt, V., R. Mehring and J. Rindert, *Berliner Geist: Eine Geschichte der Berliner Universitätsphilosophie* (Berlin, 1999).

Geuter, U. *Die Professionalisierung der deutschen Psychologie im Nationalsozialismus* (Frankfurt am Main, 1988).

Gilcher-Holtey, I. *Das Mandat des Intellektuellen: Karl Kautsky und die Sozialdemokratie* (Berlin, 1986).

Gilman, S.L. *Freud, Race, and Gender* (New Haven, 1983).

Gleason, P. 'Identifying Identity: A Semantic History', in *Journal of American History* 69(1983), pp. 910–31.

Goodwin, C.J. *A History of Modern Psychology*, third edition (New York, 2008).

Gordon, S. 'Reise westwärts, Blick ostwärts: Leipzig als Drehpunkt im Leben Martin Bubers', in S. Wendehorst, ed., *Bausteine einer jüdischen Geschichte der Universität Leipzig* (Leipzig, 2006), pp. 131–52.

Görs, B., N. Psarros and P. Ziche, eds, *Wilhelm Ostwald at the Crossroads between Chemistry, Philosophy and Media Culture* (Leipzig, 2006).

Goschler, C. *Rudolf Virchow: Mediziner, Anthropologe, Politiker* (Cologne, 2002).

Graevenitz, G. von, '"Verdichtung". Das Kulturmodell der "Zeitschrift für Völkerpsychologie und Sprachwissenschaft"', in A. Assmann, ed., *Positionen der Kulturanthropologie* (Frankfurt am Main, 1994), pp. 148–71.

Graumann, C.F. *The Individualisation of the Social and the De-Socialisation of the Individual: Floyd H. Allport's Contribution to Social Psychology* (Heidelberg, 1984).

_____. ed., *Psychologie im Nationalsozialismus* (Berlin, 1985).

Greenwood, J.D. 'Wundt, Völkerpsychologie, and Experimental Social Psychology', in *History of Psychology* 6 (2003), pp. 70–88.

Gundlach, H. 'Willy Hellpach; Attributionen', in C.F. Graumann, ed. *Psychologie im Dritten Reich* (Berlin, 1986), pp. 165–95.

_____. 'Willy Hellpachs Sozial- und Völkerpsychologie unter dem Aspekt der Auseinandersetzung mit der Rassenideologie', in C. Klingemann, ed., *Rassenmythos und Sozialwissenschaften in Deutschland. Ein verdrängtes Kapitel sozialwissenschaftlicher Wirkungsgeschichte* (Opladen, 1987), pp. 242–76.

Haar, I., and M. Fahlbusch, eds, *German Scholars and Ethnic Cleansing, 1920–1945* (New York and Oxford, 2004).

Hauschild, T. ed., *Lebenslust und Fremdenfurcht: Ethnologie im Dritten Reich* (Frankfurt am Main, 1995).

Hausmann, F.R. ed., *Die Rolle der Geisteswissenschaften im Dritten Reich* (Munich, 2002).

Hecht, J.M. 'The Solvency of Metaphysics. The Debate over Racial Science and Moral Philosophy in France, 1890–1919', in *Isis* 90(1999), pp. 1–24.

Hemecker, W.W. *Vor Freud: Philosophiegeschichtliche Voraussetzungen der Psychoanalyse* (Munich, 1991).

Hennis, W. *Max Webers Wissenschaft vom Menschen: Neue Studien zur Biographie des Werks* (Tübingen, 1996).

Hergenhahn, B.R. *An Introduction to the History of Psychology*, sixth edition (Belmont, 2009).

Herold-Schmidt, H. 'Ärztliche Interessenvertretung im Kaiserreich, 1871–1914', in R. Jütte, ed., *Geschichte der deutschen Ärzteschaft* (Cologne, 1997), pp. 43–96.

Hobsbawm, E. and T. Ranger, eds, *The Invention of Tradition* (Cambridge, 1983).

Hoeres, P. *Krieg der Philosophen: Die deutsche und die britische Philosophie im Ersten Weltkrieg* (Paderborn, 2004).

Hoeschen, A. 'Anamnesis als ästhetische Rekonfiguration: Zu Bachtins dialogischer Erinnnerungskultur', in G. Oesterle, ed. *Erinnerung, Gedächtnis, Wissen: Studien zur kulturwissenschaftlichen Gedächtnisforschung* (Göttingen, 2001), pp. 231–57.

Hoeschen, A. and L. Schneider, eds, *Herbarts Kultursystem: Perspektiven der Transdisziplinarität im 19. Jahrhundert* (Würzburg, 2001).

_____, 'Herbartianismus im 19. Jahrhundert: Umriß einer intellektuellen Konfiguration', in L. Raphael, ed., *Ideen als gesellschaftliche Gestaltungskraft im Europa der Neuzeit: Beiträge für eine erneuerte Geistesgeschichte* (Munich, 2006), pp. 447–77.

Hurch, B. 'Zum Verständnis und Unverständnis von Rudolf Trebitsch: Der Beitrag eines Ethnologen zur Baskologie', in *Österreichische Zeitschrift für Volkskunde* 62(2009), pp. 3–69.

Hutton, C.M. *Race and the Third Reich: Linguistics, Racial Anthropology and Genetics in the Dialectic of the Volk* (Cambridge, 2005).

Jacobsen, H.A. ed., *Karl Haushofer: Leben und Werk, vol. 2: Ausgewählter Schriftwechsel 1917–1946* (Boppard, 1979).

Jahoda, G. *Crossroads between Culture and Mind: Continuities and Change in Theories of Human Nature* (Cambridge, MA, 1992).

_____. 'Johann Friedrich Herbart: Urvater of Social Psychology', in *History of the Human Sciences* 19 (2006), pp. 19–38.

_____. *A History of Social Psychology from the Eighteenth-Century Enlightenment to the End of the Second World War* (Cambridge, 2007).

Janik, A. and S. Toulmin, *Wittgenstein's Vienna*, second edition (Chicago, 1996).

Jansen, C. *Professoren und Politik: Politisches Denken und Handeln der Heidelberger Hochschullehrer, 1914–1935* (Göttingen, 1992).

_____. 'Willy Hellpach: Ein antiliberaler Demokrat kommentiert den Niedergang der Weimarer Republik', in W. Schmitz and C. Vollnhals, ed., *Völkische Bewegung, konservative Revolution, Nationalsozialismus* (Dresden, 2005), pp. 209–27.

Jensen, U. *Gebildete Doppelgänger: Bürgerliche Juden und Protestanten im 19. Jahrhundert* (Göttingen, 2005).

Jones, E. *The Life and Work of Sigmund Freud*, vol. 1 (London, 1953).

Jones, R.A. 'The Positive Science of Ethics in France: German Influences on *De la division du travail social*', in *Sociological Forum* 9(1994), pp. 37–55.

Jüttemann, G. ed., *Wilhelm Wundts anderes Erbe: Ein Mißverständnis löst sich auf* (Göttingen, 2006).

Kalmar, I. 'The Volkerpsychologie of Lazarus and Steinthal and the Modern Concept of Culture', in *Journal of the History of Ideas* 48(1987), pp. 671–90.

Kaune, C.-A. *Willy Hellpach (1877–1955): Biographie eines liberalen Politikers der Weimarer Republik* (Frankfurt am Main, 2005).

Kaupen-Haas H. and C. Saller, eds, *Wissenschaftlicher Rassismus: Analysen einer Kontinuität in den Human- und Naturwissenschaften* (Frankfurt am Main, 1997).

Klautke, E. *Unbegrenzte Möglichkeiten: 'Amerikanisierung' in Deutschland und Frankreich, 1900–1933* (Stuttgart, 2003).

_____. 'Auf den Spuren des Sonderwegs: Zur Westorientierung der deutschen Geschichtswissenschaft in der Bundesrepublik', in M. Berg and P. Gassert, eds, *Deutschland und die USA in der internationalen Geschichte des 20. Jahrhunderts* (Stuttgart, 2004), pp. 98–112.

_____. 'German Race Psychology and its Implementations in Central Europe: Egon von Eickstedt and Rudolf Hippius', in M. Turda and Paul Weindling, eds, *'Blood and Homeland': Eugenics and Racial Nationalism in Central and Southeast Europe, 1900–1940* (Budapest, 2007), pp. 23–40.

Klingemann, C. *Soziologie im Dritten Reich* (Baden-Baden, 1996).

Köhnke, C. *Der junge Simmel in Theoriebeziehungen und sozialen Bewegungen* (Frankfurt am Main, 1996).

_____. '"Unser junger Freund" – Hermann Cohen und die Völkerpsychologie', in W. Marx and E.W. Orth, eds, *Hermann Cohen und die Erkenntnistheorie* (Würzburg, 2001), pp. 62–77.

_____. 'Der Kulturbegriff von Moritz Lazarus – oder: die wissenschaftliche Aneignung des Alltäglichen', in A. Höschen and L. Schneider, eds, *Herbarts Kultursystem: Perspektiven der Transdisziplinarität im 19. Jahrhundert* (Würzburg, 2001), pp. 39–67.

Krause, K. *Alma Mater Lipsiensis. Geschichte der Universität Leipzig von 1409 bis zur Gegenwart* (Leipzig, 2003).

Koselleck, R. 'The Historical-Political Semantics of Asymmetric Counterconcepts', in Koselleck, ed., *Futures Past: On the Semantics of Historical Time*, trans. K. Tribe (New York, 2004), pp. 155–91.

Kühl, S. *Die Internationale der Rassisten: Aufstieg und Niedergang der internationalen Bewegung für Eugenik und Rassenhygiene im 20. Jahrhundert* (Frankfurt am Main, 1997).

Lamberti, G. *Wilhelm Maximilian Wundt (1832–1920): Leben, Werk und Persönlichkeit in Bildern und Texten* (Bonn, 1995).

Lankenau, K.A. 'Willy Hellpach: Ein Leben zwischen Wissenschaft und Politik', in *Zeitschrift für die Geschichte des Oberrheins* 134(1986), pp. 359–75.

Lee, D.C.J. *Ernest Renan: In the Shadow of Faith* (London, 1996).

Lehmann, H. *Max Webers 'Protestantische Ethik': Beiträge aus der Sicht eines Historikers* (Göttingen, 1996).

Lenger, F. *Werner Sombart, 1863–1941: Eine Biographie* (Munich, 1994).

Lepenies, W. *Die drei Kulturen: Soziologie zwischen Literatur und Wissenschaft* (Frankfurt am Main, 2002).

_____. *Kultur und Politik: Deutsche Geschichten* (Munich and Vienna, 2006).

Levy, R.S. *The Downfall of the Anti-Semitic Political Parties in Imperial Germany* (New Haven and London, 1975).

Liebeschütz, H. *Von Georg Simmel zu Franz Rosenzweig: Studien zum jüdischen Denken im deutschen Kulturbereich* (Tübingen, 1970).

Loesch, N.C. *Rasse als Konstrukt: Leben und Werk Eugen Fischers* (Frankfurt am Main, 1997).

Lübbe, H. *Politische Philosophie in Deutschland: Studien zu ihrer Geschichte* (Munich, 1974).

Lukes, S. *Emile Durkheim, his Life and Work: A Historical and Critical Study*, second edition (London, 1992).

Lutzhöft, H.-J. *Der Nordische Gedanke in Deutschland, 1920–1940* (Stuttgart, 1971).

Mehr, C. *Kultur als Naturgeschichte: Opposition oder Komplementarität zur politischen Geschichtsschreibung?* (Berlin, 2009).

Meischner-Metge, A. '"Völkerpsychologie" oder allgemeine "Entwicklungspsychologie"? Zur Wundt-Krueger-Deklarationsdiskussion', in Jüttemann, ed., *Wilhelm Wundts anderes Erbe: Ein Mißverständnis löst sich auf* (Göttingen, 2006), pp. 81–87.

Mercury, F. *Renan* (Paris, 1990).

Métraux, A. 'Der Methodenstreit und die "Amerikanisierung" der Psychologie in der Bundesrepublik, 1950–1970', in M.G. Ash and U. Geuter, eds, *Geschichte der deutschen Psychologie im 20. Jahrhundert*, pp. 225–51.

Meyer, M.A. *Response to Modernity: A History of the Reform Movement in Judaism* (Detroit, MI, 1995).

Moscovici S. and I. Marková, *The Making of Modern Social Psychology: The Hidden History of How an International Social Science was Created* (Oxford, 2006).

Moses, A.D. *German Intellectuals and the Nazi Past* (New York and Cambridge, 2007).

Mühlmann, W.E. *Geschichte der Anthropologie*, second edition (Frankfurt am Main and Bonn, 1968).

Müller, J.W. *German Ideologies since 1945: Studies in the Thought and Political Culture of the Bonn Republic* (New York, 2003).

Neiburg, F. and M. Goldman, 'Anthropology and Politics in Studies of National Character', in *Cultural Anthropology* 13(1998), pp. 56–81.

Nicolas, S. *Théodule Ribot (1839–1916): philosophe breton, fondateur de la psychologie française* (Paris, 2005).

Nicolas S. and D. J. Murray, 'Théodule Ribot, 1839–1916, Founder of French Psychology: A Biographical Introduction', in *History of Psychology* 2(1999), pp. 277–301.

Niethammer, L. *Kollektive Identität: Heimliche Quellen einer unheimlichen Kultur* (Reinbek bei Hamburg, 2000).

Nipperdey, T. *Deutsche Geschichte 1866-1918, vol. 1: Arbeitswelt und Bürgergeist* (Munich, 1990).

Nye, R.A. *The Origins of Crowd Psychology: Gustave Le Bon and the Crisis of Mass Democracy in the Third Republic* (London and Beverly Hills, 1975).

Oberkrome, W. *Volksgeschichte: Methodische Innovation und völkische Ideologisierung in der deutschen Geschichtswissenschaft, 1918-1945* (Göttingen, 1993).

Oelze, B. *Wilhelm Wundt: Die Konzeption der Völkerpsychologie* (Münster, 1991).

Paulmann, J. 'Internationaler Vergleich und interkultureller Transfer: Zwei Forschungsansätze zur europäischen Geschichte des 18. bis 20. Jahrhunderts', in *Historische Zeitschrift* 267(1998), pp. 649–85.

Plessner, H. *Die Stufen des Organischen und der Mensch: Einleitung in die philosophische Anthropologie* (Berlin and Leipzig, 1928).

Rabinbach, A. *In the Shadow of Catastrophe: German Intellectuals, Apocalypse and Enlightenment* (Berkeley and London, 1997).

Radkau, J. *Das Zeitalter der Nervosität: Deutschland zwischen Bismarck und Hitler* (Darmstadt, 1998).

Radkau, J. *Max Weber: Die Leidenschaft des Denkens* (Munich and Vienna, 2005).

Rahden, T. van, 'Germans of the Jewish Stamm: Visions of Community between Nationalism and Particularism, 1850 to 1933', in N. Gregor, N. Roemer and M. Roseman, eds, *German History from the Margins* (Bloomington, 2006), pp. 27–48.

Raphael, L. 'Historikerkontroversen im Spannungsfeld zwischen Berufhabitus, Fächerkonkurrenz und sozialen Deutungsmustern: Lamprecht-Steit und französischer Methodenstreit der Jahrhundertwende in vergleichender Perspektive', in *Historische Zeitschrift* 252(1990), pp. 325–63.

Raulff, U., ed., *Mentalitäten-Geschichte. Zur politischen Rekonstruktion geistiger Prozesse* (Berlin, 1987).

Rebenich, S. *Theodor Mommsen: Eine Biographie* (Munich, 2002).

Reitan, R. 'Völkerpsychologie and the Appropriation of "Spirit" in Meiji Japan', in *Modern Intellectual History* 7(2010), pp. 495–522.

Remy, S.P. *The Heidelberg Myth: The Nazification and Denazification of a German University* (Cambridge, 2002).

Rieber, R.W., ed. *Wilhelm Wundt and the Making of a Scientific Psychology* (New York and London, 1980).

Ringer, F.K. *The Decline of the German Mandarins: The German Academic Community, 1890–1933* (Cambridge, MA, 1969).

Rollmann, H. '"Meet Me in St. Louis": Troeltsch and Weber in America', in H. Lehmann and G. Roth, eds, *Weber's Protestant Ethic: Origins, Evidence, Contexts* (Cambridge and New York, 1993), pp. 357–83.

Romani, R. *National Character and Public Spirit in Britain and France, 1750–1914* (Cambridge, 2002).

Rosenberg, D.J. 'Patho-Teleology and the Spirit of War: The Psychoanalytic Inheritance of National Psychology', in *Monatshefte* 100(2008), pp. 213–25.

Rosenblüth, P.E. 'Die geistigen und religiösen Strömungen in der deutschen Judenheit', in W.E. Mosse and A. Paucker, eds, *Juden im Wilhelminischen Deutschland, 1890–1914*, second edition (Tübingen, 1998), pp. 549–98.

Rössig, A. *Juden und andere Tunnelianer: Gesellschaft und Literatur im Berliner Sonntags-Verein* (Heidelberg, 2008).

Roth, K.H. 'Heydrichs Professor. Historiographie des "Volkstums" und der Massenvernichtungen: Der Fall Hans-Joachim Beyer', in P. Schöttler, ed., *Geschichtsschreibung als Legitimationswissenschaft 1918–1945* (Frankfurt am Main, 1997), pp. 262–342.

Scaff, L.A. *Max Weber in America* (Princeton and Oxford, 2011).

Schmid, H.B. '"Volksgeist." Individuum und Kollektiv bei Moritz Lazarus (1824–1903)', in *Dialektik: Zeitschrift für Kulturphilosophie* 16(2005), pp. 157–70.

Schmuhl, H.W. ed., *Kulturrelativismus and Antirassismus: Der Anthropologe Franz Boas (1858–1942)* (Bielefeld, 2009).

Schneider, C.M. *Wilhelm Wundts Völkerpsychologie: Entstehung und Entwicklung eines in Vergessenheit geratenen, wissenschaftshistorisch relevanten Fachgebietes* (Bonn, 1990).

Scholem, G. 'Juden und Deutsche', in G. Scholem, *Judaica* II (Frankfurt am Main, 1970), pp. 20–46.

Schorn-Schütte, L. *Karl Lamprecht: Kulturgeschichtsschreibung zwischen Wissenschaft und Politik* (Göttingen, 1984).

Schorske, C.E. *German Social Democracy 1905–1917: The Development of the Great Schism* (Cambridge, MA, 1955).

Schöttler, P. ed. *Geschichtsschreibung als Legitimationswissenschaft 1918–1945* (Frankfurt am Main, 1997).

Sellin, V. 'Mentalität und Mentlitätsgeschichte', in *Historische Zeitschrift* 241(1985), pp. 555–98.

Shamdasani, S. *Jung and the Making of Modern Psychology: The Dream of a Science* (Cambridge, 2003).

Sieg, U. *Aufstieg und Niedergang des Marburger Neukantianismus: Die Geschichte einer philosophischen Schulgemeinschaft* (Würzburg, 1994).

_____. 'Der Preis des Bildungsstrebens: Jüdische Geisteswissenschaftler im Kaiserreich', in A. Gotzmann, R. Liedtke, and T. van Rahden, eds, *Juden, Bürger, Deutsche: Zur Geschichte von Vielfalt und Differenz 1800–1933* (Tübingen, 2001), pp. 67–96.

_____. 'Der frühe Hermann Cohen und die Völkerpsychologie', in *Aschkenas* 13(2003), pp. 461–83.

Smith, W.D. *Politics and the Sciences of Culture in Germany, 1840-1920* (New York and Oxford, 1991).

Sprung, H. 'Hajm Steinthal (1823–1899) und Moritz Lazarus (1824–1903) und die Ursprünge der Völkerpsychologie in Berlin', in L. Sprung and W. Schönpflug, eds, *Zur Geschichte der Psychologie in Berlin* (Frankfurt am Main, 1992), pp. 83–96.

Stallmeister, W. 'Willy Hellpachs Auftritt beim Internationalen Kongreß für Philosophie in Prag 1934', in W. Stallmeister and H.E. Lück, eds, *Willy Hellpach: Beiträge zu Werk und Biographie* (Frankfurt am Main, 1991), pp. 46–58.

Stallmeister, W. and H.E. Lück, eds, *Willy Hellpach: Beiträge zu Werk und Biographie* (Frankfurt am Main, 1991).

_____, 'Die Völkerpsychologie im Werk von Willy Hellpach', in Jüttemann, ed., *Wilhelm Wundts anderes Erbe* (Göttingen, 2006), pp. 116–27.

Steinmetzler, D. *Die Anthropogeographie Friedrich Ratzels und ihre ideengeschichtlichen Wurzeln* (Bonn, 1956).

Stocking Jr., G.W. 'Franz Boas and the Culture Concept in Historical Perspective', in G.W. Stocking Jr. *Race, Culture and Evolution* (Chicago, 1982), pp. 195–233.

_____. ed., *Volksgeist as Method and Ethic: Essays on Boasian Ethnography and the German Anthropological Tradition* (Madison, WI, 1996).

Tilitzki, C. *Die deutsche Universitätsphilosophie in der Weimarer Republik und im Dritten Reich*, 2 vols (Berlin, 2002).

Tinkler, M.A. 'Wundt's Doctorate Students and their Theses, 1875–1920', in *American Journal of Psychology* 44(1932), pp. 630–37.

Toury, J. *Die politischen Orientierungen der Juden in Deutschland: von Jena bis Weimar* (Tübingen, 1966).

Trautmann-Waller, C. *Aux origines d'une science allemande de la culture: linguistique et psychologie des peuples chez Heymann Steinthal* (Paris, 2006).

Ungern-Sternberg von Pürkel, J. and W. von Ungern-Sternberg, *Der Aufruf 'An die Kulturwelt!' Das Manifest der 93 und die Anfänge der Kriegspropaganda im Ersten Weltkrieg* (Stuttgart, 1996).

Vogt, W.P. 'Un durkheimien ambivalent: Célestin Bouglé 1870–1940', in *Revue Française de Sociologie* 20(1979), pp. 123–39.

Watier, P. 'The War Writings of Georg Simmel', in *Theory, Culture, Society* 8(1991), pp. 219–33.

Watson, P. *The German Genius: Europe's Third Renaissance, the Second Scientific Revolution, and the Twentieth Century* (New York, 2010).

Wehler, H.U. *Nationalismus: Geschichte, Formen, Folgen* (Munich, 2001).

Weichlein, S. '"Qu'est-ce qu'une Nation?" Stationen der deutschen statistischen Debatte um Nation und Nationalität in der Reichsgründungszeit', in W. von Kieseritzky and K.P. Sick, eds, *Demokratie in Deutschland: Chancen und Gefährdungen im 19. und 20. Jahrhundert. Historische Essays* (Munich, 1999), pp. 71–90.

Weiler, B. *Die Ordnung des Fortschritts: Zum Aufstieg und Fall der Fortschrittsidee der 'jungen' Anthropologie* (Bielefeld, 2006).

Weingart, P. *Doppel-Leben. Ludwig Ferdinand Clauss: Zwischen Rassenforschung und Widerstand* (Frankfurt am Main, 1995).

Weingart, P., J. Kroll and K. Bayertz, *Rasse, Blut und Gene: Geschichte der Eugenik und Rassenhygiene in Deutschland* (Frankfurt am Main, 1988).

Wiedemann, A. *Die Reinhard-Heydrich-Stiftung in Prag (1942–1945)* (Dresden, 2000).

Wiedemann, F. 'Der doppelte Orient: Zur völkischen Orientromantik des Ludwig Ferdinand Clauß', in *Zeitschrift für Religions- und Geistesgeschichte* 61(2009), pp. 1–24.

Wildt, M. *Generation des Unbedingten: Das Führungskorps des Reichssicherheitshauptamtes* (Hamburg, 2002).

Zimmerman, A. *Anthropology and Antihumanism in Imperial Germany* (Chicago and London, 2001).

Zudrell, P. *Der Schriftsteller und Kulturkritiker Max Nordau: Zwischen Zionismus, Deutschtum und Judentum* (Würzburg, 2003).

Zusi, P. '"Kein abgefallenes Blatt ohn Wirkung geblieben": Organicism and Pluralism in Herder's Metaphorics of Culture', in *Der frühe und der späte Herder: Kontinuität und/oder Korrektur*, eds S. Groß and G. Sauder (Heidelberg, 2007), pp. 89–97.

Index

www.ingramcontent.com/pod-product-compliance
Lightning Source LLC
Chambersburg PA
CBHW060040030426
42334CB00019B/2418